A Gift Grows in the Ghetto

A Gift Grows in the Ghetto

*Reimagining the Spiritual Lives
of Black Men*

Jay-Paul Hinds

WJK WESTMINSTER
JOHN KNOX PRESS
LOUISVILLE • KENTUCKY

© 2022 Jay-Paul Hinds

First edition
Published by Westminster John Knox Press
Louisville, Kentucky

22 23 24 25 26 27 28 29 30 31—10 9 8 7 6 5 4 3 2 1

Unless otherwise indicated, Scripture quotations are from the New Revised Standard Version of the Bible, copyright © 1989 by the Division of Christian Education of the National Council of the Churches of Christ in the U.S.A., and are used by permission.

Book design by Sharon Adams
Cover design by designpointinc.com

Library of Congress Cataloging-in-Publication Data is on file at the Library of Congress, Washington, DC.

ISBN-13: 978-0-664-26705-6

Most Westminster John Knox Press books are available at special quantity discounts when purchased in bulk by corporations, organizations, and special-interest groups. For more information, please e-mail SpecialSales@wjkbooks .com.

Contents

Foreword

Not My Father's Jazz

A hollow gasp escaped his lungs, and he was gone. Through the doctor's pronouncement, the sorrowed wail, and the analog beep-beep of medical devices, only white noise filled my ears. As the fluorescent emergency room dulled to grey, my neurons numbed, and a steely reserve occupied my heart. Deadened to grief, I flipped the default switch to care. I figured my father would want it that way, yet as I was his firstborn son, we shared more than a name. We were friends, a privilege not granted to him by his own father.

Seven days after my father's final breath, thousands gathered for his funeral. Under the cross, I preached my father's eulogy while accompanied by a jazz cellist. Before the throngs, I reflected on the life of one born in the wilderness of the segregated South and raised in exile by a single mother. Yet within this child of patrilineal desertion a divine gift of telling stories with numbers would grow. In step with the cello's beat, we remembered his four decades of service as an accountant, his devotion to family, and his commitment to God.

Weeks after the homegoing, while sorting through a crate of dusty collectibles, I excavate my father's favorite jazz record and rush to the turntable. When the needle pricks the well-worn vinyl on the spinning plate, Grover Washington's "Mister Magic" warms the room. Yet it is not just Washington's saxophone that fills every crevice, for this familiar song conjures the ancestral presence of my father. As the syncopated tones move within me, I am transported back to the dawning hours of December 18, 1999. Awakened that morning by "Mister Magic," I found my father with closed eyes in his leather recliner. Silent tears cascaded down his grizzled beard. When the song ended, he opened his eyes and whispered, "Grover died." It was one of two times when I witnessed my father cry. Or shall I say, my father invited me to witness the vulnerability of his tears.

Since that day, the mere sound of jazz untethers emotions. So it perplexed me when the same kind of released repression occurred while reading *A Gift Grows in the Ghetto*. Uncharacteristic of many theologians, Hinds writes with lyrical complexity, unexpected crescendo, and improvisational surprise. Thus when I began drafting this foreword, I envisioned this assignment more as crafting liner notes for an album than as a preface for a book.

Though Hinds credits himself as a lover of John Coltrane, Sonny Rollins, and Charles Mingus, his style of writing is not my father's jazz. The chapter subheadings that frame this book are characteristic of an intellectual artist groomed by the grit of East Orange's ghettos in the 1980s rather than the nightclubs of Harlem in the mid-twentieth century. Hear these subheadings: "The Doryphoros Redux," "The Rage of a Hopeless Son," "Sambo Kills Uncle Tom," "No Place to Grow a Man," and "The Fantasy of the Goodie Goodies." Are these not reminiscent of album tracks? Have you heard of a pastoral theological text with such edginess?

While the subheadings sound like sensational riffs, Hinds layers his arguments with complexity and depth. I recall watching a documentary on the famed jazz pianist Thelonious Monk. In one scene, two professional pianists struggle to duplicate on two pianos a swift improvisational run that Monk made with ten fingers. Similar to Monk, Hinds demonstrates dexterity as he weaves together theories from an Egyptologist, a Hebrew scholar, a Womanist theologian, and a hip-hop icon in one chapter while paralleling the biographies of Viennese psychoanalyst Sigmund Freud and Harlem-bound protest-novelist Richard Wright in another.

Most impressive is Hinds's artistic gift of seizing his audience's attention and transporting them to another place. As he told the story of Hagar, I saw for the first time my grandmother and her children escaping under the cover of nightfall to find refuge in another state. Likewise, I could see my teenaged father enduring slights from peers who had introjected subjugation as he entered his public high school in a suit and tie with briefcase in tow. Both he and Hinds are testaments that priceless gifts grow in the ghetto.

Now, Beloved Reader, I invite you to turn the page and prepare to be moved by a sound that will alter your vision of the ghetto and the gifts therein.

Gregory C. Ellison II, PhD
Associate Professor of Pastoral Care, Candler School of Theology
Founder and Executive Director, Fearless Dialogues Inc.

Introduction

No Humans, No God, and No Gifts

The wilderness and the dry land shall be glad,
    the desert shall rejoice and blossom;
like the crocus it shall blossom abundantly,
    and rejoice with joy and singing.

—Isaiah 35:1–2

This innocent country set you down in a ghetto in which, in fact,
it intended that you should perish. Let me spell out precisely what
I mean by that, for the heart of the matter is here, and the root of
my dispute with my country. You were born where you were born
and faced the future that you faced because you were black and for
no other reason. The limits of your ambition were, thus, expected
to be set forever.[1]

—James Baldwin

In the fall of 1992, cultural theorist Sylvia Wynter wrote an open letter to her
colleagues in higher academia. Wynter had been disturbed by the events pre-
ceding, during, and following the 1992 Los Angeles riots. In March 1991, her
eyes had seen the terrifying video of Rodney King, an African American man,
mercilessly beaten by police officers while more than a dozen other officers
stood and looked, doing nothing. The fifteen-minute attack left King with
multiple skull fractures, broken bones and teeth, and, worst of all, permanent brain damage. The video caused such a national furor that four of the
officers were charged with excessive use of force. On April 29, 1992, about a
year after they were charged, all four of the officers were acquitted. Then the
riots started. According to reliable sources, the riots began at the corner of

Florence and Normandie in South Los Angeles when four young Black men attacked a white truck driver named Reginald Denny. The spark of anger that started at that intersection soon became a consuming fire of communal rage that spread throughout the city. Residents set fires, looted and destroyed stores, and continued to attack motorists for weeks. While this was happening, something else was going on about which the nightly news didn't speak. But it was something that Sylvia Wynter noticed, and she believed her colleagues needed to know about it as well.

Wynter discovered that "public officials of the judicial system of Los Angeles routinely used the acronym N.H.I. to refer to any case involving the breach of rights of young Black males who belong to the jobless category of the inner-city ghettoes."[2] What did N.H.I. mean? "No Humans Involved."[3] Wynter says that classifying the persons in these ghetto neighborhoods in this manner gave "the police of Los Angeles the green light to deal with its members [particularly young Black males] in any way they pleased."[4] This segment of the population was deemed unworthy of being treated as human beings. In his book *Wasted Lives*, sociologist Zygmunt Bauman observes that such persons are considered superfluous because of their low social status and are therefore disposable. "The American black ghetto," Bauman observes, "has turned purely and simply into a virtually single-purpose, waste disposal tip."[5] The ghetto is the home for wasted humans.

There was more to Wynter's letter, however, than making her colleagues aware of the N.H.I. controversy. In the letter she confesses that she wants to start a conversation about this disdain for Black life and, more to the point, how she and her colleagues in the academy perpetuate the problem.[6] Wynter's point is that there is a common view of Black people held among the four police officers who beat King; the mostly white, middle-class jurors who acquitted the officers; and "the best and brightest graduates of both the professional and non-professional schools of the university system of the United States."[7] There is a "system of classification" that they all adhere to, whether knowingly or unknowingly. Wynter asks,

> How did they [i.e., "the best and the brightest"] come to conceive of what it means to be both *human* and *North American* in the *kinds* of *terms* (i.e., to be White, of Euroamerican culture and descent, middle-class, college-educated, and suburban) within whose logic, the jobless and usually school drop-out/push-out category of young Black males can be *perceived*, and *therefore behaved towards*, only as the *Lack* of the human, the Conceptual Other to being North American?[8]

It's a question worth considering, even today. How, exactly, do persons who are part of the educated class, some of whom have graduated from the world's most prestigious institutions, maintain and, in some cases, build on the system of classification that created and dispersed the N.H.I. acronym? Race and racism, structural and otherwise, are integral in all of this, of course. But race is only part of an ongoing process of classification, including but not limited to class and gender, that creates an order of knowledge that differentiates the human from the nonhuman. Wynter absolves neither herself nor her colleagues, for she asks whether the N.H.I. acronym and its practice were created by persons "whom we ourselves would have educated?"[9] These educators, she claims, are at the center of the present order of knowledge that is "disseminated in our present university system and its correlated textbook industry."[10] These are used, essentially, to instill a certain point of view within students, and Black students suffer from the same miseducation.

Historian Carter G. Woodson saw the negative effects of this practice back in the early twentieth century when, in *The Mis-education of the Negro*, he wrote that the "point of view" taught in classrooms affects white and Black students differently. Black students, Carter writes, are taught to be inferior:

> At a Negro summer school two years ago, a white instructor gave a course on the Negro, using for his text a work which teaches that whites are superior to the Blacks. When asked by one of the students why he used such a textbook the instructor replied that he wanted them to get that point of view. Even schools for Negroes, then, are places where they must be convinced of their inferiority.
> The thought of the inferiority of the Negro is drilled into him in almost every class he enters and in almost every book he studies.[11]

In the end, though, Woodson attests that this miseducation is harmful to those designated as inferior because it "kills one's aspirations and dooms him to vagabondage and crime."[12] As for white students, Woodson states,

> It is strange, then, that the friends of truth and the promoters of freedom have not risen up against the present propaganda in the schools and crushed it. This crusade is much more important that the anti-lynching movement, because there would be no lynching if it did not start in the classroom. Why not exploit, enslave, or exterminate a class that everybody is taught to regard as inferior?[13]

Psychoanalyst Erik Erikson, who wrote extensively on youth and identity, pointed out that, in the classroom and beyond, whites are instructed not only that they are superior but that it is their exclusive right to maintain this superiority, at any means necessary. "It is true that the [white male] is offered special chances and privileges in order to make him define his own identity in the narrow and uniform terms demanded by the system."[14] This is a pivotal point for Wynter, particularly in relation to the state-sanctioned violence against young Black males. Three decades since Wynter issued the letter to her colleagues at Stanford University and throughout higher academia, and nearly a century since Woodson's *The Mis-education of the Negro*, a question hangs in the air: "Has anything changed?"

NO GOD IN THE GHETTO

On May 25, 2020, Minneapolis police officers arrested George Floyd, a Black man, after a convenience-store employee called 911 to report that Floyd had bought cigarettes with a counterfeit twenty-dollar bill. About twenty minutes later, the first group of police officers arrived on the scene. Derek Chauvin, one of the police officers, pinned Floyd to the ground, keeping his knee on Floyd's neck for more than eight minutes, all while Floyd gasped for air. Chauvin kept his knee on Floyd's neck as a sign of his disregard for Floyd's humanity (i.e., N.H.I.) and refused to remove it until well after his death. The following day protesters took to the streets of Minneapolis-St. Paul, but it was only the beginning of the unrest. Minneapolis was the flashpoint that sparked a series of fiery responses to the murders of unarmed Black men and women, such as Rayshard Brooks in Atlanta; Aubrey Ahmad in Brunswick, GA; and Breonna Taylor in Louisville, KY, to name but a few. Almost thirty years after the brutal beating of Rodney King and the ensuing Los Angeles riots in 1992, it is evident that we are still being miseducated into the point of view that categorizes Black people—especially young Black men—as nonhuman.

Perhaps N.H.I. is no longer officially used by law enforcement, but the tragic events of 2020 prove that the disdain for young Black males hasn't changed. Doubtless many of the concerns raised by Sylvia Wynter back in 1992 are relevant to our current situation. Has the "misrecognition of human kinship," to use Wynter's phrase, improved over the last three decades?[15]

As an educator in the theological academy, I wonder how Wynter's letter applies to those of us educating the "best and the brightest" church leaders, that is, those trained in seminaries, divinity schools, and so on throughout the United States. How did the strong adherents of the doctrines of racial inferiority use theology and Scripture to classify young Black males as the accursed other? William A. Jones Jr., who pastored a church in the Bedford-Stuyvesant neighborhood of Brooklyn for more than forty years, writes in *God in the Ghetto* that "the black man's relationship to God was the cause of serious debate during the early years of American slavery."[16] He also adds that "preachers, many of whom were slaveowners, sought to develop a theological justification for the profitable institution of human slavery."[17] The end of slavery didn't stop this form of theology, however. It persisted well into the twentieth century.

African American theologian Willie James Jennings recounts when his mother, Mary Jennings, a devout Christian, was approached by two white men from a local church, doing some evangelizing it seems, whom he could tell doubted his mother's faith or, put another way, her relationship with God.[18] Before walking into the backyard of the Jennings's home and greeting his mother, the two white men had already categorized the family as non-Christian. Jennings shares that he "thought it incredibly odd that they never once asked her if she went to church, if she was Christian, or even if she believed in God."[19] Jennings admits that his own theological quest has been inspired by such experiences, which, as he claims, is "fueled [by] a question that has grown in hermeneutic force for me: Why did they not know us? They should have known us very well."[20] *But how could they?* The two white men who did not recognize Ms. Jennings's faith *knew* all too well, due to their own Christian miseducation, that she could not be a real Christian. Why would they think otherwise? Viewing Ms. Jennings's faith as equal to their own would have meant that her humanity was just as valuable as theirs—a notion unacceptable to them. Similar to the public officials and juridical system in Los Angeles that created and utilized the N.H.I. acronym, these two white men had been instructed to believe that when encountering a Black person, they were not to regard such persons as the chosen, that is, as persons having a relationship with God. I propose that this misrecognition is deadlier than the N.H.I. acronym, for in such acts it is being announced, in essence, that there is a category of persons, living in certain locales, that God has abandoned. Perhaps we should think of a new acronym: N.G.I., meaning "No God Involved." This is the classification used when considering the spiritual lives of Black people in the ghetto, particularly young Black males. Please note, however, that this is not a white Christian church problem alone. The Black Christian church is guilty of using the same mode of classification as well.

In their foundational text *Black Metropolis*, sociologists St. Clair Drake and Horace R. Cayton mention how inner-city churches disparaged residents of the community. They share that in the Bronzeville district of Chicago there were "500 churches, at least 300 of these being located in definitely lower-class neighborhoods."[21] According to the authors, the churches in Bronzeville were sustained by a faithful few who were instructed to reject the "Devil" and the "Sin" that were plaguing the city's streets. A sermon by a local pastor conveys his church's view of the neighborhood's residents:

> Why, the people have lost all self-respect, and most of our children are brought up in homes where there is strife, anger, and viciousness

all the time. Some of you people lie down mad and get up mad. Just cursing and swearing all the time over the children. I sometimes wonder can't you that live that sort of life find a place for Jesus in your homes. That's where to start a remedy, right in your home life.[22]

The message: Your life would be better if God were present—really present—in your home. Some of the more derisive sermons, though, were directed toward the city's Black men. Another local pastor remarks, "You lazy, kidney-kneed men are too lazy to work. You have these poor women out in some white person's kitchen or laundry, and you go out for your meals, and then stand around the corners the rest of the day being sissies."[23] The congregants who heard these sermons drew a stark distinction between themselves and those outside the walls of the church, many of whom were trapped in the patterns of disorganization identified with ghetto life. Drake and Cayton remark that "to some lower-class people, however, identification with the church is considered the better alternative of a forced option: complete personal disorganization or 'serving the Lord.'"[24]

Novelist James Baldwin, who confesses that he "fled into the church" to avoid the streets, describes the seemingly godless environs of his youth in Harlem:

> The wages of sin were visible everywhere, in every wine-stained and urine-splashed hallway, in every clanging ambulance bell, in every scar on the faces of the pimps and their whores, in every helpless, newborn baby being brought into this danger, in every knife and pistol fight on the Avenue, and in every disastrous bulletin: a cousin, mother of six, suddenly gone mad, the children parceled out here and there; an indestructible aunt rewarded for years of hard labor by a slow agonizing death in a terrible small room; someone's bright son blown into eternity by his own hand; another turned robber and carried off to jail.[25]

Baldwin, who was a holiness preacher during his teenage years, was a member of the Fireside Pentecostal Assembly on 136th Street, a fundamentalist church. In *Harlem: The Making of a Ghetto 1890–1930*, historian Gilbert Osofsky says that leaders of these nontraditional Black churches in Harlem preached "a fundamentalism which centered around the scheming ways of Satan, who was everywhere, and the terror and joy of divine retribution, with an emphasis on terror."[26] The place congregants in these churches feared most was the immediate environment—the street and the people—outside the sacred four walls of the church.

Sociologist Omar McRoberts points out that for "these churches, the street was the world urbanized, and the world was not only 'profane' but full of evil."[27] R. Drew Smith, a scholar of urban ministry, explores the various ways the urban poor are isolated from church. In his essay "Churches and the Urban Poor: Interaction and Social Distance," Smith argues that scholars have focused "on the ways that churches have extended themselves to the urban poor but generally not on whether, in doing so, they have actually connected with them."[28] To better understand the situation, Smith observed two large, low-income public housing complexes in Indianapolis, Indiana. The public housing complexes were within a mile of fifty churches, all of which, Smith notes, were predominately Black. The data from his research revealed that "churches, though an important spiritual and social resource for some low-income families, have not been a significant factor in the lives of the majority of the families in the housing complexes surveyed in Indianapolis."[29] And why? "Churches, on their part, fail to grapple with the life-worlds of socially marginalized and disaffected populations to the point of being challenged on the exclusive conceptions of community prevailing among many of these congregations," writes Smith.[30] There are congregations that do have interactions with the immediate environment through charitable organizations and events (food pantries, clothing drives, etc.), but Smith identifies these as *indirect* forms of interaction. In sum, they do not directly interact with the people from the streets in such a way that these persons feel included in the church's community and, by extension, God's community. Needless to say, it matters little whether it is Harlem, Compton, or the South Side of Chicago—these are neighborhoods where it is believed no God is involved (N.G.I.), not only in the streets but even more so in the lives of the people.

What is often overlooked is that these negative classifications also lead to a host of harmful acts. N.H.I., says Wynter, gave law enforcement officials in Los Angeles considerable latitude to use excessive force when interacting with ghetto residents. In other instances, officers faced no punishment if they chose not to respond to an emergency in certain N.H.I. neighborhoods. Similarly, one could argue that N.G.I. gives Christian clergy and laypersons the authority, so to speak, to enact spiritual violence against those deemed godless. What does this spiritual violence look like? And who are its most noticeable victims?

THE BIGGER PROBLEM

Bigger Thomas is a problem. The main character of Richard Wright's *Native Son* remains a model not only of the dangers of life in the ghetto but of how such a life makes a person dangerous. Bigger's life has become the cautionary answer to W. E. B. Du Bois's harrowing inquiry "How does it feel to be a

problem?"[31] Wright biographer Margaret Walker says that "his great achievement in his novels is his application of modern psychology and philosophy to
black and white racial patterns and human personality, and to the black male,
who is seen as an outcast, criminal, or marginal man."[32] In his analysis of Bigger in "How Bigger Was Born," Wright explains that in his own life he had
encountered a number of Biggers. These were real-life, young, Black males
who exhibited the characteristics of the fictional Bigger Thomas.[33] They were
angry young men. They also suffered from unstable emotional lives, moving
back and forth between "moods of intense elation and depression."[34] The
melancholy was brought on by the "impossibility of his ever being free."[35]
Because of this lack of hope, Wright saw something else when diagnosing the
problem with these real-life Biggers. Their spirits were broken. For many of
them the ghetto had become more than their location. It had become their
way of life; it was all consuming and evident, as one person told Wright, that
"the white folks won't let us do nothing."[36] Wright claims that the person
who said this to him went crazy, literally, and was "sent to the asylum for the
insane."[37] The white folks wouldn't let him do anything.

A similar claim of hopelessness is made in *Native Son* by the fictional Bigger Thomas during a conversation with his friends:

> "Look!" Bigger said.
> "What?"
> "That plane writing up there," Bigger said, pointing.
> "Oh!"
> They squinted at a tiny ribbon of unfolding vapor that spelled out
> the word: USE . . . The plane was so far away that at times the strong
> glare of the sun blanked it from sight.
> "You can hardly see it," Gus said.
> "Looks like a little bird," Bigger breathed with childlike wonder.
> "Them white boys sure can fly," Gus said.
> "Yeah," Bigger said, wistfully. "They get a chance to do everything."[38]

Later in the conversation, Bigger laments,

> "Goddammit!"
> "What's the matter?"
> "They don't let us do nothing."
> "Who?"
> "The white folks."[39]

Wright encountered numerous Biggers in the South during his youth and
then later in Chicago, where he worked with young men at the South Side
Boys' Club, and then in Harlem, where he helped establish the Lafargue
Mental Hygiene Clinic. He discovered that these young Black men were

unable "to belong, to be identified, to feel that they were alive as other people were."[40] Other people could fly. Other people had hope. Other people were alive. Not the Biggers. Their lives were consumed by what Wright describes as "an objectless, timeless, spaceless element of primal fear and dread . . . a fear and dread which exercises an impelling influence upon our lives."[41]

The most perplexing issue, though, is that, based on bad faith, many believe that neither Bigger Thomas nor the countless other Biggers have the spiritual resources to contend with and, ultimately, overcome this hopelessness. These Biggers, according to Wright, have been subjected, repeatedly, to a spiritual violence that has left them feeling absolute estrangement, not only from their community but from God. "Estranged from the religion and folk culture of his race," as Wright puts it.[42] Bigger was trapped in a world wherein "metaphysical meanings had vanished; a world in which God no longer existed as a daily focal point of men's lives; a world in which men could no longer retain their faith in an ultimate hereafter."[43] All of Bigger's focus, it seems, was on the white boys who "get a chance to do everything."[44] This was his ultimate concern—his faith.

At the core of the spiritual violence, though, is the belief that these young Black males, the Biggers, are not worthy of relationships. Given what has been purported about his character (e.g., depraved, lazy, salacious, etc.) and what he has been called (e.g., Nigger, Sambo, "the goddamn scum of the earth"[45]), who, I ask, would want to be in a relationship, of any kind, with a Bigger? The truth is, however, that no Bigger is truly alone. Let's just use the example of the interactions between young Black males in the ghetto and law enforcement. When excessive police force, which often leads to death, is deemed the only means by which the Bigger can be dealt with, what these officers fail to consider—in their "reflex anti-Black male behavior-prescriptions"[46]—is that they are traumatizing and, in some instances, destroying a web of relationships. They forget that Bigger is someone's son, husband, brother, nephew, friend. They forget—or choose to ignore—that Bigger—no matter his perceived fallenness—is someone's *gift*.

UNDERSTANDING SPIRITUALITY AND THE GIFT

N.G.I. is a spiritual crisis for young Black men. It therefore requires a spiritual remedy. By framing the crisis in this manner, I am not suggesting that neither the socioeconomic nor the psychological challenges confronting African American men be set aside. Rather, by claiming the value of spirituality, I am uplifting a mode of existence that, when allowed to grow, is a communally oriented, culturally relevant, and effective means of responding creatively to the destructive isolation of the ghetto. This book contends that the spirituality of Black men must be reimagined as grounded in and nourished by their identity as a gift. But what is meant by the word *spirituality*? *Merriam-Webster* provides the following definitions: 1) "something that in ecclesiastical law belongs to the church or to a cleric as such"; 2) "clergy"; 3) "sensitivity of attachment to religious values"; 4) "the quality or state of being spiritual."[47] Spirituality is more than what this definition suggests, however. Kenneth Pargament, a scholar of religious belief and health, suggests that whereas religion is "restricted to institutionally based dogma, rituals, and tradition," spirituality "is generally described as a highly individualized search for the sense of connectedness with a transcendent force."[48] Yet spirituality is more than what Pargament suggests. Scholar of Christian spirituality E. Glenn Hinson points out that spirituality in the Protestant tradition has various contemporary expressions, such as secular and charismatic forms of spirituality. Charismatic spirituality, for instance, "emphasized experiential religion, speaking in tongues or glossolalia being only one, though an important, expression."[49] According to Hinson, one of the problems with contemporary expressions of spirituality is its focus on the individual. "Protestants," Hinson attests, "have placed responsibility on the shoulders of individuals and have de-emphasized corporate means and duties."[50]

Other shades of spirituality further problematize the definitions offered by Pargament and Hinson. Contrary to Pargament's definition, for instance, African American spirituality does not uplift the "connectedness to a transcendent force" exclusively but also endeavors to be in relationship with an immanent God. In the *Spirituality of African Peoples*, Christian ethicist Peter J. Paris notes, "The 'spirituality' of a people refers to the animating and integrative power that constitutes the principal frame of meaning for individual and collective meanings."[51] Paris's point underscores the ways in which the African communal ethos influences African American spirituality. According to Paris,

> Because each person is an essential part of family and the larger community, each significant event in the individual's life is at one and the same time an important occasion in the life of the whole community. As the latter is affected for good or ill by the unfolding drama of the individual's life, times of happiness or grief are invariably shared by the community. . . . Contrary to the thinking of many Western peoples, this communal view of personhood does not imply the devaluation of individuality. Rather it implies that the value Africans bestow on individuals is not the primary good.[52]

Theologian Dwight N. Hopkins comments that in the spirituality of African American women there are "values of connectedness" whereby bonds are formed "to the poor black woman herself; to her immediate community; to her broader community; and to nature." As for their connection to the immediate community, Hopkins states that African American women are committed to maintaining the close spiritual bonds they have with others. He sees this communally focused spirituality in the stories of novelist Toni Morrison, wherein women "display a resilient will to involve themselves in liberated relationships, despite the continual presence of the Thing's spirituality (that is, the evil and damning forces of gender, racial, and economic discrimination)."[53]

Archie Smith Jr., a scholar of pastoral theology and pastoral care, brings to light another facet of African American spirituality by noting its "creative responses to radical evil in the community of the faithful and in personal experience."[54] Smith emphasizes the dialectic between the individual and the communal, noting that "personal or internal spiritual experience is essential preparation for external struggle."[55] It in no way minimizes the fact that African American spirituality is "relational or communal in character."[56] Smith maintains that radical evil is a traumatizing suffering that is not only personal but also reaches throughout the community and across generations. The lingering effects of slavery and Jim Crow on African Americans are identifiable instances of radical evil. These are traumatizing historical events to which African Americans responded with a creative spirituality that could alleviate their oppression and transform their sorrow into hope. But this spirituality is not a given. In *Navigating the Deep River: Spirituality in African American Families*, Smith warns that the African American community is experiencing an emergence of "spiritual refugees."[57] These are persons who have been "rejected, traumatized, or ousted by powerful forces that operate in church and society."[58] A similar theme is found in pastoral theologian Edward Wimberly's *Relational Refugees*. Unlike Smith, however, Wimberly views such persons as relational refugees who have not been ousted but instead have decided to separate themselves from "family, community, and past generations."[59] Therefore, whether by force or by choice, these spiritual and relational refugees, because of their intense isolation, lack the necessary spiritual resources to respond creatively to the radical evil encountered in their daily lives.

As with *spirituality*, the term *gift* is a signifier that is loaded with complexities and is therefore difficult to define. Sociologist Marcel Mauss's *The Gift* examines the custom of gift exchanges in primitive societies. Mauss proposes that what was being exchanged in primitive societies was not simply economically useful objects, what he termed "the potlatch," but "everything," material and nonmaterial, in an ongoing effort to form social ties.[60] In such societies, there is an obligation to give and to receive, and failing to do either is viewed unfavorably. "To refuse to give, to fail to invite, just as to refuse to accept, is tantamount to declaring war; it is to reject the bond of alliance and communality," writes Mauss.[61]

The most-noted critique of Mauss's theory of the gift has come from philosopher Jacques Derrida, who argues that the gift is an impossibility. Derrida writes that "for there to be a gift, there must be no reciprocity, return, exchange, countergift, or debt."[62] The gift places one in a cycle of return from which neither the giver nor recipient can escape. Sociologists Alain Caillé and Jacques Godbout critique Derrida for placing the gift strictly within an economic system and not sufficiently emphasizing that it is part of a "social system concerned with personal relationships."[63] These networks established through the gift are necessary for communal survival. However, according to Caillé and Godbout, Derrida omits this point entirely in his account of the gift. Caillé and Godbout note that in some communities, "there still remains, as the least resort, that network of interpersonal relations consolidated by the gift and mutual aid, which alone enables one to survive in a mad world."[64] Another significant feature of the gift mentioned by Caillé and Godbout is that it marks our individuality within our social networks. The gift protects us from the decaying effects of conformity and unanimity and is an essential part of one's identity. The authors caution that as modern society endeavors to replace the significance of the gift by making everything subject to production, it "aims to produce everything so that nothing will be created, nothing emerge, nothing come into the world that is not produced."[65] Unfortunately, the weakening of the gift and gift exchange also brings about the weakening of communal bonds, without which the community cannot survive. What happens, for instance, when a community no longer exchanges what I would categorize as humanizing gifts, such as recognition, forgiveness, friendship, love, and inclusion? These gifts not only improve our humanity, but they also build the kind of communal trust necessary to respond creatively to radical evil.

There is a spiritual dimension to the gift as well. In 1 Corinthians 12:7–11, the apostle Paul identifies several spiritual gifts:

> To each is given the manifestation of the Spirit for the common good. To one is given through the Spirit the utterance of wisdom, and to another the utterance of knowledge according to the same Spirit, to another faith by the same Spirit, to another gifts of healing by the one Spirit, to another the working of miracles, to another prophecy, to another the discernment of spirits, to another various kinds of tongues, to another the interpretation of tongues. All these are activated by one and the same Spirit, who allots to each one individually just as the Spirit chooses.

Thomas R. Blanton, scholar of early Christianity, considers how the gift functioned within the early church, most specifically in the letters of Paul.[66] The social context of the time is important to Blanton's argument, as it was a time, not dissimilar to our own, during which social stratification was prevalent throughout Greco-Roman cities like Corinth. Wealth designated a person of high social status. "Wealth, especially if displayed in conspicuously stylish ways, might count more heavily than religious purity," writes biblical scholar Wayne Meeks.[67] Theologian Pheme Perkins provides the following account of the social stratification in Corinth:

> When the Corinthians met to celebrate the Lord's Supper, which took place during a meal, some people were eating well and even becoming drunk. Others, the poor members of the community, were being left out and going hungry. We know that in the society of the time a wealthy person might give a banquet in which his special friends were served good food and wine but lesser associates of the host or of his friends would be served small portions of poor food and wine.[68]

Blanton claims that Paul would have been among those designated as a poor member of the community because he was an "impoverished and homeless itinerant, [and] was accorded shame and dishonor."[69] In an attempt to invert his low social status, Paul employed a "rhetoric of inversion" to persuade the church of Corinth to believe that the gifts of the spirit are more valuable—and bestow more status—than the material things associated with honor and prestige. "The gift of the spirit," Blanton writes of Paul's rhetoric of inversion, "enables humans to perceive 'the things of God'—including the 'deep things of God.' . . . Similar knowledge of things divine is not available to those who have received only the 'spirit' of the world.'"[70] Through this inversion, Paul sought to construct a new evaluative scheme whereby the powerless in society would be empowered not by wealth but through their spiritual gifts. These gifts signified that they had a relationship and were being empowered by God. Blanton states that "[Paul] proposed a system in which the weak of the world—as he himself appeared to be—were accorded higher honors that the world's 'strong' or socio-politically dominant."[71] The weak are made strong by the gift.

REIMAGINING THE SPIRITUALITY OF AFRICAN AMERICAN MEN: THE GIFT OF ISHMAEL

A Gift Grows in the Ghetto reimagines the spiritual lives of African American men *first* by making a correlation between the modern ghetto and the biblical wilderness. Each of these locales has been designated as the abode of the outcast, that is, society's rejects. Sociologist Loic Wacquant states that a "ghetto can be characterized ideal-typically as a bounded, ethnically uniform sociospatial formation born of the forcible relegation of a negatively typed population—such as Jews in the principalities of Renaissance Europe and African Americans in the United States . . . to a reserved territory."[72] The biblical wilderness has similar characteristics. Hebrew Bible scholar Shemaryahu Talmon remarks that "due to its remoteness from settled land and its terrifying desolation, the wilderness becomes the chosen refuge of outlaws and fugitives."[73]

The *second* necessary correlation is between the negative characterization of Black men in the American ghetto and the biblical character Ishmael in the wilderness. Sociologist Elijah Anderson observes that "living in areas of concentrated ghetto poverty, still shadowed by the legacy of slavery and second-class citizenship, too many young black men are trapped in a horrific cycle that includes active discrimination, unemployment, poverty, crime, prison and early death."[74] He adds that "people—black as well as white—necessarily avoid [the young Black male], and through their avoidance behavior teach him that he is an outsider in his own society."[75] The young Black male is an outcast who is in constant conflict with everyone. Ishmael suffered a similar fate. In Genesis 16:12 the angel of the Lord tells Hagar, regarding her son, Ishmael,

> "He shall be a wild ass of a man,
> with his hand against everyone,
>   and everyone's hand against him;
> and he shall live at odds with all his kin."

Hebrew Bible scholar Gregory Mobley points out that due to Ishmael's life in the wilderness he is depicted as a "onager-man" (onagers are a race of the Asian wild ass native to northern Iran), which allows him to function narratively in the Genesis account "as the 'feral double' of the patriarch Isaac."[76]

The *third* correlation notes that although giftlessness can condemn young Black men to a life consumed by the despair of the ghetto, Ishmael's growth as a gift allowed him to creatively find new life in the wilderness. Remembering the story of Bigger Thomas is useful here, for Bigger is the model of giftlessness. In *Spiritual Empowerment in Afro-American Literature*, theologian James H. Evans Jr. argues that Bigger endeavors to be the "creator of his own destiny."[77] He has taken matters into his own hands, so to speak, but is devoid of the necessary ethical and moral compass to give his actions life-giving direction. Bigger operates solely on his own vision of the good, nothing else. Evans observes,

> As a moral agent Bigger distinguishes between good and evil based on the *breadth of his vision* [italics mine]. . . . The fundamental weakness of

> Bigger's character . . . is his failure to recognize the contingent nature of his reality, the ambiguity of his moral decisions, and the finitude of his person. Thus, the promise of historical agency is unkept. Instead of instilling hope into the life of Vera, he merely whets her sense of grief. Instead of pulling Bessie out of her unconscious oppression, he takes her life. Instead of politicizing his race, Bigger becomes the solitary rebel.[78]

Bigger desires to change his status, to become empowered in the ghetto, but he wants to do this on his own, that is, to transform himself by his own hands. Ultimately, all Bigger can do is harm himself and others in this finite act of self-creation. He is giftless.

The story of Ishmael differs in that his transformation begins in and is nourished by his relationship with God. Genesis 21:20 states that "God was with the boy, and he grew up; he lived in the wilderness, and became an expert with the bow." First, Ishmael's growth as a gift functioned to protect not only himself but Hagar, his mother, in the wilderness at a time when they were vulnerable. He was a gift to Hagar. Second, in acquiring the skills of an expert bowman, Ishmael attained a new identity that radically altered his low social status. Finally, Ishmael's relationship with the God of his mother, El Roi (the God who sees me), allowed him to discover resources beyond "the breath of his vision" and therefore create a unique way of life in the wilderness.

Following this introduction, the rest of this book explores the spiritual lives of young Black men by using an interdisciplinary approach. The overall methodology for this study is the correlational method. Theologian Frederick L. Ware says that in African American theology "correlation is applied within a complex web of connections between religion and experience."[79] Ware cautions that correlation is problematic because the Black experience and, by extension, Black religion are so diverse. For instance, he states that the religious life (or lives) of African Americans includes "Roman Catholic and Orthodox conceptions of Christianity, Islam, Judaism, African-derived religions . . . eclectic spiritual traditions, Hinduism, and Buddhism," and "secular worldviews" are to be considered as well.[80] Yet despite these challenges, the value of the correlational method is affirmed by Paul Tillich, who attests that it "explains the contents of the Christian faith through existential questions and theological answers in mutual interdependence."[81] The first three chapters of this book present a series of existential questions, or problematics, concerning young Black men.

The first chapter, "'I WAS A MAN NOW': The Problematic Manhood of African American Men," interrogates the dominant images—and models—of African American manhood. There is the image of the Sambo, the dutiful slave, who would obey the slave master even to the point of harming others within the slave community. Also emerging during this time was the image of Uncle Tom, who was equally dutiful but, as I shall argue, would not view his fellow slaves through the slave master's evaluative logic. Uncle Tom was no Sambo. To negate these negative images of African American men, the race man emerged during the late-nineteenth and early-twentieth centuries, evinced in such figures as Booker T. Washington and W. E. B. Du Bois, the Black messiah type. These men were models of a redeemed Black manhood, but this model also proved insufficient, for it was, in many ways, a willful parroting of white patriarchal manhood. It was, I argue, so focused on declaring, "I am a man" that it never discovered and practiced new modes of being human.

Chapter 2, "The Hero's Sorrow: A Gift Yet Unwrapped," further explores the problem of manhood by looking at the father-son relationships of Sigmund Freud and Richard Wright. Although some readers might think it odd to include Freud in a study on Black men, my reason for doing so is not that Freud developed the Oedipus-complex theory, though that is important; it is that his failed relationship with his father negatively affected his identity as a son and, by extension, his ability to hope. Freud was giftless. As the chapter will demonstrate, Freud made several attempts to create for himself a relationship whereby he could feel himself a beloved son, that is, truly cared for by someone he deemed a heroic father. But this never happened. His dear friend and later enemy Wilhelm Fliess ultimately failed to fill this role, and his own father, Jacob Freud, did not exemplify the kind of heroic manhood Freud could admire. The unfortunate result is that he felt abandoned during his greatest achievement: his visit to the Acropolis. Freud had lifted himself from the shame of his childhood in the Leopoldstadt ghetto to become a renowned theorist of the human mind, but, in the end, he still suffered from what pastoral theologian James Dittes terms the "sorrow of incompleteness."[82]

Richard Wright's experience is somewhat different from Freud's, but the end result is the same: giftlessness. His father, Nathan Wright, abandoned his family after failing to make a better life for them in Memphis, Tennessee. During their time in Memphis, however, Richard noticed that his father was changing, and not for the better. His soul was succumbing to life in the ghetto. Worst of all, Richard saw his father's situation deteriorating because of Nathan's growing sense of spiritual abandonment—Nathan wanted to be a preacher but never received a call from God. Soon after, Nathan went into spiritual ruin, an aching hopelessness that led him back to the Natchez plantation he tried to escape. This terrified his son Richard—so much so that Richard would never allow himself to feel the need for the gift of sonship. He adopted the attitude that to embrace the vulnerability of sonship would lead him to sacrifice the only thing that he could truly depend on: himself, Richard Wright.

Chapter 3, "Ghetto Grown," analyzes the crisis of the ghetto by using the scholarship of noted sociologists, such as Mitchell Duneier, Elijah Anderson, William Julius Wilson, Horace R. Cayton, and St. Clair Drake. The ghetto is not an American original. It was created in Europe to segregate the Jewish community, particularly those who were unacculturated, from the rest of society. Furthermore, the ghetto was not always a place of desolation but was perceived as a safe space, so to speak, wherein the segregated population could maintain its unique cultural heritage. The American ghetto during the early-twentieth century, due to the Great Migration that brought millions of African Americans up north from the south, changed not only the racial makeup of the ghetto but also its public image. The data provided by sociologists portray the ghetto as an utterly hopeless place, ravaged by crime, violence, and a host of other social ills. A primary characterization of the ghetto put forth by Daniel P. Moynihan and others (for instance, psychologist Kenneth B. Clark) is that it is full of disorganized families, that is, single-family households headed by Black women. The result is that Black women are the true power brokers in the ghetto, whereas Black men are weakened because they cannot assume their supposed natural mantle of authority in the home. The disorganization of the ghetto household leads Black men to assert their manhood status in other areas. The work of aforementioned sociologist Elijah Anderson details how young Black men develop an alternative way of life—the code of the street—to provide them with a sense of meaning amidst the chaos in the ghetto. Such efforts, however, do not help Black men overcome the many challenges of ghetto life.

Chapter 4, "The Wilderness: Where Our Gift Grows," shifts the focus from existential questions (or problematics) to theological answers. A guiding question for the chapter is "How does the theology of the biblical wilderness provide an answer to the existential question of the modern ghetto?" There are diverse views of the wilderness provided by biblical scholars. It is portrayed as a place of utter desolation wherein it is impossible for anything to grow as well as a place of divine encounter, a unique space where spiritual transformation occurs. Chapter 4 examines the struggles, survival, and liberation of Hagar and Ishmael in the wilderness. Unfortunately, Hagar's story of survival in the wilderness remains undervalued, even within African American theology, because biblical scholars focus instead on the wilderness in the Exodus narrative. However, among Black feminist/womanist theologians, such as Delores Williams, Hagar's story details how God sees and nurtures our gifts in order to provide a means for our survival, particularly when confronted with inescapable suffering. The chapter argues that this process of gift development was contingent on God's care-*full* development of Hagar's gift—her son, Ishmael. God's recognition of and ongoing interaction with Ishmael (e.g., "God was with the boy, and he grew up" [Gen. 21:20]) demonstrates that the wilderness environment, though hostile, will not overwhelm Hagar. She will live because God has given her a gift.

Chapter 5, "Talking about Our Gifts," argues that the gift is a theological answer to the current spiritual crisis afflicting Black men. Currently, a primary diagnosis is that the problems of Black men in the ghetto can be attributed to poor mental health. John Head, for instance, maintains that racism has led to high rates of depression among African American men. What chapter 5 suggests is that, besides mental health and other factors, another significant contributor to the crisis is the absence of an awareness of one's gift. For many young Black men in the ghetto, there is little that affirms the presence of God. Is there a way for them to know that God is with them? A theological answer is provided by examining Ishmael's initiation into manhood in the wilderness, which is marked by his acquiring expertise as a bowman, thereby providing him a new identity. Ishmael never underwent a weaning ceremony while living in the house of Abraham; thus he never had a communal ritual to affirm his transition into manhood. This must have been terrible for his self-identity. One could imagine Ishmael asking himself, "Who am I?" during the early stages of his wilderness experience. Moreover, without this ceremony, despite his age, Ishmael was still viewed as a boy. His initiation in the wilderness, however, not only gave him an identity but also provided him with the necessary skills to live in the wilderness. What would happen if African American men in the ghetto could hear Ishmael's story? Would it inspire them to discover how a relationship with God could help them find life—not just despair—in the ghetto?

Chapter 6, "Warning: God Don't Like Ugly," offers the concluding reflection regarding the commonalities between the wilderness and the ghetto, between Ishmael and young Black men. It begins with an overview of the ways in which the wilderness was viewed as a place of spiritual encounter in the African American religious tradition, which teaches that the African American religious experience is rooted in rejecting normative ways of viewing the wilderness. Therefore, one discovers in the African American literary tradition a number of works that portray a character finding refuge in environments set apart from society—sewers, cellars, subways, and so forth. An example of this is found in Richard Wright's novel *The Man Who Lived Underground*, wherein Fred Daniels, the main character, has an epiphany of self-discovery while living underground in an urban wilderness.[83] The problem with Daniels is that his experience in the underground is void of divine encounter. He discovers himself and nothing else. Daniels and those who seek refuge in wilderness settings like the underground have been taught that these are grotesque locales, ugly places that are disapproved by God. A further problem is that not just the location but the people themselves are deemed too ugly for God to be with them. What are the intracommunal implications for persons who, within a given inner-city community, embody the very ills of the ghetto? Does such a person ever have a chance to grow as a gift in the ghetto? And if not, what is the true cause of their demise?

1

"I WAS A MAN NOW"

The Problematic Manhood
of African American Men

> In an important sense there is only one complete unblushing male in America: a young, married, white, urban, northern, heterosexual Protestant father of college education, fully employed, of good complexion, weight, height, and a recent record in sports. Every American male tends to look out upon the world from this perspective, this constituting one sense in which one can speak of a common value system in America. Any male who fails to qualify in any of these ways is likely to view himself—during moments at least—as unworthy, incomplete, and inferior.
>
> —*Erving Goffman*[1]

BE YE PERFECT . . .

Perfect. What does it mean to be perfect? In Matthew 5:48 Jesus encourages his listeners to "be perfect, therefore, as your heavenly Father is perfect." So then, according to Scripture, God is perfect. God meets all the requirements of perfection by being omniscient, omnipresent, and omnipotent. In *Church Dogmatics*, theologian Karl Barth adds to these qualities by stating that God's perfection "consists in the fact that He is the One who loves in freedom."[2] For Barth, this love is grounded in the Trinity: "Since God is Father, Son and Holy Ghost, i.e., loves in freedom, every perfection exists essentially in him."[3] But there is something else suggested in the abovementioned Scripture. God's people can (and should) be perfect too. How can this be? Are we to expect, in any way, our frail humanity to mimic the divine qualities of God? Who among us is omniscient, omnipresent, and omnipotent? No one. All-loving?

Zero. But the desire to attain God's perfection remains, albeit in perverse forms. Barth states that "all that [man] does when he arrogantly assaults the limits marked out for him is attain a pseudo-divinity" and in so doing only "secretly worships himself."[4] Theologically, the word *perfect* doesn't describe an ideal state—that is, flawless—but rather conveys such meanings as whole or mature. Nevertheless, even in the Christian tradition this sense of the word *perfect* is often overlooked, and it has been this way for centuries.

Christian ethicist Reinhold Niebuhr contends that the Renaissance was the era when the idea of humankind achieving perfection in history began to flourish. The "perfectionist impulse," as Niebuhr calls it, was expressed in religious and social movements that believed in the fulfillment of life in history. For Niebuhr, "the chief agent of this development was undoubtedly the new confidence in developing reason, in cumulative knowledge and experience and in the rational conquest of nature."[5] He adds,

> The guiding principle of the philosophy which underlies the idea of progress is that of an immanent logos which is no longer believed to transcend history as an eternal form, but is thought of as operating in history, bringing its chaos gradually under the dominion of reason.[6]

Inspired by this belief, Christian sects purported that the conquest of nature included overcoming the vices of human nature. These perfectionist Christians, Niebuhr argues, proclaimed that those who do not live up to this perfectionist idea of salvation "fail to achieve perfection only because they do not try hard enough or do not define perfection as the goal of Christian life with sufficient rigor and consistency."[7] Theologian Paul Tillich identifies this perfectionist impulse in Calvinism, which "has produced a Protestant ethics in which progressive sanctification is the aim of life."[8] Perfectionism provides evidence of the believer's development in the Christian life. Tillich warns, however, that this striving for perfection "leads to continuous explosions of the repressed and only superficially admitted forces in the totality of man's being . . . and such explosions are personally and socially destructive."[9] Therefore, he attests that, despite the potential for perfection, humankind, due to its inherent ambiguity, also has the "liability to the greatest imperfection."[10]

Theologian David Tracy notes that a cadre of early-twentieth-century theologians began to criticize the remnants of the Renaissance's perfectionist impulse that remained in the twentieth century. Neo-orthodox theologians—such as Karl Barth, Reinhold Niebuhr, and Paul Tillich—were repulsed by the "evolutionary optimism and . . . the now oppressive modernist model of autonomous man's possibilities widespread in the late nineteenth- and early twentieth-century liberal periods."[11] These theologians lived through a terribly violent period of history—world wars, the rise of National Socialism, and so on—that evinced not man's progress toward perfection but rather a decline into chaos, particularly as international conflict, economic upheaval, and racial oppression became more pronounced. Tracy remarks that the notable growth of the human community's imperfections galvanized the neo-orthodox theologians to critique the "illusions and naivete of the liberal or Enlightenment attitude."[12] Unfortunately, by the early-twentieth century, due in large part to the colonizer/colonized relationship during the eighteenth and nineteenth centuries, the idea of human perfection had been firmly tethered not only to reason but even more so to an image of the perfect man that was constructed within the ideologies of race and racism. Cultural theorist Sylvia Wynter provides an invaluable insight when she observes that "race was therefore to be, in effect, the non-supernatural but no less human ground (in the reoccupied place of the traditional ancestors, gods/God, ground) of the answer that the secularizing West would now give to the . . . question as to the who, and the what we are."[13] This shift created a new doctrine for perfection: Be ye perfect as the (self-) exalted man of the world is perfect (Matt. 5:48, paraphr.).

THE DORYPHOROS REDUX

The ancient Greek sculptor Polykleitos of Argos created the first sculpture depicting the perfect human figure. Art historian J. J. Pollitt shares that Polykleitos's artworks differed from those of his predecessors in that his principle of *symmetria* (i.e., the harmony of parts in sculpture) aimed to express "*to eu*, the perfect or the good, and what others seemed to have called the beautiful."[14] His most-renowned sculpture is the Doryphoros (the *Rule*), which, according to Pollitt, was a display piece that stood in a "public place as part of a votive or sepulchral monument."[15] The Doryphoros embodied the Pythagorean system of harmony that Polykleitos used "to give expression to an ideal conception of human nature, a divine pattern which expressed the essential nature of man."[16]

Centuries later, philosopher Immanuel Kant claimed that the Doryphoros remained the model of human beauty. An extensive review of Kant's philosophy of beauty and taste, as provided in his *Critique of Judgment*, is beyond the scope of this study, but worth mentioning is Kant's definition of the normal idea of beauty:

> The normal Idea of the figure of an animal of a particular race must take its elements from experience. But the greatest purposiveness in the construction of the figure, that would be available for the *universal standard* [italics mine] of aesthetical judgment upon each individual

of the species—the image which is as it were designedly at the basis of nature's Technic, to which only the whole race and not any isolated individual is adequate—this lies merely in the Idea of a judging [subject]. And this, with its proportions, as an aesthetical Idea, can be completely presented *in concreto* in a model.[17]

After making this claim, Kant adds the caveat that, based on experience, "a Negro must have a different normal Idea of the beauty of the [human figure] from a white man, a Chinaman, a European, etc."[18] It seems agreeable—doesn't it?—that there should not be a single model of beauty for the entire human race. Kant's supposed nod to a postmodern view belies his conviction that there remains a universal model of the perfect human figure. Kant explains:

> It is by no means the whole archetype of beauty in the race, but only the form constituting the indispensable condition of all beauty, and this merely *correctness* in the [mental] presentation of the race. It is, like the celebrated *Doryphoros of Polycletus*, the *rule*. . . . It can therefore contain nothing specifically characteristic, for otherwise it would not be the *normal Idea* for the race.[19]

This statement confirms that well into the eighteenth century, at the apex of the Enlightenment, Polykleitos's Doryphoros remained influential. Unlike Polykleitos's era, however, Kant's had developed a rationale about the perfect representation of the human figure supported by theories of race and racism.

More than a decade before writing the *Critique of Judgment*, Kant penned an essay titled "Of the Different Races of Man." For Kant, the four races were 1) the white race, 2) the Negro race, 3) the Hun race (Mongul or Kalmuch), and 4) the Hindu or Hindustani race.[20] Philosopher Emmanuel Chukwudi Eze argues that, according to Kant, the superior races have specific geographical, physiological, and psychological advantages over those deemed inferior.[21] For instance, Kant claims that the iron content in the blood causes the different colors of the human races.[22] The volatility of iron is a problem for persons of red, black, or yellow skin, but for whites, "these acids and the volatile alkaline content are not reflected at all because the iron in the bodily juices has been dissolved, thereby demonstrating both the *perfect* [italics mine] mixing of these juices and the strength of this human stock in comparison to others."[23] In his reading of Kant's writings, Eze finds sufficient evidence to suggest that Kant believed "blacks are never thought of as capable of moral, intellectual, or aesthetic experience."[24] One finds support for Eze's hypothesis in Kant's "On the Different Races of Man," wherein he states that, due to their residence in an extremely warm climate, Negroes (as he refers to them) develop negative physical and psychological characteristics, such as when he says that "he [the Negro] . . . is lazy, indolent, and dawdling."[25] Furthermore, Negroes can never be viewed as the perfect representation of the human figure. Instead, the Negro, in essence, is posited as the anti-Doryphoros, that is, antiperfection. Kant asserts that, unlike the Doryphoros and the race that most resembles it, the Negro has "thick fatty lips . . . oily skin, which weakens the nourishing mucus necessary for the growth of hair," along with a host of other physical deficiencies.[26] Suffice it to say, opinions espousing the differences of the races persisted—and in many ways became more prominent—well after the Enlightenment era.

Sociologist Erving Goffman comments that "the Greeks, who were apparently strong on visual aids, originated the term *stigma* to refer to bodily signs designed to expose something unusual and bad about the moral status of the signifiers."[27] Persons who possessed these signifiers—such as slaves, criminals, or traitors—were perceived as damaged and were to be avoided in public spaces. According to Goffman, there are three types of stigma. *First*, there are physical stigmas—that is, "abominations of the body"—such as physical deformities. Second, stigmas of character, such as "weak will, domineering of unnatural passions . . . dishonesty, homosexuality, etc." *Third*, there are group stigmas attributed to one's family group, race, ethnicity, religion, and so on.[28] Conversely, says Goffman, "those who do not depart negatively from the particular expectations at issue I shall call the *normals*."[29] Who is the model of the normal? The epigraph provided at the beginning of this chapter is Goffman's definition of the normal—that is, the white, urban, northern, heterosexual male. Goffman notes that there are two responses to the norm of the perfect human. The first is that one can conform to the norm by supporting its verity while at the same time recognizing that one will never achieve it. The other response is to rebel by rejecting the norm and alienating oneself from the community that upholds it as a standard.[30] Neither response eases the shame of knowing oneself to be less than human, no matter how hard one tries to reach perfection.

Two opposing figures emerged during the late-nineteenth and early-twentieth centuries in response to the fact that Black men could not achieve this standard of perfection. One conformed. One rebelled. The first is the Sambo, who so embodied the antithesis of the norm that his image was used to dispense negative ideas about Black men. The other is the Black messiah, the anti-Sambo, who served as the model for Black men because his life was devoted to uplifting the Black race. In the end, however, neither the Sambo figure, no matter how much he conformed, nor the race man, no matter how much he rebelled, removed the Black man's desire to reach the perfection of the Doryphoros model in the American context: the white male.

THE UNDERDEVELOPMENT OF SAMBO

In his article "Myths and Stereotypes: The African Man in America," sociologist William H. Turner remarks that "reality itself is often defined within the context of the myths and stereotypes developed to account for it."[31] There are, of course, several myths and stereotypes about Black men that, through various efforts, have been ingrained within the American mind. Their purpose, according to Turner, is "to lessen the cognitive-load of modern man inasmuch as we must codify and categorize the infinite amount of information on which reality itself is based."[32] Given Turner's argument, it is easier, then, for white America to categorize all Black men as lazy, childlike, angry, and libidinous than it is to consider the realities of Black life that delegitimize such labels. Turner has it that the original "proper personification" of the Black man in America was the mythic Sambo figure. The Sambo myth had such a hold on the white imagination, even well into the twentieth century, that folklorist Patricia A. Turner suggests that "the white public's love affair with Sambo . . . undermined the efforts of African Americans to achieve equality."[33] What was it about Sambo, in mythology and reality, that made him so beloved by white America and, at the same time, so harmful to the image of Black men?

Historian Joseph Boskin's *Sambo: The Rise and Demise of an American Jester* offers a thorough overview of how Sambo became so popular in American culture. For Boskin, Sambo's rise was due to the fact that this figure was the first "truly indigenous American humor character throughout the culture, transcending region and ethnicity."[34] Humor was just one part of the Sambo's appeal. Another trait that contributed to the Sambo's rise was the belief that he was incapable of feeling sorrow. There were countless stories told by slave masters of the melancholy and suicidal tendencies of slaves who had been torn from their homeland and brought to toil on foreign land. Boskin maintains that there were slavers who admired the way that, in their opinion, some slaves could suffer with merriment, that is, "that people so oppressed could sing and dance."[35] Eventually, these demonstrations of joyful suffering were transformed into readily available entertainment for the slave-owning class. "On the plantations, it was expected that one of the slaves' primary tasks was to entertain their whites," writes Boskin.[36] What the whites enjoyed as meaningless entertainment, however, was far more serious to the slaves. These were expressions of the slaves' boundless creativity.

Sterling Stuckey, historian of African American religion and art, argues that these creative expressions—songs, dances, and so forth—were often used during festivals to celebrate "the slaves' gratefulness to forces bigger than man."[37] The harvest festival is an example. Stuckey states,

> Harvest festivals were excellent occasions for passing on African cul-
> tural traits from one generation to the next. Some of the best dancing
> and music took place then, because of the high purpose of the occa-
> sion. Aware that few if any whites understood the deeper purpose of
> the festival, blacks found it an ideal situation, within the context of
> oppression, for them to give full expression to their Africanity. . . .
> Slave celebrations were regarded by whites, who allowed them to take
> place, as "innocent pleasures," though harvest festivals had existed
> for centuries in Africa before blacks had arrived in North America.[38]

Locations like the slave quarter, the forests, and hush harbors were cherished
safe spaces where culturally specific ceremonies occurred.[39] Sometimes, however, in order to maintain a close relationship with the slave master, these
sacred rituals and the practices that were integral to them were turned into
minstrelsy, and the Sambo was the quintessential minstrel figure.

Slavery was founded and maintained through the paternalistic master-
slave relationship. The master wanted to be seen as a divine figure to whom
slaves pledged absolute obedience. Historian Kenneth Stampp remarks that
to accomplish "perfect submission" the slave master had to be a "keen student
of human psychology"[40] There was no universal set of rules for how masters
sought to control their slaves. Some were terrifyingly brutal whereas others
were surprisingly caring. No matter the methodology, the goal was the same:
the absolute submission of the slave. Slave-owner Bennet Barrow kept a diary
detailing how he controlled the estimated two hundred slaves on his cotton
plantation in Louisiana. While Barrow provides a glimpse of the organization
of labor on the plantation, the psychological control of the slaves is the focus
of his diary entry on May 1, 1838:

> The very security of the plantation requires that a general and uniform
> control over the people of it should be exercised. Who are to protect
> the plantation from the intrusions of ill-designed persons when every
> body is abroad? Who can tell the moment when a plantation might be
> threatened with destruction from fire—could the flames be arrested if
> the negroes are scattered throughout the neighborhood, seeking their
> amusement. Are these not duties of great importance, and in which
> every negro himself is deeply interested to render this should exist on
> the plantation as to make it necessary for a negro to leave it. . . . *You
> must, therefore, make him as comfortable at Home as possible, affording
> him What is essentially necessary for his happiness—you must provide for
> him Yourself and by that means create in him a habit of perfect dependence
> on you* [italics mine].[41]

The reward for instilling dependence within the slave is that "the Negro
who is accustomed to remain constantly at Home, is just as satisfied with the
society of the plantation as that which he would find elsewhere."[42] As with any

home, the plantation had rules for acceptable behavior. These were created by the slave master, the sole authority figure. Abolitionist Frederick Douglass, who experienced slavery firsthand, shares that most slaves were in awe of the master's power, and most believed that their masters were "invested with a sort of sacredness."[43] At a young age, Douglass realized that in order to survive, the slave had to view the slave master as the powerful father. He testifies that he received "a regular whipping from old master, such as any heedless boy might get from his father."[44] In *Sambos and Minstrels*, Sylvia Wynter contends that the construction of the Sambo was essential to the master-slave relationship, stating that "representing the identity of Sambo as childlike, by instituting processes of infantilization, the slave master constituted himself as *Paternal Father*."[45] The inequitable power structure of the plantation ensured that the slave master could produce dependent, Sambo-like behavior in slaves.

Minstrelsy, the emergence of the song-and-dance man, was the chief means by which the Sambo mythology was made real, and it persisted well after slavery. Boskin writes that the minstrel show began promulgating the Sambo image in 1827 when white entertainer George Washington Dixon and others, such as Thomas D. Rice (Daddy Rice), who popularized the famous song "Jump Jim Crow," put on black face to present themselves as "plantation darkies."[46] Minstrel performances received thunderous applause from captivated audiences that believed they were viewing accurate depictions of the inept Sambo figure. The minstrel shows, however, never sought to convey the limitless creativity of the African American folk tradition as expressed through song and dance. Therefore, cultural practices that slaves used to creatively transform their lived conditions became, through minstrelsy, "harmless entertainment."[47] Wynter claims that "the marginalization of creative cultural activity was therefore carried out through the . . . Sambo/minstrel stereotype."[48] Moreover, as the Sambo figure spread through American culture, it served as a model of the Black man as the antithesis of white manhood. Therefore, not only slave masters but *all* white men could believe themselves the paternal father who, in order to secure his own sense of manhood, needed a dependent and obedient child, the Sambo.

The Sambo's dependency on his master was limitless. Historian Stanley Elkins argues that there were significant and, in many ways, long-lasting changes made to the slave during the era of chattel slavery. Elkins avers that the unique personality types found among slaves were created due to what he terms "the closed system" of the plantation, a system that was so complete because everything concerning the slave's life was under the master's control. Living under such extreme regulation created the Sambo personality type, which Elkins defines as follows:

The characteristics that have been claimed for the type come principally from Southern lore. Sambo, the typical plantation slave, was docile but irresponsible, loyal but lazy, humble but chronically given to lying and stealing; his behavior was full of infantile silliness and his talk inflated with childish exaggeration. His relationship with his master was one of utter dependence and childlike attachment: it was indeed this childlike quality that was the very key to his being. Although the merest hint of Sambo's "manhood" might fill the Southern breast with scorn, the child, "in his place," could be both exasperating and loveable.[49]

Elkins's study focuses on how the closed system of the plantation "could sustain infantilism as a normal feature of behavior."[50] He notes that the slave's identification with the absolute power of the slave master was integral to maintaining the system. To make his point, Elkins compares the closed system of the plantation to that which existed decades later in Nazi concentration camps. By reading personal accounts detailing life in the concentration camps, Elkins formulates the thesis that the prisoners had developed an "intensive identification with the SS,"[51] which was necessary for the prisoner's complete adjustment to the concentration-camp environment.

Using Austrian psychologist Bruno Bettelheim's essay "Individual and Mass Behavior," Elkins states that "a prisoner had reached the final stage of adjustment to the camp situation when he had changed his personality so as to accept as his own the values of the Gestapo."[52] Physician Elie Aron Cohen, who recounts his experience at the Auschwitz concentration camp in his book *Human Behavior in the Concentration Camp*, confesses that "for all of us [the prisoners] the SS was a father image."[53] To this, Elkins responds that "the closed system, in short, had become a kind of gross patriarchy."[54] Elkins finds a similar form of patriarchy in the closed system of the American plantation, which, due to its extended duration, lasting for several generations, was even more effective. Elkins explains:

> The plantation offered no really satisfactory father-image other than the master. The "real" father was virtually without authority over his child, since discipline, parental responsibility, and control of rewards and punishments all rested in other hands; the slave father could not even protect the mother of his children except by appealing directly to the master. . . . From the master's viewpoint, slaves had been defined in law as property, and the master's power over his property must be absolute. . . . Absolute power for him meant absolute dependency for the slave—the dependency not of the developing child but of the perpetual child. For the master, the role most aptly fitting such a relationship would naturally be that of the father.[55]

Slave masters who were diligent in maintaining this perverse father-son relationship, and did so with a balance of timely harshness and care, expected their slaves to exhibit all the characteristics of the dutiful son, the Sambo. John W. Blassingame, a historian, confirms that "the master and slave lived and worked together on such intimate terms that they developed an affection for each other, and the slave identified completely with his master."[56] It is not hyperbole to suggest that the Sambo's self-identity and self-esteem depended on how much his outlook and way of existing were in line with the slave master's. Wynter suggests that there exists "the need to be master in order to experience oneself as the Norm, as human."[57] Unfortunately, if this is correct, it means that the Sambo's own sense of self-worth was based on engaging in the process of producing childlike behavior in those of the same status, fellow slaves, especially Black men. And violence was essential to this process of creating the childlike, utterly dependent Sambo.

SAMBO KILLS UNCLE TOM

Stanley Elkins's psychohistorical analysis of the Sambo type underscores the Sambo's childlike docility. Over the years, no other image of the Sambo type has come to represent this more than Uncle Tom.[58] Uncle Tom was popularized as a Sambo type due in large part to the success of Harriet Beecher Stowe's novel *Uncle Tom's Cabin*. Historian Jason Richards states that "black face minstrelsy and *Uncle Tom's Cabin* were mutually constitutive phenomena," adding that "minstrelsy and Stowe's novel were, in many ways, conjoined cultural twins."[59] Published in 1852, *Uncle Tom's Cabin* became the proof text for several claims made about the Uncle Tom figure seen in various minstrel stage shows. Patricia A. Turner, scholar of African American literature, states that the stage shows altered the complex image of Uncle Tom found in the novel by depicting Uncle Tom caricatures as "thoroughly subservient individuals who willingly betrayed their black brethren in order to please their white masters."[60] Even today, the stereotype remains effective as Uncle Tom is a name ascribed, for instance, to Black men considered overly supportive of conservative policies and social causes that are harmful to Black people (e.g., anti–affirmative action). But is that the real Uncle Tom?

Historian Wilson Jeremiah Moses contends that "the character of Uncle Tom was not originally intended to be pejorative."[61] He also suggests that those who hold a negative view of Tom have never read Stowe's novel.[62] There remains a great deal of debate about the novel and its main character. For example, considering its influence on minstrelsy, is the novel a racist or an antiracist text? Does the main character, the spirit-filled Christian slave, hurt or help the cause of Black liberation? Surveying the extensive literature on the debate regarding *Uncle Tom's Cabin* is beyond the scope of this study. Rather, I want to offer a different view of Uncle Tom as depicted in Stowe's novel: First, he did not display absolute obedience to his slave master, Simon Legree. Though instructed to do so by Legree, Uncle Tom, even to save his own life, would not commit violent acts against his fellow slaves. Second, due to his spirituality, Tom did not demonstrate absolute dependence on his slave master—evinced when he says, "My soul an't yours, mas'r. . . . It's been bought and paid for by the One that's able to keep it."[63] Finally, due to his beliefs, Uncle Tom was despised and ultimately murdered by those who most identified with and, by extension, sought to imitate Legree, his two "principal hands," the slaves Sambo and Quimbo.

Harriet Beecher Stowe provides the factual basis of her depiction of slavery in *A Key to Uncle Tom's Cabin.* As though presaging the thesis of Elkins's *Slavery*, Stowe tells of the slave master's desire for absolute power over the slave: "Only this office of master . . . contains the power to bind and loose, and to open and shut the kingdom of heaven, and involves responsibility for the soul as well as the body."[64] This incredible power, she claims, is often wielded by men without honor. "No Southern law requires any test of Character from the man to whom the absolute power of master is granted," writes Stowe.[65] Southern law supported malevolent slave masters, such as Legree, who used any method available in their attempt to achieve total control of their slaves. Stowe's diagnosis even assesses the slave master's poor spiritual condition: "How many souls of masters have been ruined through it! How has this absolute authority provoked and developed wickedness which otherwise might have been suppressed! How many have stumbled into everlasting perdition over this stumbling stone of IRRESPONSIBLE POWER!"[66]

During a telling episode in the novel, Legree, believing himself a deity, requires that Tom pay him obeisance. Legree shouts, "Now, Tom, get right down on yer knees and beg my pardon." Tom, refusing to kneel, responds, "I'll be a true and faithful servant to ye. I'll give ye all the work of my hands, all my time, all my strength; but my soul I won't give up to mortal man."[67] Tom, like so many other slaves, would not allow Legree to have *complete* authority over him. There were slaves, however, who did submit to the will of and were therefore absolutely dependent on the slave master.

Legree had two slaves named Sambo and Quimbo, and the novel attests that he "had trained them in savageness and brutality as systematically as he had his bulldogs; and, by long practice in hardness and cruelty, brought their whole nature to about the same range of capacities."[68] On the plantation, there was agreement, particularly among slaves, that those male slaves who had close relationships with the slave master were especially cruel toward fellow slaves. According to John Blassingame, these men were "called whip-ping men, overlooker, whipping boss, foreman, and overseer by the slaves" and were "generally described by bondsmen as being as 'mean as the devil.'"[69] The close relationship between Legree and his two most-trusted hands instilled within them a palpable hatred for anyone who failed to revere the slave master. Therefore, Sambo and Quimbo, the slaves closest to Legree, despised Uncle Tom. Legree tested the faithfulness of his slaves by having them commit acts of violence against one another. This facet of the Sambo type is not mentioned enough. Sambo, yes, was a minstrel figure, but when commanded to do so, he could also be violent, particularly in harming his fellow slaves. Just before the novel ends, Tom is chastised by Legree for not flogging a female slave named Lucy. When he purchased Tom, Legree hoped that he could make him into another trusted driver, a Sambo. But Tom's constant refusal to obey his master's commands comes to a head at the end of the novel. Tom was found ill-equipped for the position of overseer, first, for not flogging a fellow slave, and later on for not revealing the location of two runaway slaves, Casey and Emmeline. Though it is Legree who engages in a series of verbal battles with Tom, all of which end with Tom's voicing his unyielding faith in God's absolute redemptive power, the overseers, Sambo and Quimbo, are the ultimate "instruments of cruelty,"[70] for Legree's two trusted slaves kill Tom.

It is evident that, due to the infantilizing process of slavery, the Sambo, the perfect slave, as represented by Sambo and Quimbo in *Uncle Tom's Cabin*, desired the absolute power of the paternal father, the slave master. To achieve it, though, the Sambo must move from minstrelsy to murder. To be truly empowered, like his father on the plantation, the Sambo must rule over and destroy Black life.

BLACK MESSIAHS AND THE NEW NEGRO

The Sambo figure and its variants were not the only slave characters to emerge in the antebellum South. Blassingame mentions that Nat was depicted as the other side of Sambo. Whereas Sambo was quintessentially docile, Nat was "revengeful, bloodthirsty, cunning, treacherous, and savage."[71] The myth of Nat is based on the life of preacher and revolutionary Nat Turner, who had garnered fame for leading the most violent and successful slave revolt in U.S. history, as told in *The Confessions of Nat Turner*.[72] Before the Turner-led insur-rection, numerous slave revolts were inspired by the Haitian San Domingo revolt (1791–1804) led by general Toussaint Louverture as well as the revolt led by Denmark Vesey in 1822. Moreover, during the 1820s, the South was on edge because of a host of antislavery materials that included but was not limited to David Walker's *Appeal*, published in 1829. But nothing terrified the South's slave-owning class more than the Nat Turner rebellion. There was a supernatural element to Turner's rebellion that adds to the mythology of not only the event but the man himself. Scholar of African American literature William L. Andrews points out that before the start of the revolt on August 21, 1831, Turner (or Prophet Nat) received a series of "heavenly" visions between the years of 1825 and 1831. In the vision of May 12, Turner "learned of his *messianic* [italics mine] task: to 'fight against the Serpent' in the approaching eschaton."[73] These visions led to the violent acts that, when completed, left dozens of whites dead and, in Andrews's words, "traumatized the white South."[74] The symbol of Turner as "Prophet Nat" became a model for a type of Black manhood that was uncompromising in its pursuit of manhood rights. Wilson Jeremiah Moses contends the Nat Turner was "superficially reminiscent of the wrathful, retributive messiah."[75] The mythology of Turner as a Black messiah cannot be separated from the rise of millennialism in the South during the early 1800s.

James Moorhead, a scholar of American church history, shares that "under the slave regime, the spirituals promised deliverance and a final judgment when the last would be first."[76] African American history has been filled with figures, mostly men, who have been seen as messiahs, that is, modern-day deliverers who would save Black people from oppression. The biblical leader Moses, for instance, has been a source of inspiration for African Americans who likened their condition to that of the Israelites enslaved in Egypt. Moses is not a messiah figure, however. The hoped-for Black messiah is not just a deliverer but is also supposed to render God's final judgment by punishing those who oppress God's people. Black messianism was inspired by the Black folk hero who, according to historian Lawrence Levine, was able to manipulate those in power and reverse "as far as possible the normal structure of power and prestige."[77]

Wilson Jeremiah Moses suggests four different patterns of messianism: 1) "The expectation or identification of a personal savior—a messiah, a prophet, or a Mahdi [messianic figure in Islam]"; 2) "The far more important theme of racism messianism—a concept of the redemptive mission of the black race . . . the theme of *Uncle Tom's Cabin*"; 3) "Messianic symbolism—journalistic and artistic representations of certain black individuals as symbolic messiahs"; and 4) "'Prophetism' and 'prophetic movements'—anyone with a special mission from God."[78] Moses also defines *messianism* as "the perception of a person or group, by itself or by others, as having a manifest destiny or a God-given role to assert the providential goals of history and to bring about the kingdom of God on earth."[79] The Hebrews created the term *messiah* as a means to express their belief that a great deliverer would be sent to accomplish God's will on earth. Scholar of ancient religions Peter Schäfer finds that the Son of Man–Messiah "*fights* for this dominion and brings final redemption to the people of Israel."[80] The Son of Man–Messiah is described as a warrior who has come to engage in life-and-death battle with the enemies of God's people, and he is supernaturally equipped to do so. Though the Son of Man–Messiah engages in battle with the enemies of God's people, he himself is not an earthly figure. Schäfer proclaims that the Son of Man–Messiah is a "heavenly savior who from the beginning is hidden with God; although he acts on God's behalf, he virtually acts as God when his time has come."[81] But this creates a problem. Schäfer notes that the Son of Man–Messiah takes on tasks that are usually reserved for God. Even worse, due to his successful battles against Israel's oppressors, "rather than coming to God, the nations are now coming to the Messiah—or else the Messiah is God."[82]

In *The Black Messiah*, Christian minister and civil rights activist Albert B. Cleage Jr. is unwavering in his conviction that the Black Christ is the only messiah who would lead "a Black Nation to freedom."[83] There were undoubtedly exemplary leaders, such as Marcus Garvey, who had led Black nationalist movements, but Cleage did not uphold any of these leaders as the Black messiah. Nevertheless, distinguishing between the heavenly messiah and earthly Black messiah would be a recurring problem, particularly during an era when the struggle to achieve the freedom of Black people was being led by a new—some would say redeemed—Black manhood, the New Negro. Cultural historian Richard A. Long suggests that the New Negro evolved during the first three decades of "the twentieth century, receiving the most attention during the peak years of the Harlem Renaissance."[84] The New Negro sought to weaken the lingering effects of the negative stereotypes of Black men. In his 1924 essay "The New Negro," critic, educator, and philosopher Alain Locke contrasts the Old Negro and the New Negro. Describing the psychological transformation of the New Negro, Locke says, "The mind of the New Negro seems suddenly to have slipped from under the tyranny of social intimidation and to be shaking off the psychology of *imitation* [italics mine] and implied inferiority."[85] No longer, Locke attests, would the New Negro devoutly mimic the ways of the white world but would achieve something new, which Locke likens to a "spiritual emancipation."[86] Locke goes on to infuse his claim with the language of messianism when he says that this new era comes with "the promise and warrant of a new leadership."[87] These new leaders are to receive the respect and, in some instances, admiration of the oppressed masses awaiting deliverance. The absolutely dependent figures of the past are gone, as Locke alleges that the "day of 'aunties,' 'uncles,' and 'mammies' is equally gone. . . . Uncle Tom and Sambo have passed on."[88]

Historian August Meier underscores the radical nature and protest orientation of the New Negro—the Black race's new ideal. In "The Social and Intellectual Origins of the New Negro," Meier provides a statement about the New Negro from Leslie Pinckney Hill of the Cheyney Institute (now the Cheyney University of Pennsylvania), who remarks that this new leader must spare no effort to achieve "full untrammeled American citizenship, or go down in the midst of a glorious warfare for it."[89] Historian Leon F. Litwack remarks that "if the image of a New Negro brought pride to many blacks as a sign of the race's regeneration, that same image frightened whites into thoughts of racial degeneration. . . . Worst of all the New Negro violated white expectations of black people, confounding their feelings of superiority, and violated stereotypes long assimilated into the white psyche."[90] Most frightening of all, the New Negro possessed a manhood that whites feared, one that had "lost in large measure the traditional and wholesome awe of the white race which kept the Negroes in subjection."[91] Various character types were prominent in the protest literature created by the New Negro, but no one represented this new manhood more than the Black political leader, the race man, the embodiment of the Black messiah.

Because no one person is the model of Black leadership, there are potentially a multitude of Black messiahs. Political scientists Ronald W. Walters and Robert C. Smith contend that there are, in fact, several leadership types. The authors begin with economist Gunnar Myrdal's two-fold construct of Black leaders who were either accommodationist or protest oriented.[92] In surveying other studies on Black leadership Walters and Smith discovered that a number of studies done in the 1960s categorized leaders using such labels as *liberal, moderate, conservative, radical, Uncle Tom,* and *race men.*[93] The authors suggest that coming to a finalized classification of the Black leader is difficult, however, because so much of the leader's approach depends on how he is perceived by whites. Furthermore, the authors support political scientist Everett Carll Ladd's argument that "the limits and contents of the styles are determined by prevailing patterns of race relations which vary with time and place."[94] Complexifying the Black leadership typology in this manner is important because it demonstrates that a person can be viewed as a Black militant in the white community and, at the same time, as an Uncle Tom in the Black community. Walters and Smith also underscore a dichotomy in Black leadership, evident in the difference between individual and collective leadership. The individual leader is, in essence, the Black messiah type, represented by such figures as Frederick Douglass, Booker T. Washington, W. E. B. Du Bois, and Marcus Garvey. Conversely, in collective leadership, groups of men and women come together to form organizations to address the oppression of Black people. Although collective leadership has maintained a pivotal role in the fight for equality, the spotlight has always been on the individual leader. The oppressed Black masses, some believe, need a Black leader, a Black messiah.

The religious overtones of the Black leader's role, most notably within the Black church, cannot be ignored, a point emphasized by Christian ethicist Peter J. Paris, who contends that "black churches constituted the primary agency for the development of social cohesion and social organization in the Black community . . . they nurtured, trained, and launched virtually every credible Black leader."[95] Paris, too, rejects the notion that there exists one model within the Black-religious-leader tradition. Rather, he suggests there are four ideal types: priestly, prophetic, political, and nationalist.[96] No matter the type, the leader is expected not only to motivate the Black masses to fight for change but also to present the community's interests to the dominant political structure. The leader's role, especially during the era of the New Negro, went far deeper than political leadership, however. He was to represent the best of the race. For example, in providing remarks on the death of Frederick Douglass, the Presbyterian minister Francis James Grimke implored the Black race to "stand up for a pure leadership; honor the men, and the men only, whose character you can respect, and whose example you can command to your children."[97] Martin Luther King Jr. also expressed the need for exemplary Black male leadership when he stated, "God give us leaders . . . leaders who can stand before a demagogue and his treacherous flatteries without winking! Tall leaders, sun crowned, who live above the fog in public duty and private thinking."[98] Nothing was more of an indicator of the Black leader's messianic qualifications than his manhood. In fact, there was something redemptive about the attainment of this cherished manhood.

In *My Bondage and My Freedom*, Frederick Douglass shares the story of his encounter with his owner Edward Covey, referred to as the Negro-breaker. In a letter written from Scotland in 1846 to abolitionist William Lloyd Garrison, Douglass states that the conditions on Covey's plantation were so terrible that "[his] soul was crushed and [his] spirits broken."[99] But something happened that changed Douglass. Douglass discusses his miraculous transformation from the enslaved "ordinary Negro," Frederick Bailey, to the freeman Frederick Douglass, who was a new, empowered man.[100] What brought about this transformation? Douglass confesses that his battle with Covey was the turning point in his life because, through violent confrontation with his master, he received "a sense of [his] own manhood."[101] He goes on to claim, "I was a changed being after that fight. I was nothing before; I WAS A MAN NOW."[102] Douglass likens the acquisition of his slave master's power-filled manhood to a redemptive religious conversion:

A man, without force, is without the essential dignity of humanity. Human nature is so constituted, that it cannot honor a helpless man, although it can pity him; and even this it cannot do long, if the signs of power do not arise. . . . After resisting him [Covey], I felt as I had never felt before. It was a resurrection from the dark and pestiferous tomb of slavery to the heaven of comparative freedom. I was no longer a servile coward, trembling under the frown of a brother worm of the dust, but my long-cowed spirit was roused to an attitude of manly independence.[103]

One must not forget that three years prior to his fight with Covey, Douglass, at the age of thirteen, had experienced a "change of heart which comes by . . . having faith in Jesus Christ."[104] But was he truly born again? After this conversion, the young Douglass began to see "the world in a new light."[105] His later testimonial suggests that this early conversion to Christianity did not give Douglass what he desired most: the slave master's manhood. Historian John David Smith argues that "[Douglass's] confrontation with Covey released Douglass from the chains suppressing his will and identity and gave him self-confidence to act on his own regardless of the circumstances."[106] Douglass biographer S. William McFeely maintains that Douglass's victory over Covey was not his alone but rather, given his antislavery audience, was "on behalf of the cause."[107] It was a victory for the Black race. Douglass's message of redemptive manhood would become the leitmotif for Black leaders who wanted to protest the oppression of Black people. From then on, acquiring a power-full manhood would be associated with authentic liberation. Only a true man was free. But this, too, proved problematic for Black manhood, as it constructed a model overvaluing a patriarchal, violence-laden, and overly self-reliant form of manhood.

THE CHARISMATIC RULE

In order to demand the devotion of his followers, the Black messiah must be charismatic. Sociologist Max Weber defines *charisma* as "a certain quality of an individual's personality which is considered extraordinary and treated as endowed with supernatural, superhuman, or exceptional powers and qualities."[108] Charisma endows leaders with undeniable messianic qualities in that their characteristics "are not accessible to the ordinary person, but are regarded as of divine origin . . . and on the basis of them the individual concerned is treated as the leader."[109] Weber contends that it doesn't matter whether or not the leader actually possesses these qualities but that "followers" or "disciples" believe in the person's charismatic authority.[110] Charismatic leaders are not assured of their status, however. Proof of their heroic powers must be reaffirmed and reasserted continuously. Weber notes that "if proof and success elude the leader for long, if he appears deserted by god . . . if his leadership fails to benefit his followers, it is likely that his charismatic authority will disappear."[111]

In order to maintain power, the charismatic leader engages in what Weber terms *charismatic domination*, done in three phases.[112] First, the charismatic leader is to be followed because of extraordinary capacities that create an inner devotion in the leader's disciples. Second, the charismatic leader is able to mobilize followers because the leader's message is associated with revolutionary change (a radical break with the past), which makes the charismatic leader very appealing during times of crisis. The third phase is when charisma must undergo a change due to an external circumstance and adjust to the everyday needs of its followers (e.g., the question of succession). An additional type of charismatic domination must be considered when discussing the Black messiah. That is, the Black messiah as the *Rule*, a calibrated Doryphoros, must be emulated by his followers. Hence, there arose a firm belief, almost a doctrine, that if one truly wanted to be free, then one must attain the supernatural manhood of the charismatic leader, the Black messiah.

Literary scholar Erica R. Edwards argues that within Black social movements there has long existed the idea that "freedom is best achieved under the direction of a single charismatic leader."[113] Focusing on the single charismatic leader, the Black messiah, such as Frederick Douglass, Malcolm X, Martin Luther King Jr., or Huey Newton, "reduces a heterogenous black freedom struggle to a top-down narrative of Great Man leadership."[114] Edwards's careful analysis of the dangers of Great Man leadership in Black social movements is instructive, but it is her focus on the damage that it does to Black men that is most relevant to this study. Charisma, Edwards says, is "a mode of representation, a figural process that works precisely as a masculinist mode of inscription and ascription—charismatic leadership is written violently on the masculine as much as it is represented against the feminine." She then adds that it is "a prescription for men . . . to prescribe mean[ing] to freeze in representation."[115] Unfortunately, it is an outmoded and ineffective model of Black manhood that remains influential for far too many, even today.

For instance, in *Visions for Black Men*, Afrocentric psychologist Na'im Akbar states that his vision "of the black man is going to be defined by a group of unquestionable *models* [italics mine] of black manhood."[116] Akbar is confident that these models are to be emulated because "if we want to begin to understand how to be African American men . . . they have ideas and aspects and qualities which are worthy of imitation."[117] Included in Akbar's pantheon of exemplary Black men are Martin Luther King Jr., a man of courage; the

Honorable Elijah Muhammad, a man of defiance and self-determination; Booker T. Washington, a man who had a strategy for economic development; Paul Robeson, a man of integrity; and Cheikh Anta Diop, a man of immense scholarship.[118] My critique of Akbar's argument here is not that the Black men he has chosen are not to be admired but rather that he designates them as sufficient models of Black manhood. This is not Akbar's fault alone. Activist and actor Ossie Davis, for example, extols the manhood virtues of Malcolm X. Davis says that Malcolm X "was always the rarest thing in the world among us Negroes: a true man."[119] Elsewhere Davis claims that "Malcolm spoke directly to the emasculation of the black male in particular. . . . He wanted to teach us how, in spite of that, to be men again."[120]

Though there were numerous women, such as civil rights activist Ella Baker,who condemned the patriarchal ethos modeled by Black male leadership, some women remained captivated by the charismatic manhood of certain Black leaders. For example, poet and activist Sonia Sanchez admired Malcolm X's ability to speak in a "very manly fashion" and also shared that he "became the man that most African American women have wanted their man to be: strong."[121] *But is there anything truly new about this model of Black manhood?* Those who have become disillusioned with the often patriarchal and paternalistic manhood of these models discover that this new manhood still mimics the destructive manhood of the purported only true man in America, described by Goffman as the "only . . . complete unblushing male in America"[122]: the perfect American white male.

FROM AN OLD MODEL TO A NEW MODE

What happened to the Black messiah? Political scientist Robert C. Smith observes that the peak of the Black messiah's reign lasted between 1905 to 1968, an era that coincided with several peaks and troughs of Black nationalism. However, in Smith's estimation, "by 1980 the radical wing of the [civil rights] movement was in disarray and retreat, and the historic black freedom struggle was largely co-opted into routine institutions and processes of American political life."[123] Essential to the demise of the Black messiah is, according to Smith, the way in which co-option compromises and weakens leadership. Smith defines *co-option* as the "process of absorbing new elements into the leadership-determining structure of an organization as a means of avoiding threats to its stability."[124] Smith identifies two types of co-option: formal and informal. Formal co-option occurs when the dominant system offers an attractive benefit to tempt the public figure who is a threat to the established order.

An example of this form of co-option is W. E. B. Du Bois's being offered a position in the United States Military Intelligence. Joel E. Spingarn, the man who approached Du Bois with the offer, desired to recruit African American agents "to win the war for democracy in Europe and for civil rights in America."[125] The result of Du Bois's co-option was his writing the now-infamous "Close Ranks" editorial, in which says,

> We of the colored race have no ordinary interest in the outcome. That which the German power represents today spells death to the aspirations of Negroes and all the darker races for equality, freedom, and democracy. Let us not hesitate. *Let us, while this war lasts, forget our special grievances and close our ranks shoulder to shoulder with our white fellow citizens and the allied nations that are fighting for democracy* [italics mine]. We make no ordinary sacrifice, but we make it gladly and willingly with our eyes lifted to the hills.[126]

It's hard to accept that these words are from the same person who ten years prior wrote in "The Color Line Belts the World" that "we have a way in America of wanting to be 'rid' of problems," particularly "our most sinister social problem, the Negro."[127] Therein, Du Bois states that it is "dangerous, because it fails to realize the most significant fact of the opening century. . . . [that] the Negro problem in America is but a local phase of a world problem."[128] But that is what he is requesting Black people do in "Close Ranks"—that is, to "forget our special grievances."

The reaction to Du Bois's remarks was swift and harsh. A scathing rebuke was given by writer and political activist Hubert Harrison, who underscored that Du Bois had demonstrated an immense failure of leadership—or, one could argue, failed in his role as the Black messiah. "Dr. Du Bois has failed," Harrison writes, "and neither his ungrateful attack on Emmett Scott nor his belated discovery of Wilsonian hypocrisy will, we fear, enable him to climb back into the saddle of race leadership."[129] For Harrison, though, Du Bois's hypocrisy was only a symptom of a more significant disease plaguing Black leadership: the dominant structure's approving who is a qualified leader for Black people. Harrison does not approve of the "good white friends who are selecting our Negro leaders."[130] August Meier uses the language of co-option when describing the leadership role of Martin Luther King Jr.: "King thus gives white men the feeling that he is their good friend, that he poses no threat to them."[131] This was essential to King's "sustaining his image as a leader of heroic moral stature in the eyes of white men."[132] By the end of the civil rights era, there had been several Black messiahs, but the promised redemption of the Black race had not occurred. Yet the Black messiah model remains influential. However, some Black men proclaim that what is needed is not a model but a new mode of Black manhood.

Rudolph P. Byrd, a scholar of African American literature, finds a new mode of Black masculinity in the African American folklore figure High John the Conqueror. John is committed to liberation and survival. He is a hope bringer. John is not trapped within patriarchal forms of sexuality and is independent without sacrificing relationships. John is open to change and improvisation. Byrd maintains that this mode of Black masculinity "potentially poses the greatest danger to empires, in whatever form and whatever place, as well as to the fossilized notions of Black masculinity."[133] John is portrayed as a "redemptive and transgressive" figure in the writings of anthropologist and novelist Zora Neal Hurston. In Byrd's interpretation of Hurston, he finds an example by which Black men can develop the spiritual resources to overcome obstacles, or "make a way out of no way."[134] Manhood in the tradition of John cannot affix itself to an existing model of manhood. "There is no established picture of what sort of looking man this John de Conqueror was," notes Hurston.[135] He was a figure always open to transformation, always open to improvised ways of being. It was necessary for John as he was the "supreme antagonist of 'Old Mass' and the various hegemonic structures he and his descendants have created."[136] John, then, is the antithesis of the pervasive model of dominative patriarchal manhood. According to Byrd, "such a masculinity is mired in the slavery of misogyny that prizes the outmoded but still powerful values of patriarchy."[137] Byrd's argument, though convincing, still leaves one questioning if emulating John is the answer to the problematic manhood of African American men. Does John "meet the exigencies of modern forms of slavery by which many of us are trapped"?[138] Probably not. But that is why John is a mode, not a model, of Black masculinity. John is not supposed to be the answer. Instead, John inspires African American men to search for more ways of being human than he alone could ever provide.

2

The Hero's Sorrow

A Gift Not Yet Unwrapped

A hero is a man who stands up manfully against his father
and in the end victoriously overcomes him.
—*Sigmund Freud*[1]

THE RAGE OF A HOPELESS SON

The previous chapter's discussion regarding insufficient models of manhood
continues in this chapter but now with a focus on the most-significant model
of manhood in a man's life: the father. Of course, there are countless stories written by not only men of renown but also men of little reputation, in
works of fiction and nonfiction, telling of fathers who failed to live up to their
sons' expectations; and, doubtless, these fathers failed for various reasons. For
example, there are sons who believed that their fathers were never truly alive.
The father was, so to speak, a dead man walking. For instance, German com-
poser Karlheinz Stockhausen's memories of his father were of a man who, as
he states, "just wanted to die."[2] From the son's purview, the father had given
himself wholeheartedly to the German military, serving in various wars, all
at the expense of developing his own sense of self-worth. "My father," says
Stockhausen, "had talent and it was unrealized."[3] But more than this, Stockhausen recalls his father's failings as a father, which is encapsulated in the last
time he saw his father, who said, "I won't come back [home]; now take care
of yourself."[4] What was Stockhausen's reaction to this? He states with an
uncanny self-assurance that "the more that was taken away from me [by his
father's abandonment and later death] the stronger I became."[5] Stockhausen
was convinced that he could make something of himself, find his own way in
the world, all on his own, without his father.

Not every story depicts a son's valiant triumph over the failed father, however. Other sons confess that their father, particularly the model of manhood he exemplified, was far too powerful to overcome. In "Letter to His Father" novelist Franz Kafka writes the following about his relationship with his father: "I am afraid of you. . . . I have always hidden from you, in my room, among my books, with crazy friends, or with crackpot ideas." Throughout the letter Kafka notes the many ways his father was "too strong" for him, mainly due to his father's intellectual and physical superiority. In the end, so as to not be overwhelmed by his father's power, Kafka had to escape from his family. But this move resulted in a great loss. Kafka says to his father, "Not only did I lose my family feeling, as you say; on the contrary, I did indeed have a feeling about the family, mostly in a negative sense, concerned with the breaking away from you (which, of course, could never be done completely)."[6] Kafka's escape included a failed attempt to find refuge in Judaism, but it was, in the end, the Judaism of his father, which was for Kafka, given his father's example of religious life, a "mere nothing, a joke," a religious tradition that the son wanted to be rid of as soon as possible.[7] The father's religion, on the son's observation, was used to cement his position of authority within society and, most specifically, within the Kafka household, and nothing more. It was not a religion that facilitated a spiritual kinship between father and son but one that moved Kafka further away from his father, turning him inward to find refuge in his most cherished possession, something that he himself could truly trust: his writing.

Melvin R. Lansky, a psychiatrist specializing in family systems theory, argues that our desire for fathering has a unique characteristic in that it is related to a "wish to master the world and to face challenges."[8] Therefore, when a son cries out, "I want my father," what is hoped for is a sense of control over what is perceived as a chaotic or intrusive environment "rather than a more regressive wish to be cared for and exempted from responsibility that is connected with a wish for mothering."[9] This need for the father or, more to the point, fathering underscores the son's sense of vulnerability in the face of a daunting task, which for a man is the recognition that he is, in fact, a man, even a heroic man. Pastoral theologian James Dittes notes that there are religious dimensions to the quest for manhood that are often ignored. According to Dittes, "To deem a man religious is to claim his serious earnest engagement with the potentials and the limitations of the human experience."[10] Men are engaged in a constant quest to encounter and overcome the horizons of their given experiences, but they cannot do this alone. Dittes suggests that a man needs fathering: "A full term of sonship is the right of every male, son to a father—genuine sonship, not apprenticeship for fatherhood, not a junior manhood, most urgently not a pretend manhood."[11] Without the gift of an authentic sonship, men are left anxious, always worrying if someone, whether a stranger or a loved one, will discover they have never achieved manhood. Another harmful result of the loss of sonship is that a man becomes "a patriarch . . . [who] tries too hard, works too hard, frets too much, commands too much, judges himself (and others) too cruelly."[12] The man without sonship is extremely cruel when judging his father.

This chapter uses the life histories of psychoanalyst Sigmund Freud and writer Richard Wright in order to explore the damaging effect that giftlessness has on a son's life. Neither Freud nor Wright had fathers who could provide their sons with a sense of mastery over the world or an ability to face life's challenges; moreover, the needed experience of sonship was absent. Rather, these sons viewed their fathers as unheroic, that is, as fathers who model what it means to be defeated by the world, unable to meet life's challenges in a heroic manner. Worst of all, Freud and Wright held that their only means of achieving a heroic status of their own was to defeat and, in some instances, terminate their fathers. The act of patricide is the root of Freud's well-known Oedipus-complex theory, which Dittes refers to as the "epitome of the male experience, the prototypical man in [Freud's] canon."[13] The danger, however, particularly for young Black men, is that it perpetuates a cycle of overvalued (and, in many instances, sacralized) self-reliance that denigrates the need for the gift of sonship, especially in a man's life-long quest for identity, independence, and, most of all, hope. Lansky warns that this intergenerational cycle creates failed fathers who maintain a fantasy of power by attempting to control the world through violence but who are themselves "prone to shame, narcissistic vulnerability and proneness to humiliation"[14] These are men who gain "power by rage and intimidation rather than generativity and guidance."[15] For Freud and Wright, this rage was turned toward the person who had failed them the most: the father. Nevertheless, in the end, it was also turned toward anyone who demanded filial piety—the duty of a faithful son—whether it be an earthly father or the Father in heaven. The absence of the hope granted by sonship leaves a man with what Dittes terms "the sorrow of incompleteness," as though his life were "a gift not yet unwrapped."[16]

FREUD'S SEARCH FOR A HERO

On January 29, 1936, Sigmund Freud, the progenitor of psychoanalysis, penned an open letter to celebrate his dear friend Romain Rolland's seventieth birthday. Rolland was an accomplished French novelist who, in 1925, won the Nobel Prize for literature. Historian and Freud biographer Peter Gay reports that the two men had maintained a "cordial, mutually admiring correspondence since 1923."[17] Most of their conversations, it seems, were centered on religion. Rolland suggested to Freud that the source of religion was a "particular feeling" that provided a "sensation of eternity . . . a feeling of something boundless, as it were, oceanic."[18] Needless to say, Freud, who often referred to himself as a godless Jew, would not admit that he had ever experienced such feelings. Nevertheless, Freud did agree that, in the development of culture, human beings did develop various "oceanic" devices to help us deal with and, at times, escape the challenges of everyday life. He discusses this idea in his book *The Future of an Illusion*.[19] Discussions on religion aside, Freud had a deep admiration for Rolland as a truth seeker and a writer, as expressed in the letter when he writes,

> My Dear Friend,
> I have been urgently pressed to make some written contribution to the celebration of your seventieth birthday and I have made long efforts to find something that might in some sense be worthy of you and might give expression to my admiration for your love of the truth, for your courage in your beliefs and for your affection and devotion towards humanity; or, again, something that might bear witness to my gratitude towards you as a writer who has afforded me so many moments of exaltation and pleasure.[20]

After adorning Rolland with a garland of praise, Freud shifts attention to himself by providing a synopsis of what he and his admirers deem his most admirable quality: the creation of psychoanalysis.

Freud asserts that the "aim of [his] scientific work was to throw light upon unusual, abnormal or pathological manifestations of the mind—that is to say, to trace them back to the psychological forces operating behind them and to indicate the mechanisms at work."[21] Freud's discovery of psychoanalysis was an isolated and intrapersonal endeavor: "I began by attempting this [psychoanalysis] upon myself and then went on to apply it to other people and finally, by a bold extension, to the human race as a whole."[22] But much remained a mystery to Freud regarding his own mind. Even at the advanced age of eighty, he remained perplexed by an unresolved problem. It was a deeply personal issue that required further self-analysis. Freud tells Rolland that "during the last few years, a phenomenon of this sort, which I had experienced a generation ago, in 1904, and which I had never understood, has kept recurring to my mind."[23] The pivotal event is described to Rolland in this very letter. The first decade of the twentieth century was a time of great accomplishment for Freud. Though the *Interpretation of Dreams* had drawn the attention of admirers when it was published in 1899, Freud's fame increased immensely during the following period due to the publication of several manuscripts: *The*

Psychopathology of Everyday Life (1901), *Three Essays on the Theory of Sexuality* (1905), *Jokes and Their Relation to the Unconscious* (1905), to name a few. In addition to these major works, Freud also published three significant case histories: "Dora Case" (1905), "Little Hans" (1909), and "Rat Man" (1909). His immense output proved that Freud was committed to making a contribution that would change the scientific and cultural attitudes of the Westernized world. These external successes belied an inner turmoil, however. Psychoanalyst and Freud biographer Max Schur suggests that Freud's deteriorating relationship with his friend Wilhelm Fliess, a physician, was causing him great distress. Schur states that "it is not surprising that Freud's self-analysis during this whole period was still related to his complex relationship with Fliess."[24]

Complexes were not only integral to how Freud interpreted the mind; complexes—Oedipus and otherwise—were also essential to his interpersonal relationships. "An intimate friend and a hated foe have always been necessary to my emotional life; I have always been able to create for myself fresh embodiments of both, and not infrequently my childhood ideal went so far that friend and foe coincided in the same person," writes Freud in *The Interpretation of Dreams*.[25] Freud declares that his adult relationships with friends are, in his words, "incarnations" of his childhood love-hate relationships with family members. No other person was more important to Freud's emotional life during his adult years than Wilhelm Fliess, but it was a complex relationship. Fliess was more than a friend—he was a father figure. And in the end, as their relationship deteriorated, Freud viewed Fliess just as he did any father representation: an enemy to be defeated.

There were notable similarities between the two men. For one, Freud and Fliess were both Jews who faced a hostile anti-Semitic environment in fin-de-siècle Vienna. Cultural historian Carl E. Schorske explains that increased ideological and class antagonism had created "virulent nationalism and Christian socialism" among the lower middle class and peasantry.[26] All this led to the 1895 election of avowed anti-Semite politician Karl Lueger. Schorske says that all of this was "a stunning blow to the bearers of liberal culture, Jew and Gentile. The forces of racial prejudice and national hatred, which they had thought dispelled by the light of reason and the rule of law, reemerged in terrifying force as the 'century of progress' breathed its last."[27] Freud believed that this racially hostile environment was holding him back professionally. In *The Interpretation of Dreams*, he shares the story of two colleagues being denied promotion at the University of Vienna because of "religious considerations" (i.e., their Jewishness) and Freud's realizing that, eventually, he, too, would be denied for the same reason.[28] Wilhelm Fliess, however, seemed to thrive in this environment. Fliess represented, in many ways, what Freud wanted to become—but couldn't. Fliess was a man of science, a true man of the West, and was respected by his peers. Peter Gay remarks that Fliess's "scientific learning was wide-ranging and his scientific ambition vast; he impressed others . . . with his appearance, his cultivation, his erudition."[29] Fliess also provided Freud with a father figure, an object of his affection, which he had desired since his youth. Gay says, "Fliess was precisely the intimate he needed: audience, confidant, stimulus, cheerleader, fellow spectator shocked at nothing."[30]

Freud was fascinated with Fliess. His attitude toward him bordered on hero worship. There is ample evidence in early letters between the two to prove the point. Of particular interest is a series of letters written between November 24, 1887, and September 13, 1894. Jeffrey Moussaieff Masson, editor of the Freud-Fliess letters, argues that these letters mark the beginning and intensification of the friendship between the two men. For example, in a letter dated August 1, 1890, Freud tells Fliess, "When I talked with you and saw that you thought well of me, I even used to think something of myself, and the picture of absolutely convincing energy that you offered was not without its effect on me."[31] As the relationship became more intense, so too did Freud's appreciation of the uncanny intimacy between the two, evident in a letter written in May 1894 in which, according to Peter Gay, Freud refers to Fliess as "the only Other . . . the alter."[32] Certainly, the letters covered a host of topics—ranging from Freud's ruminations about patients, his new theories, and even his smoking habits—but, for the most part, they were expressions of Freud's overwhelming affection for Fliess. On January 1, 1896, he writes,

> Your kind should not die out, my dear friend; the rest of us need people like you too much. How much I owe you: solace, understanding, stimulation in my loneliness, meaning to my life that I gained though you, and finally even health that no one can give back to me. It is primarily through your example that intellectually I gained the strength to trust my own judgement, even when I am left alone—though not by you—and, like you, to face with lofty humility all the difficulties that the future may bring. For all that, accept my humble thanks! *I know that you do not need me as much as I need you, but I also know that I have a secure place in your affection* [italics mine].[33]

Freud was immensely private. He destroyed countless documents in an attempt to keep his secrets hidden from others. Peter Gay contends that, though regarded as one of his more self-revealing texts, *The Interpretation of Dreams* is evidence of a clash within Freud between "self-revelation and self-protection."[34] Confessions of his own dependency—his need for an intimate relationship—are seldom found in Freud's oeuvre. It is why his letters to Fliess are so profound. They are an avowed declaration of filial piety. Fliess was the heroic father Freud desired.

JACOB (RE-) INTERRED

Clinical psychologist and Freud biographer Peter M. Newton provides compelling evidence that Freud attempted to maintain the "secure affection" of Fliess not only through letters but also through a series of one-on-one encounters or, as they referred to them, congresses.[35] Twenty meetings between the two occurred between 1887 and 1904, the bulk of which, about fourteen, occurred between 1894 and 1900.[36] During those six years, when the frequency of congresses increased, two life-changing events occurred in Freud's life: 1) the death of his father, Jacob Freud, in 1896; and 2) the publication of *The Interpretation of Dreams* in 1899. Freud seldom expressed immense grief over the death of Jacob Freud, but in the preface to the second edition of *The Interpretation of Dreams*, published in 1908, he confesses that a father's death is "the most significant event, the most decisive loss, of a man's life."[37] Given his grief, it is understandable that Freud sought out the secure affection of Fliess, who was a trusted companion during this challenging time of personal loss. Above all, Fliess provided the intellectual and emotional support Freud needed during the development of the revolutionary science of psychoanalysis. Fliess, and in many instances Fliess alone, gave Freud fathering, in the abovementioned way that Melvin Lansky uses the term—that is to say, by giving Freud the confidence to pursue theories and practices considered outside the bounds of normative medical inquiry and practice. As Freud was advancing controversial ideas on the relationship between sexuality and neurosis, Fliess had already put forth arguments that "sexual disturbances could manifest themselves in the nose . . . in fact, according to Fliess, some nasal troubles stemmed from neurasthenia, a disorder he . . . believed was due to sexual abuse."[38] Such theories have led many to question how Freud could have been so captivated by Fliess, whom Peter Newton refers to as a "crackpot."[39]

The Emma Eckstein tragedy, which occurred in 1895, is a telling example of just how much Freud willingly ignored Fliess's incompetence as a physician. Eckstein was a patient of Freud's who suffered from hysterical anxiety symptoms and bloody secretions from her nose. Though Freud thought that her symptoms were caused by psychological disorders, he still requested that Fliess examine her in case there was a biological reason for her illness. Given that Fliess's conviction that the nose, not the mind, was the source of neurosis, he viewed Eckstein's blood secretions as proof that a nose operation—not psychoanalysis—was the only solution. The operation was a total disaster. Eckstein experienced severe hemorrhaging from her nose due to Fliess's "inadvertently leaving a half-meter strip of iodoform gauze" in her nasal cavity.[40] Eckstein had to undergo numerous reparative surgeries, all while experiencing "persistent pain, fetid secretions, and some bleeding."[41] Schur reports that Fliess departed for Berlin immediately after the operation in February of 1895, leaving Freud alone to deal with the results, most of all the guilt and shame, of the botched operation.[42] It was so bad that Freud attempted to work out the trauma of the event unconsciously through a dream, now referred to as the "Irma dream." In the dream Freud admits that he may have "over-looked an organic illness after all," thus confirming, through his interpretation of the dream, his previous need for Fliess's expertise.[43] Freud also finds that the dream is used to absolve himself of any guilt for Eckstein's condition.

> The last part of the dream has for its content the idea that the patient's pains derive from a serious organic infection. I sense that all I want with this is to shift the blame from myself. The psychological treatment cannot be held responsible for the persistence of a diphtheritic condition. But I still feel troubled at having invented for Irma a serious illness wholly and solely to exonerate myself. It seems so cruel.[44]

Freud also sought to absolve Fliess of any blame as well. In a letter written on May 17, 1896, more than a year after the operation, Freud suggests that Eckstein's ongoing poor condition is all her fault. "She had always been a bleeder, when cutting herself and in similar circumstances; as a child she suffered from severe nosebleeds," writes Freud.[45] The worst of Freud's allegations against Eckstein was when he alleges that she "had an old wish to be loved in her illness."[46] Simply stated, Freud suggests that Eckstein was using her sickness to be romantically involved with him; thus he reports, "She renewed the bleedings, as an unfailing means of arousing my affection."[47]

Freud was willing to do anything, even something immoral, to remain Fliess's beloved son. Peter Gay contends that Freud was "caught in a severe transference relationship with Fliess."[48] Psychoanalysts Bernard Fine and Burness Moore define *transference* as "the displacement of patterns of feelings and behavior, originally experienced with significant figures in one's childhood, to individuals in one's current relationship."[49] They also comment that "parents are usually the original figures from whom such emotional patterns are displaced."[50] In his 1912 essay "The Dynamics of Transference," Freud suggests that transference is usually related to one's libidinal attachment to the father imago, an infantile imago (or image). Freud, however, viewed this as occurring in the analyst-analysand (or physician-patient) relationship whereas Fine and Moore's definition suggests that transference is not restricted to the patient-physician relationship. It can occur with anyone, which is apparent in the relationship between Freud and Fliess. Freud "idealized Fliess beyond measure," and even though Fliess was two years younger than Freud, he was the one to whom Freud "poured out his innermost secrets."[51]

Fliess's most significant contribution to Freud was his unwavering and unrivaled support of Freud's unconventional theories when they were being rejected by the scientific community and those closest to him. Peter Gay states that Freud's family was not supportive of his scientific endeavors; for example, Freud's wife, Martha Bernays, thought them "a form of pornography."[52] Isolated from the scientific community and misunderstood by his family, Freud could always turn to Fliess. "The family did not assuage his dismaying sense of isolation," writes Gay, "that was Fliess's task."[53] Fliess's affection, his fathering, was a trusted citadel that protected Freud against the criticisms of the outside world and gave him a sense of control over the chaotic theories floating about within his own mind. Fliess was his secure base. But, as Freud eventually discovered, Fleiss's affection would not last forever.

It ended the way it started, with a letter. Freud's colleague Ernest Jones, a psychoanalyst who founded the British Psychoanalytic Society, claims that the letter, written on January 27, 1904, was an indictment claiming that Freud had not given sufficient credit to Fliess for the theory of bisexuality.[54] After some back and forth, Freud finally admitted, in a letter written on July 27, 1904, that Fliess has "always (since 1901) been the author of the idea of bisexuality."[55] Nothing changed, however. Fliess's letter served as his formal declaration that their relationship had fallen apart, and Freud was powerless to put it back together. Ernst Jones observes that Freud admitted he "must have been influenced by his wish to rob Fliess of his originality, a wish presumably compounded of envy and hostility."[56] There were signs, though, that Fliess had been breaking away from Freud long before this letter. For instance, in the letter, Freud provides evidence that communication between the two had slowed considerably, hence the following remark: "The fact is that *in the past few years* [italics mine] . . . you have no longer showed an interest in me or my family or my work."[57] But Freud, rather than show his desire to maintain the relationship, affirms his independence, declaring, "By now I have gotten over it [i.e., Fliess's secure affection] and have little desire for it any longer; I am not reproaching you and ask you not to reply to this point."[58] Put another way, Freud tells Fliess, "I don't need you anymore!" Overall, the most disingenuous part of the letter is that Freud attempts to deny how important Fliess was to his personal development. Fliess was with Freud, supporting his theories and affirming his genius, when few others were. Now the relationship was over.

Ernst Jones claims that the relationship started to deteriorate during the final Freud-Fliess congress (or meeting), held in the summer of 1900 in Munich. Though the particulars about the congress are not provided by Jones, he suggests that after Freud offered some criticism of Fliess's "periodic law" theory, Fliess criticized Freud's own expertise as a psychoanalyst, alleging that he "read his own thoughts into his patients."[59] Such a statement was not only a resounding rejection of Freud as a scientist but even more so of psychoanalysis as a science. Freud, in his own way, also began to move away from Fliess. He had abandoned the seduction theory,[60] which was influenced by Fliess's views of sexuality, for the Oedipus complex. Schorske provides a compelling analysis of the ways in which Freud's theoretical shift was due to his rebellion against authority. According to Schorske, the unfolding drama of his rebellion occurred in three acts: professional, political, and personal. His professional rebellion was caused by his long wait—seventeen years in total—to secure a professorship at the University of Vienna. His political rebellion was caused by the above-mentioned election of Karl Lueger in 1895, which was only a part of the rise of a New Right across Europe, all but securing an official platform for anti-Semitic rhetoric and, more damaging, policies. His personal rebellion centered on the death of his father, which, according to Schorske, awakened in Freud "a crisis of professional failure and political guilt."[61]

Freud's theory of the Oedipus complex was his attempt, first through self-analysis, to resolve these crises. But it required his father, who died in 1895, to die once more in a psychological act of patricide. And Fliess's rejection of Freud was necessary for this to occur. Ernst Jones suggests that the "swelling undercurrent of hostility toward Fliess was connected with the unconscious identification of him [i.e., Fliess] with his father [i.e., Jacob Freud]."[62] In a cunning psychological move, Freud, through transference, used Fliess to keep Jacob alive just so he could kill Jacob himself. Freud's act of patricide is the fulfillment of the oracle's prophecy to Oedipus. Freud accepted it as a heroic man's destiny as well. This act would secure his absolute independence, but it also terminated his sonship. Hence, the revelatory remark at the end of "The Dynamics of Transference" when he says,

> This is the ground on which the victory must be won, the final expression of which is lasting recovery from the neurosis. It is undeniable the subjugation of the transference-manifestations provides the greatest difficulties for the psycho-analyst; but it must not be forgotten that they, and they only, render the valuable service of making the patient's buried and forgotten love emotions actual and manifest; for in the last resort *no one can be slain in absentia* or *in effigie* [italics mine].[63]

It had to be done. He had to cut all ties—be totally independent—if he wanted to prove to himself that he needed no one. Not Fliess. Not Jacob. Not any father.

THE INCOMPLETE HERO AT THE ACROPOLIS

"Nothing will come of the boy."[64] Why did these words haunt Freud throughout his life? The damning prophecy was uttered during an unforgettable accident that occurred during Freud's childhood. At the age of seven, Freud made the terrible mistake of relieving himself (urinating) in his parents' bed-room, in their presence.[65] Jacob Freud was so displeased with his son that he remarked, "Nothing will come of the boy." Looking back on this later in life, Freud admits, "It must have been a terrible blow to my ambition, for allusions to this scene recur in my dreams again and again and are invariably connected with enumerations of my successes and achievements."[66]

There is another event, however, that would have an equally harmful effect on Freud's ambition. It, too, occurred during his childhood years and would intensify Freud's belief that he would never be a success due to his unheroic patrimony. Jacob Freud, at least in his son's eyes, was no hero. Financially, the family's extreme poverty was due to his father's failed endeavors as a wool merchant. Marianne Krull, a psychologist and Freud biographer, shares that the Freud family resided in Leopoldstadt, the Jewish district of Vienna regarded as a ghetto.[67] This environment was far different from the peaceful surroundings of his younger days in the Moravian town of Freiberg. Freud admitted that he "never really felt comfortable in the city."[68] Culturally, Jacob could not assimilate to Viennese society, primarily because of language. Jacob spoke Yiddish, which was looked down on by assimilated Western Jews, so much so that Jewish political activist Theodor Herzl referred to Yiddish as "repressed ghetto language."[69] But nothing shaped Freud's negative view of Jacob more than his father's unheroic disposition. Freud shares the following story:

> I must have been ten or twelve years old when my father began to take me with him on his walks and in conversation tell me his views on things of this world. In this vein, to show me how I had been born into better times than he had, he once told me: "When I was a young man I went for a walk on a Saturday in the town you were born in, wearing my best clothes and with a new fur cap on my head. Then a Christian comes along, knocks my cap in the mud with a single blow, and shouts: "Jew, get off the pavement!"—"And what did you do?"—"I stepped into the road and picked up my cap," came the impassive reply.[70]

When offering a response to this, Freud says of his father's actions: "They did not seem to me very heroic of the big, strong man who was leading me by the hand."[71]

Psychoanalyst Lydia Flem concludes that the story of his father's unheroic behavior greatly diminished Freud's view of Jacob, but it also had a negative effect on "his own narcissism."[72] This episode motivated Freud to avenge his father's disgrace by becoming a great man, indeed a hero, himself. To do so, however, he had to overcome his identification with Jacob Freud, whom Flem refers to as a "humiliated Jew."[73] It must be noted that, in the Jewish culture of Freud's milieu, rebelling against one's father was regarded as an act of transgression. To become a great man, though, required that Freud reject Jacob and the form of Jewishness he represented, which was, for Freud, the primitive ways of Eastern Europe. Freud wanted to be a man of the West. Flem argues that, for Freud, "Athens represents the primal scene of the West, the birthplace of the language and reason of Europe: its foundational myths, its ideal values."[74] Of course, the Oedipus theory, his most cherished theoretical accomplishment, is derived from a Greek legend, retold by Sophocles in his play *Oedipus Rex*. Psychologist Patrick Mullahy states that the resolution of the Oedipus complex represents a struggle for freedom, as its resolution means that the son can "put away childish things and take his place as an adult member of society."[75] Later, Mullahy observes that the hero is the one who has succeeded in overcoming his reliance on the father.[76] He notes,

> The masses have a strong need for an authority which they can admire, to which they can submit, and which sometimes dominates and abuses them. But one may wonder why the masses have such (an alleged) need. Freud's answer is that the need springs from a longing for the father, the father who lives in each of us from childhood. It is the same father, he says, whom the hero of legend boasts of having overcome.[77]

Freud had to overcome his need for a man who acted in such an unheroic manner, even if Jacob had what Newton describes as "millennia of paternal authority on his side."[78] The only option for Freud was to rebel against his father's authority. Jacob had warned his son that an act of such rebellion would never be looked on favorably. The following story is provided by Newton:

> A contemporary of young Freud's named Rosenthal told of arguing with his own father in the street when Jacob came along. "What," Jacob exclaimed, "are you contradicting your father? My Sigmund's little toe is cleverer than my head, but he would never dare contradict me!"[79]

Philosopher Max Horkheimer claims that the kind of authority Jacob Freud wielded over young Sigmund was used to convince the son that "the father is, in the last analysis, always right where his son is concerned."[80] Jacob's word would always be correct. Ernest Jones remarks that what Jacob represented to his son were the "principles of denial, restraint, restriction, and authority; the father stood for the reality principle."[81] But Freud could not submit himself to this. His visit to the Acropolis was to be the culmination of his achievements as an independent man. No longer would Freud be beholden to the words of his father or any other idealized father figure—not a man, not a god—but would instead attempt to make himself into the hero his father failed to be. Freud visited the Acropolis in the summer of 1904, only a few weeks after his break with Fliess. Remember, it was in that final letter, written on July 27, 1904, that Freud proclaimed he no longer needed Fliess's affection.[82] Though claiming victory over the pain of Fliess's rejection, Freud still must have approached the Acropolis with a heavy heart. For the first time in his life, he was his own man—totally independent, alone. Jacob was dead. The relationship with Fliess was over. Freud was free, or so he thought. In his 1909 essay "Family Romances," a brief but insightful reflection he contributed to Otto Rank's book *The Myth of the Birth of the Hero*, Freud begins by saying,

> The freeing of the individual, as he grows up, from the authority of his parents is one of the most necessary though one of the most painful results brought about by the course of his development. It is quite essential that this liberation should occur and it may be presumed that it has been to some extent achieved by everyone who has reached a normal state. Indeed, the whole progress of society rests upon the opposition between successive generations. On the other hand, there is a class of neurotics whose condition is recognizably determined by their having failed in this task.[83]

Freud goes on to explain his conviction that during the maturation process we no longer look on our parents as the "only authority and source of all belief."[84] The reason for this increased lack of faith in the parents' authority is quite telling. Freud suggests that during childhood, a child feels a "sense that his own affection is not being fully reciprocated then finds a vent in the idea . . . of being a step-child or an adopted child."[85] He goes on to state that "a boy is far more inclined to feel hostile impulses towards his father . . . and has a far more intense desire to get free of him."[86] The cause of the antagonism between the generations is the unequal affectional bond between father and son. The son loves his father more than the father loves him. As a result, the son feels as though he is a "step-child."[87] Nevertheless, it is a loss that must be overcome if a boy wants to become a heroic man.

Freud's initiation into heroic manhood occurred on September 3, 1904. He and his brother Alexander, ten years his junior, took a trip to Athens. Much of Freud's description of the trip in the aforementioned 1936 letter to Romain Rolland focuses on his experience of derealization, a psychological defense used to keep undesirable material away from one's conscious mind. Ernest Jones points out that the beauty of the Acropolis so overwhelmed Freud that he wrote back home to tell his family that "the experience there had surpassed anything he had ever seen or could imagine."[88] But this didn't last. Freud's resounding joy soon turned into a rigorous self-analysis. Freud began to ask himself why he felt unworthy of the successes that allowed him to reach the magnificent Acropolis.

Yes, finally, at the age of forty-eight, Freud was able to fulfill his childhood desire to behold "the sight of Athens with [his] own eyes."[89] But his eyes did not convince him that it was all real: "By the evidence of my senses I am now standing on the Acropolis, but I cannot believe it."[90] During his self-analysis, Freud discovers that his inability to grasp the reality of the Acropolis is because he was unable to accept the "possibility that [he] should travel so far—that [he] should 'go such a long way.'"[91] Childhood poverty is the explanation Freud gives as to why a trip to Athens was not previously possible for him. *Had he truly gone from the dregs of the Leopoldstadt ghetto to glory of the Acropolis?* That is not the entire story, however. Something else had put limitations on Freud's ability to "go such a long way." Since the age of seven or eight, Freud had lived under the shadow of Jacob's damning prophecy, "Nothing will come of the boy." The Acropolis had proven that Freud had come a long way—something did come of the boy. But Freud could not enjoy his great accomplishment. "It seems as though the essence of success," he writes, "were to have got further than one's father, and as though to excel one's father were still something forbidden."[92]

Recall that Jacob declared, "He [young Sigmund] would never dare to contradict me!"[93] Although Freud recognizes at the Acropolis that he was indeed superior to Jacob, he also realizes that it was the ultimate sign of his contradicting Jacob's authority. At the end of the letter to Rolland, Freud, who was now eighty years old, looks back with sorrow at his victory over Jacob. He hoped the most hallowed citadel, the Acropolis, would make him feel that he had reached the heavens, but it only served to teach him a painful lesson: He was a hero who had slain the father; the Oedipus complex was complete, but at what cost? He was all alone at the Acropolis. Thus writer Maynard Solomon describes the "Disturbance of Memory" essay as "a lamentation, not an ode to joy."[94] For Solomon, Freud cannot escape the supposedly "passive-feminine components of his nature"[95]—he remained a son who needed a relationship with his father. Even at the age of eighty, the heroic father of psychoanalysis—the man credited with creating a new language for the inner workings of the human mind—remained, in many ways, a young boy who yearned for the gift of Jacob's secure affection. "I want my father," to use Lansky's phrase, is what Freud wanted to express as he reached the Acropolis, still realizing he was in need of someone to help him master the world and face the many life challenges that remained. But he was just a lonely hero suffering from "the sorrow of incompleteness."[96]

The unyielding desire to become a heroic man comes at a great cost. For Freud, achieving heroic status demanded that he renounce his sonship by overcoming his reliance on his father and anything that possessed the authority of the father. His shallow self-mastery, however, meant that at times of great vulnerability, and even success, he was alone. He was his own source of protection, the only one he trusted to manage the chaos both within himself and the world. Yet even with his accomplishments, Freud could not overcome his identification with his father. He realized that no matter his efforts, whether by reaching the Acropolis or some act of patricide, he would always need fathering, whether from Jacob, Fliess, or someone else. He would always be a son in need of a father.

A similar version of Freud's story of sorrow at the Acropolis would be retold in another place and at another time by novelist Richard Wright. Wright, too, lifted himself from a humble background to become not a man of science but a man of letters who used his words as a weapon to fight against oppression. Wright's ascension, like Freud's, was inspired by the downfall of his father, Nathan. Wright regarded his father as the symbol of failed (hu)man, a man who was controlled by and not in control of his environment, and thus a man incapable of fathering a son. Literary scholar Abdul R. Jan-Mohamed refers to such a person as the death-bound-subject. That is to say, his father was the "'black boy' virtually reduced to the status of an animal and ruled by the rhythms of an unconscious tethered to the cycle of natural seasons, etc.'"[97] Nathan's way of being-in-the-world is enveloped by death. Thus neither Nathan nor the sons in relationship with him can grow into manhood. Richard, however, was determined to make himself, despite Nathan's failure to provide him the gift of sonship, more than just another Black boy.

DYING FOR THE CALL

Although Richard was born a Wright, everything about his birth, despite his surname, seemed wrong. Wright biographer Michel Fabre suggests that Richard Wright was so ashamed by the fact that he was the descendant of slaves that "he preferred to have come out of nothing."[98] Though Wright never provided an in-depth analysis of his family background in his works, not even in his autobiographical novel *Black Boy*, biographers have been able to acquire sufficient information to confirm and challenge some of Wright's negative opinions regarding his heritage. It is indisputable that the Wrights were born on the fertile soil of the Mississippi Delta. His grandparents were slaves who worked the cotton trade when Natchez, Mississippi, was deemed a Southern utopia. Wright biographer Hazel Rowley detects some honor, a bit of good blood perhaps, in the family's background. For instance, in an act of bravery, Wright's maternal grandfather, Richard Wilson, fled a Natchez plantation to join the Union Army during the

Civil War. Wilson was "militantly resentful of slavery," and on completing his service in the army, he returned to Mississippi where he was an active participant in the fight for freedom. For instance, "he used to stand armed guard in front of ballot boxes to protect blacks who were voting."[99]

On the other side of the family, Wright's paternal grandfather, Nathaniel Wright Sr., according to Fabre, "was one of the few freed slaves in the region who . . . was given by the military government the plot of land which he had worked as a slave."[100] This was no small feat for a Black man in the Old South. Fabre adds that Nathaniel Wright "was able to make a living at the beginning of the century on this small farm . . . about twelve miles east of Natchez."[101] Moreover, Nathan Wright Sr., much like Richard Wilson, fought against injustice: "He was respected in the community because he had succeeded in combating certain cunning white neighbors who had tried to cheat him out of his piece of land."[102] The moderate successes that were gained by Black men like Richard Wilson and Nathaniel Wright were diminished—if not eliminated—by the emergence of the Lost Cause creed.

The Lost Cause creed helped white residents throughout the South get over the traumas of the Civil War and, most specifically, Reconstruction. Historian Jack E. Davis suggests that the Lost Cause creed "helped make life in the postbellum South somewhat familiar and predictable again for whites."[103] Historian Charles Regan Wilson maintains that the Lost Cause, which he defines as a civil religion, reinstilled a sense of race superiority within whites. This iteration of race superiority went beyond the gentility of the antebellum period.[104] Wilson writes,

> In *The Lost Cause* (1866), the Richmond editor Edward A. Pollard called for a "war of ideas" to retain the Southern identity. The South's religious leaders and laymen defined this identity in terms of morality and religion: in short, Southerners were a virtuous people. Clergymen preached that Southerners were the chosen people, peculiarly blessed by God. "In a word," says Samuel S. Hill, a leading historian of Southern religion, "many southern whites have regarded their society as God's most favored. To a greater degree than any other, theirs [Southern society] approximates the ideals the Almighty has in mind for mankind everywhere."[105]

There were moderates (or paternalists) who proclaimed that free Blacks needed the guidance of the chosen Southerners, particularly the former planter class. Others, however, used violence to ensure that Blacks knew their place and would pay a deadly price for crossing social boundaries. The violence used by militia groups like the Ku Klux Klan was justified, particularly among racist clergymen, because they "prevented greater bloodshed in the lawless, disordered world of Reconstruction,"[106] a world where Blacks dared to view themselves the equals of whites. This was also when the number of lynchings in the South grew at an alarming rate. Sociologists Stewart Tolnay and E. M. Beck suggest that lynchings reached a zenith "during the bloody '90s'" (i.e., 1890s).[107] But these acts of mob violence remained prevalent in the early twentieth century. The death of Eli Hilson in the winter of 1903 serves to make the point. Hilson, a resident of Lincoln County, Mississippi, was a prosperous Black landowner who would not forfeit his property and, because of his unwillingness to leave, was murdered by a white mob. According to Tolnay and Beck, Hilson was murdered not so much for the land but rather because "he did not limit his aspirations to laboring for whites, and this independence was unacceptable."[108] There are too many similar tales to recount here of how any sign of independence by a Black person was an unacceptable offense to the social order. Of course, many chose to rebel, but there were also many who yielded *completely* to this deadly oppression. The testimony of his eldest son, backed by reliable historical evidence, suggests that Nathan Wright, Richard Wright's father, was such a person—a dependent Black boy. But was he always this way?

During his younger years, Nathan Wright attempted to become independent by leaving home to be a sharecropper. Doubtless, he wanted to make a life for himself and be respected like his father, "Old Man Nathan," who, according to Michel Fabre, was considered a patriarch.[109] But sharecropping limited Nathan's ability to become much of anything. Sharecropping, a common social arrangement in Natchez, maintained a system of dependency between Black tenant farmers and white landowners. In sharecropping parlance, Nathaniel was a "halfer," meaning that he gave half of the farm's yield to the landowner, but it never covered the cost of renting the land and farm equipment, resulting in Nathan's being stuck in and overwhelmed by a cycle of poverty and debt. But what else could he do? Nathan didn't know anything else. Sharecropping was in his blood. Wright biographer Constance Webb attests, "The soil was all that Nathan knew."[110] Remaining tied to the soil, both literally and symbolically, also ensured that Nathan would never threaten the established order. Sharecropping kept him in his place. Many Black men chose to live this way to protect not only themselves but their loved ones as well. Hazel Rowley notes that "if a black man did not know his place—if he came over as sassy or biggity—he would endanger his own life and put others in the black community at risk."[111] Whippings and hangings were commonly used to keep disrespectful Black sharecroppers in their place. A prominent white planter attests,

> There was one black tenant out our way not long ago—he was on a place near ours—who was getting too smart. I told my sons that if he

didn't behave, they ought to take him out for a ride and tend to him, and tell him that if he didn't stop talking and acting so big, the next time it would be a bullet or a rope. That's the way to manage them when they get too big.[112]

During the early twentieth century, mob violence remained a threat in the minds of any Black man who crossed the boundaries assigned to him. In *Black Boy*, Richard Wright shares his own experience of living under this threat, confessing that he felt helpless, totally unprotected, because there were "men against whom [he] was powerless, men who could violate [his] life at will."[113] He saw this violation take place, firsthand, with his father, Nathan Wright. In Natchez, Nathan would always be a sharecropper, the true calling for a Black boy. Perhaps, things would be better for Nathan if, somehow, he could free himself from the clutches of this place.

Nathan Wright did try to make things better for his family when, in 1914, they boarded the *Kate Adams*, a Mississippi River steamboat, to leave Natchez for the city of Memphis, Tennessee. Even at a young age, Richard Wright was aware that the economic opportunities in Memphis came at a terrible cost. For one, the city lacked Natchez's natural beauty, which made the city seem dead. The family's living conditions were also far different from those in Natchez. The Wright family lived in a small tenement apartment, wherein the family of four was cramped into a very small space.[114] But that wasn't the biggest problem. Wright noticed that life in Memphis was changing Nathan, and not for the better. Nathan worked nights as a porter at a local drugstore, but this work, though not sharecropping, still relegated him to a life of poverty. Physically, he was deteriorating, as he was no longer the tall, handsome man he had once been in Natchez. Worse of all, Nathan's mood began to emulate his environment. He became lifeless, dark and moody, and domineering. Fabre remarks that Richard "came to regard his father solely as an incarnation of authority . . . and in no way saw him as an example to follow or a figure to be proud of and love."[115] Nathan became such a distant figure that Richard comments that his father was "a stranger . . . always somehow alien and remote."[116] Richard looked on with horror as Nathan's despair spiraled out of control. Life in the Memphis ghetto was killing Nathan.

Literary critic Addison Gayle suggests that Nathan's inner turmoil was being caused by more than just his failures in Memphis. Nathan's "true ambition," Gayle suggests, "seemed to lay . . . in the ministry; and he waited in vain for the sign, *the call* [italics mine], that would ordain him as one of the chosen."[117] According to Gayle, "a preacher was a respected individual in the black community." The "call" would give Nathan new life. If nothing else, it would be a sign that God was with him. Nathan's family looked on with anxiety as "no star appeared directing him to the pulpit; no prayers were strong

enough to move the intractable heavenly host."[118] The (called) preacher
maintains a unique position in the African American community, one that
bestows immense power and recognition. In his essay "Of the Faith of the
Fathers," W. E. B. Du Bois writes, "The Preacher is the most unique person
developed by the Negro on American soil. A leader, a politician, an orator,
a 'boss,' an intriguer, an idealist,—all these he is, and ever, too, the centre
of a group of men, now twenty, now a thousand in number."[119] Du Bois's
analysis focuses on the social position of the preacher but doesn't mention
how the call to the ministry itself was so integral to the personal development
of some African Americans seeking a way to improve their low social status.
Clarence Snelling, a theologian, argues that when looked at developmentally,
the call to ministry "may represent an attempt to create a sense of self in the
face of radical self-doubt and emptiness, to confirm personal worth against
feelings of low self-esteem . . . to gain love and respect from peers, or power
over them."[120] At a time when he was, by all accounts, failing to improve life
for himself and his family, it is plausible that Nathan Wright was convinced
that a call from God was the only thing that would give him self-worth and,
of equal importance, make him valuable to his family. Nathan experienced a
slow spiritual death, however, waiting for the call. It was as though God had
abandoned him. In an early draft of *Black Boy*, Wright describes the family's
reaction to Nathan's spiritual pain:

> He [Nathan Wright] prayed and brooded, indulged in gloomy mono-
> logues that were the despair of my mother and cowed me and my
> brother to silence. . . . The anxiety that came into my mother's face
> whenever he complained about not being "called" made me conceive
> of it as something dreadful, an event that would leave me and my
> mother and brother alone in the world.[121]

Where was the call? Gayle notes that "even [Nathan's] God had made him feel
unworthy."[122] It seemed that God wanted nothing to do with someone like
Nathan Wright.

In *Divine Callings*, sociologist Richard N. Pitt points out that "most Protestant denominations affirm the idea that there must be a specific encounter with God that leads people to devote their lives to the ministry."[123] The
encounter that initiates the call is the beginning of an invaluable and irreplace-
able relationship between the minister and God. "Call experiences," says Pitt,
"are always described as a personal journey where the only other participant
is God."[124] Thus without the call, Nathan felt bastardized, a man unloved
and unprotected—in other words, fatherless. Nathan's inner angst, an intense
spiritual hunger, was turned into rage that was directed toward his two sons,
who themselves were also made to endure the torment of abandonment. The

streets of Memphis's ghetto soon became Nathan's preferred abode as he stayed away from his family for longer periods of time until, eventually, one day, he never returned.

THE FIGHT AGAINST FAITH

Richard knew something was wrong. For days, he experienced a new hunger that his mother was not able to satisfy. He begged his mother for something to eat, and, after growing weary of his persistent pleas for food, she tells him, "You'll just have to wait . . . for God to send some food."[125] Though his mother was not someone who had received the call to ministry, Richard knew that Ella Wright was a woman of sincere faith. Her deep—and, in some instances, fanatical—faith, along with that of her mother, Margaret Wilson, would influence Richard's views on religion, often in a negative way. While Ella had faith in the Scriptures' promise "I have never seen the righteous forsaken, nor his seed begging bread" (Ps. 37:25, KJV), Richard grew even more skeptical of a God who let his family suffer starvation. God alone was not to blame, however. Richard knew the family's hunger was being caused by Nathan's absence. "Where's your father?" asks Ella.[126] The question was troubling, for certain, but it was made even more unbearable because his mother asked it with tears in her eyes. The question and attendant emotions signaled an alarm within Richard, as he now recognized that his father's absence meant that he would not eat. Hunger. Hunger. Hunger. Ella would soon warn her sons that their lives would be different. Yes, food would be hard to come by, but something far more significant would be missing as well. "Sometimes, when she was in despair," confesses Richard, "she would call to us and talk to us for hours, telling us that we now had no father, that we must learn as soon as possible to take care of ourselves."[127] Richard would have to learn to be on his own. Ella's cautionary talk left them feeling "a vague dread."[128] The term of his sonship was over.

When Nathan deserted the family, Richard was no more than five or six years old, far too young to understand what it meant to take care of oneself. But Ella had no choice. To support the family, she started working as a cook, leaving the boys home alone for most of the day. The streets of Memphis soon claimed Richard as a son; they would provide the fathering he needed. The streets taught him to fight and steal; he roamed the streets and eased his pain with alcohol. He had friends, or associates, but he knew his relationship with a local gang of children was doing him more harm than good. Richard admits that he was "wandering farther and farther away from home each day."[129] Wright's hunger for healthy companionship, an authentically caring relationship, fathering, soon supplanted his want of food. But he didn't want to be Nathan's son. Richard was so embittered by his father's absence that he "didn't want to think of him . . . didn't want see him."[130] Wright biographer Margaret Walker states, "This period of life in Memphis was the beginning of an adult suffering . . . the scars of the separation [Nathan's abandonment], the complete despair of a helpless and innocent child full of pride and full of anger, impotent rage . . . would remain for a lifetime."[131] In Memphis, the family's financial and emotional state became so untenable that Ella could no longer care for her two sons. "Half sick and in despair" is how Richard describes his mother's condition when, after failing to pay the rent in their tenement apartment, she was forced to take her sons to Settlement House, a Methodist orphanage located near Memphis.

Wright describes Settlement House as a rather unsettling place, a haunt for homeless children who were made to suffer severe discipline and malnourishment. Richard had another problem at the orphanage, however. Constance Webb alleges that a Miss Simon, the orphanage's caretaker, described as a "tall, gaunt, mulatto woman," made improper sexual advances toward Richard.[132] During his six-week stay at the orphanage, Richard made numerous attempts to escape, but policemen would capture him and return him to be "beaten sadistically" by Miss Simon.[133] Already abandoned by his father and, now, his mother, Richard could not help but become more distrustful of his environment. He could trust only himself. A radical individualism became Richard's view of the world. Ella did return, eventually, to free her sons from the terror of Settlement House, and she would take them through a series of visits with family members before settling in with Richard's grandmother, Granny Wilson, in Jackson, Mississippi. Ella hoped the stability of her mother's religious home, guided by the teachings of the Seventh Day Adventist Church, would provide her sons, especially Richard, with a nurturing environment that could make amends for the severe isolation they experienced in Memphis. What occurred instead was a systematic effort to break Richard's strong individualism by forcing him to receive a call not to the ministry but to a fanatical form of Christian discipleship. In Margaret Wilson's home, it was believed that God would make Richard change his wicked ways.

Before the move to Jackson, Ella's health had started to deteriorate. A stroke at the age of thirty-five had left her so incapacitated that she had to travel on a stretcher all the way to her mother's home. Ella never fully recovered physically, remaining in bed for about ten years. Emotionally, she moved in and out of bouts of intense despair. For Richard, his mother's overall state—the noticeable absence of well-beingness—became a symbol for the inescapable dreadfulness of life. He writes,

My mother's suffering grew into a symbol in my mind, gathering to
itself all the poverty, the ignorance, the helplessness; the painful, baf-
fling, hunger-ridden days and hours.[134]

Richard felt hopeless, and Ella was aware that her physical and emotional condition weakened if not all together incapacitated her ability to
care for her sons. There would be periods when her health improved, but
not for long. She was convinced, though, that what Richard needed was a
call from God—*he needed to be saved*. It was his only hope. Rowley reports
that at the final night of a local Methodist revival Ella, limping and crying,
took her son's hand and brought him to the front of the church. "Come,
son, let your old mother take you to God. . . . I brought you into the
world, now let me help to save you," Ella said to Richard.[135] But his strong
individualism, fueled by his distrust of others, would not allow Richard to
submit. He didn't want God's call. He didn't want God at all. For Richard, to accept this call was nothing more than a public display of "how
much [he] had in common with other people."[136] If he were converted—
then what?—he would be expected to be like everyone else. Would he be
like the other Black men in the church? Just another "saved" Black boy?
He went along with his mother's wishes; the baptism was completed; but
he confessed to Ella nothing had really changed. "Mama," he tells her,
"I don't feel a thing."[137] His grandmother also attempted, repeatedly, to
bring Richard to God. Her failed attempts, however, resulted in what he
describes as the "greatest shame and humiliation of her religious life."[138]
Her most significant rebuke of Richard came when he decided that in
order to earn money he would work on Saturday, an act forbidden by his
grandmother's Seventh-Day Adventist[139] faith, to which she responded,
"You left the church . . . *you are dead to me, dead to Christ* [italics mine]."[140]
But religion, at least this form of it, was not the answer for Wright, no
matter his family's insistence.

In his essay "Richard Wright's Blues," novelist Ralph Ellison argues that
Richard's family environment was but a microcosm of the American South,
wherein African Americans were to "accept the role created for them by the
whites and perpetually resolve the resulting conflicts through the hope and
emotional catharsis of Negro religion."[141] On the other hand, notes Ellison,
"they could reject the situation, adopt a criminal attitude, and carry on an
unceasing psychological scrimmage with the whites, which often flared forth
into physical violence."[142] Richard's attitude was in line with the latter option,
particularly as he rejected the "pre-individualistic" values upheld by his family and other African Americans throughout the South. Ellison remarks that
"to wander from the paths of behavior laid down for the group is to become

the agent of communal disaster."[143] The primary means of keeping the community safe is for African American parents and caretakers to make sure "the impulse towards individuality is suppressed" in their children.[144] There is ample evidence in *Black Boy* to support Ellison's hypothesis, for throughout the text, whether on the plantation in Natchez, the ghetto in Memphis, or the prison of his grandmother's home, it was through violence, whether physical punishment or religious coercion, that his family sought to make Richard surrender his selfhood to his environment. Ellison observes that what made Richard Wright so unusual was that he "recognized and made no peace with its [i.e., the family's] essential cruelty."[145] All Richard saw in the lives of those who used their religion as a means to conform to social norms was an inner ruin, a terrifying spiritual death. In later years, Wright looked back on his childhood with dismay, writing,

> After I had outlived the shocks of childhood, after the habit of reflection had been born in me, I used to mull over the strange absence of real kindness in Negroes, how unstable was our tenderness, how lacking in genuine passion we were, how void of great hope, how timid our joy, how bare our traditions, how hollow our memories, how lacking we were in tangible sentiments that bind man to man, and how shallow was even our despair.[146]

Richard's family had sought to destroy his individual hope so that he would embrace, instead, what they had hoped for him. But what was their hope for Richard? What did they really believe he could become? Whose footsteps did they envision he would follow? Richard saw a warning, not hope, in his family's heritage; nothing of value had been passed down throughout the generations. There was no one he could connect with. Richard was giftless.

BLACK BOYS FOR LIFE

Scholar of African American literature Robert Stepto writes that Richard considered his father, along with other elder kinsmen, "warnings," not "examples," of a life lived in spiritual ruin, that is, a life devoid of the "flight and ascent" necessary to achieve a life beyond the restrictions of places like the plantation and the ghetto.[147] Richard was faced with the warning of Nathan's failed life when, after leaving Mississippi to live in Memphis and Chicago, he returned to Natchez once again, after twenty-five years, to see his father, face to face. During this time, Richard had become his own man, a hero who had raised himself up from nothing. But he was alone. Richard even admits, "In all my life . . . I had not had a single satisfying sustained relationship with another human being."[148] He had great faith, however, that his individualism had transformed him from a Black boy into a self-made man. Anthropologist Allison Davis contends that Wright was an "artist of miraculous talent, who by genius and hard work transcended the enormous obstacles raised by deep Southern racism."[149] But Wright's talents did not enable him to transcend one inescapable fact: he was, in the end, the son of a Black sharecropper. His father was a Black boy.

Twenty-five years had passed since Richard last saw Nathan, and the years had not been kind to his father. Richard vividly describes Nathan's physical decline:

> That day a quarter of a century later when I visited him on the plantation—he was standing against the sky, smiling toothlessly, his hair whitened, his body bent, his eyes glazed with dim recollection, his fearsome aspect of twenty-five years ago gone forever from him.[150]

Nathan's decrepit physical condition is surpassed by the irreversible destruction of his inner world. Richard, who had fought valiantly to keep the South's toxic social environment from contaminating his soul, was distressed to see Nathan's complete submission to the call of the graceless and rapacious gods of the Natchez plantation. Richard remarks that "from the white landowners above him there had not been handed to him a chance to learn the meaning of loyalty, of sentiment, of tradition."[151] Nathan had received nothing during his years on the plantation that he could give to his son. All he had was the misery of sharecropping. He could not even engage in a relationship that would make Richard view himself as a son. There was no fathering to be had on this plantation. Richard laments,

> A quarter of a century, during which my mind and consciousness had become so greatly and violently altered that when I tried to talk to him I realized that, though ties of blood made us kin, though I could see a shadow of my face in his face, though there was an echo of my voice in his voice, we were forever strangers, speaking a different language, living on vastly different planes of reality.[152]

Richard had hoped the trip back home to Natchez would allow him to become reacquainted with this father, but he soon found that differing life experiences, one becoming a man while the other remained a boy, had permanently severed the father-son bond. Rather than empathize with his father's lowly condition, Richard claims a resounding victory over Nathan, declaring an Oedipal triumph as it were, stating that his father was "a black peasant who had gone to the city seeking life, but who had failed in the city . . . that same city which had lifted me in its burning arms."[153] And he accomplished all of this alone, that is, by being "aggressively independent."[154] Whereas

Nathan waited the rest of his life for a call from God that would redeem his self-worth, Richard relied on himself alone to reach "alien and undreamed-of shores of knowing."[155] Allison Davis observes that Richard was "a strong man, an independent and self-directing man, [and] one must add that he was also a man in conflict, a suffering man."[156] Richard's was a pyrrhic victory. For all his accomplishments, Wright was a giftless man. Nothing could help him get over the fact that he desired to be his father's son. "He was never able," writes Davis, "to resolve the conflict in his feelings for his father."[157] Richard needed his father, even if, at least in his son's eyes, he was only a Black boy.

Both Sigmund Freud and Richard Wright earnestly sought to rid themselves of the sorrow of incompleteness. Throughout their lives they wanted to overcome the vulnerability of sonship by claiming the fullness of manhood on their own. But they failed to do so. Certainly what has been discussed in this chapter attests to their ability to will themselves to greatness, to reach the pinnacle of their given fields, to be looked on as great men by their contemporaries and following generations; and yet, something was missing, they still felt a sense of lack—a hunger—that could not be satiated. It is worth returning to Dittes's statement regarding the sorrow of incompleteness:

> *Is that all there is?* The sorrow of incompleteness is man's from the outset—part of creation, not a symptom of sin or fall. . . . This sorrow of incompleteness, life chronically destined, is what is offered to man as the avenue to wholeness and holiness. Life in want; life detoured, in a closet, a gift not yet unwrapped.[158]

Freud and Wright were enraged because their fathers never provided them with the gift of heroic manhood. Dittes offers us a different perspective that provides a more dire warning, and it is this: Freud and Wright never recognized that they themselves—not Freud's theories and writings on psychoanalysis nor Wright's novels and other literary works—were gifts. Due to the absence of sonship in their lives, they painfully searched for someone, ideally a trusted father, who could over a period of time, with love and care, unwrap and nurture the gift of sonship within them. Who is to blame for this? Should Jacob Freud (or Wilhelm Fliess) and Nathan Wright be absolved for their failure as fathers? No. Not at all. But other factors must be taken into consideration to explain why many sons remain, as Dittes states, "a gift not yet unwrapped."[159] For many young Black men, the problem of the gift not yet unwrapped is compounded by the problem of the American ghetto. The ghetto has become the place where gifts, both fathers and sons, are cast away to suffer the sorrow of completeness left unwrapped, unloved, and unfulfilled.

3

Ghetto Grown

THE MESSAGE: GETTING TO KNOW THE GHETTO

Whose is the most trusted voice about life in the ghetto? Over several decades, noted sociologists, such as Louis Wirth, W. E. B. Du Bois, Horace R. Cayton, St. Clair Drake, and, more recently, Mitchell Duneier and Elijah Anderson have studied the various social dynamics of ghetto life. Their works have been cited as reliable sources on the ins and outs of the ghetto by politicians, educators, and other public figures, but few sociologists have ever called the ghetto their home. Other experts, however, have provided an account of the ghetto. Historian and journalist Jeff Chang observes that during the early to mid-1980s hip-hop artists emerged as the "voices of their generation."[1] These artists were viewed as the ones with *the message* about the ghetto. "Advocates often cite rap's stories as proof of the music's truth-telling capacity, its prophetic voice for everyday people," writes literary critic Adam Bradley.[2] In the summer of 1982, South Bronx hip-hop artists Grandmaster Flash and the Furious Five released their hit song "The Message." The song provided informative social commentary on the urban decay of the ghetto. In 1982, *Rolling Stone* writer Kurt Loder claimed that "The Message" was a "detailed and devastating report from underclass America."[3] Loder underscores that the song's lyrics are not about the South Bronx alone but rather provide "startling images of life in the universal ghetto."[4]

"The Message" talks about the ghetto's deteriorating physical landscape: "Broken glass everywhere / People pissin' on the stairs."[5] The reality depicted in the song's lyrics were matched by the images portrayed in the music video. Cheryl L. Keyes, a scholar of ethnomusicology, remarks that "The Message" was the first mainstream rap music video, and it was the director's intent to bring viewers into the "harsh realities" of the ghetto.[6] The song also mentions the sociopolitical challenges of life in the ghetto. Therefore, in the video one sees that "behind the song's main MC, Melle Mel, and the other members of Grandmaster Flash and the Furious Five, dilapidated buildings appear. . . . Documentary style footage of a homeless woman, tow truck, and a street arrest reinforce the gravity of ghetto life."[7] "The Message" is about not only the ghetto as a place but also its people—that is, the way they live, how they relate to one another, and even what they hope for. "The Message" is a haunting meditation on the ghetto because it talks about the challenges of growing up (or down) behind ghetto walls:

> A child is born with no state of mind
> Blind to the ways of mankind
> God is smilin' on you but he's frowning too
> Because only God knows what you'll go through
> You'll grow in the ghetto livin' second-rate . . .
> You'll admire all the number-book takers
> Thugs, pimps and pushers and the big money-makers
> Drivin' big cars, spendin' twenties and tens
> And you'll wanna grow up to be just like them.[8]

The pressures of living in the ghetto create an unsettled psychological state that has residents always on edge; as the song says, "So don't push me 'cause I'm close to the edge. . . . I'm trying not to lose my head."[9] But "The Message" does more than portray the grim reality of the ghetto. Bradley argues that the stories of rap songs like "The Message" serve as "occasions to imagine alternate realities."[10] Though "The Message," says Bradley, "offers a powerful description of urban plight," it does not eliminate rap's focus on "imagining possible realities [rather] than with simply recording urban experiences."[11] Although rap poetics seek to challenge perceptions of the ghetto and its residents, a dominant image of ghetto life, as depicted in "The Message," remains fixed within the American mind. The message is clear: Nothing good grows in the ghetto.

In *Poverty and Place*, scholar of public policy Paul A. Jargowsky contends that the images of the ghetto don't capture the fact that most residents in the ghetto do not live "underclass lifestyles"—that is, they "go to work each day, avoid the street for fear of crime, and do not hang out on street corners."[12] He also mentions that researchers "may have contributed to a truncated and overly negative image of ghetto . . . residents."[13] Even so, Jargowsky notes that there are indeed specific negative characteristics found in America's ghettoes. To the casual observer, the first characteristic of the ghetto is the dilapidated housing, which is "the most visible sign of neighborhood poverty and abandonment."[14] Whether it is a tin-roof shack located in Jackson, Mississippi, or a deteriorating housing project in Camden, New Jersey, ghetto housing is symbolic of a place that few people want to call home. Another characteristic of the ghetto, according to Jargowsky, is economic distress. The unemployment rates in ghetto neighborhoods, especially for men, are very high; and even when men are working, they are not making enough money to support a family.[15]

The absence of work can also lead to negative behavioral outcomes, a point made by sociologist William Julius Wilson when he says, "Work in the formal economy . . . provides a framework for daily behavior because it readily imposes discipline and regularity."[16] Wilson is a proponent of the significant influence that structural forces have in creating concentrated poverty in the inner city, but he does so without disputing the influence of culture, that is, the processes of meaning making in the ghetto. The culture of the ghetto is the last characteristic discussed by Jargowsky, who says that the social pathologies of the ghetto are disturbing to observers, who "view them as the symptoms of a much more general deterioration of American society and culture."[17] At the center of the ghetto's social pathology is what some analysts have defined as the Black family's "disorganized" structure, primarily caused by the prevalence of single-parent households. "The widely noted breakdown of the family," says Jargowsky, "is characteristic of poor neighborhoods, particularly ghettoes."[18]

Unfortunately, residents in the inner city often use harmful coping strategies to deal with these social pathologies. For example, scholar of urban health Sara F. Jacoby and her research associates found that when single parents, all mothers, were asked to share their coping strategies, they not only reported healthy activities like journaling and exercise but also used unhealthy strategies (or health-detracting behaviors) such as binge eating and social isolation. Their sense of being cut off from their own community and the larger society was most distressing to the interviewees. In fact, participants shared that they believed their conditions would improve if they could "develop social support networks in their daily lives."[19] The authors point out that "focus group participants emphasized the importance of social support to mitigate the disadvantages of their income and housing instability; participants identified enhanced social connections as a primary strategy through which they believed they could better manage their stress."[20] Distrust of the environment makes it so that single mothers do not pursue these relationships, as the authors report that these single parents "choose not to interact with neighbors."[21] Even more disturbing, there is a lack of healthy social connections among residents in their homes. Therefore, in some cases, you have parents isolated from one another and from their own children. The ghetto is where isolation is the norm not only among its inhabitants but between its inhabitants and the rest of society—and it was created for that very reason.

THE BIRTH OF THE GHETTO:
THE WORD AND THE PLACE

The ghetto is not an American original, neither the word nor the place. *Merriam-Webster* provides three definitions of *ghetto*: 1) "a quarter of a city in which Jews were formerly required to live"; 2) "a quarter of a city in which members of a minority group live especially because of social, legal, or economic pressure"; and 3) "an isolated group."[22] Sandra Debenedetti-Stow, a scholar of Italian-Jewish dialect and comparative literature, writes that the term *ghetto* was first used in 1516, and it came "to specify zones of Jewish residence throughout Italy up to the middle of the nineteenth century."[23] She traces the origin of the term to the Hebrew *get*, which means "divorce, or separation."[24] Furthermore, in various Venetian writings of that era, the words *geto* and *getto* were used to designate Jewish areas isolated from the rest of the city. Though much debate remains regarding the origin of the term *ghetto*, what is indisputable is that "the Jews had come to view their *ghetto* enclosure as divorcing them from Roman society as a whole."[25]

An extensive reflection on the word *ghetto* is provided in historian Daniel B. Schwartz's *Ghetto: The History of a Word*. Similar to Debenedetti-Stow, Schwartz identifies 1516 as the year when Venetian authorities ordered Jewish residents to reside in a segregated section of the city. He claims that this was the first "enduring experiment with residential segregation of Jews, at least in Italy."[26] These were to become exclusively Jewish spaces that would, for the first time, be associated with a specific word, as Schwartz explains:

> The Venetian Republic ordered that the Jews of Venice be restricted to a small island on the northern edge of the city. Christian inhabitants of this area were compelled to vacate their homes; all outward-facing doors, windows, and quays of the island were to be bricked over, and gates were to be erected in two places, to be locked at sunset. The new Venetian enclave was hardly the first example in history of the "Jewish street" or "Jewish quarter," which dated to the origins of the Jewish Diaspora in antiquity. . . . Yet the establishment of an enforced and exclusive residential space for the Jews of Venice was a historical beginning in at last one respect. It marked the start of a fateful link between the idea of segregation and a particular word: "ghetto."[27]

Schwartz points out that *ghetto* is derived "from the Venetian verb *gettare*, meaning to throw or to cast."[28] History informs us that, far after the word *ghetto* originated and flourished in Venice, this notion of throwing or casting a particular population within a confined space, rhetorically and otherwise, is a common theme when the word *ghetto* is used. Venice, according to Schwartz, viewed itself as a "city of God" and a "new Jerusalem" that had been protected from military overthrow and various natural disasters by "divine protection."[29] Christian residents believed that in order to ensure God's protection over the city, the Jewish population would either have to convert to Christianity or face expulsion. This view is evident in a proclamation that supported the Jews being sent into the *Ghetto Nuovo* [the new ghetto], which stated,

> No godfearing subject of our state would have wished them [the Jews], after their arrival, to disperse throughout the city, sharing houses with Christians and going wherever they choose day and night, perpetuating all those misdemeanors and detestable and abominable acts which are generally known and shameful to describe, with grave offense to the Majesty of God and uncommon notoriety on the part of this well-ordered Republic.[30]

The Jewish presence, principally, was a threat to the established (Christianized) order of Venetian society, and this idea would become a common theme throughout Europe well into the twentieth century.

Scholar of Jewish history David Vital remarks that "from the end of the eighteenth century, the tendency in all the major continental states of Europe was to aspire to a powerfully centralizing, rationalized, internal ordering of society."[31] To achieve this social coherence, however, a sociopolitical doctrine was created dictating that "the Jews could no longer be allowed—for their own good, but more especially for the good of society at large—to continue in their set and ancient manner."[32] To address this conundrum, various European states created a "defined, fixed, and intelligible place" for their Jewish residents who were either unwilling or incapable of joining the move toward "social uniformity."[33] What was created in Europe was a ghetto system that, in Vital's view, comprised "locked and barred night-time urban cages" that had "profound sociopsychological consequences."[34] Fear of the world outside the ghetto was the most common result of residing in the segregated section of the city, as Vital explains: "A venture into the wider, unfamiliar, intimidating, world of the gentiles . . . was not only fraught with immense practical difficulty, but was for the overwhelming majority no less than unthinkable."[35] The ghetto was their home.

The ghetto, the word and the place, would make its way across the Atlantic and, though beginning as an exclusively Jewish settlement, it would later become associated with America's most outcast population: the urban Black poor. "For most of the nineteenth century, the word *ghetto* was foreign to

Americans," writes Schwartz.[36] Much of this changed due to a surge of Jewish immigration to the United States during the late nineteenth century. According to Schwartz, "between 1881 and 1924, more than two-and-one-half million Jews left Eastern Europe for America."[37] Once stepping onto American soil, these Jewish immigrants settled in neighborhoods that provided them with the needed isolation to reconstruct the communal enclaves of the European ghettoes. They segregated themselves from the rest of society, but note that this was a voluntary segregation. According to sociologist Herbert J. Gans, *voluntary* segregation creates "enclaves [that] are seen as places settled by racial, ethnic, religious, or other minorities that are not stigmatized by the white majority but self-segregate themselves . . . because they share a language, culture, or nationality."[38] Conversely, *involuntary* segregation is based on the "othering process," which, according to Gans, is "the selection of minorities who are stigmatized, discriminated against, racialized, and ghettoized."[39] Gans cautions that distinguishing between the two is not always clear-cut. For instance, he notes that "sometimes the involuntarily segregated participate in their own exclusion," and this "[enables] family and friends, as well as culturally similar and like-minded people, to live together."[40]

In his 1928 article "The Ghetto," sociologist Louis Wirth states that the term *ghetto* designates "those areas where the poorest and most backward groups of the Jewish population, usually the recently arrived immigrants, find their home."[41] The sense of community within the ghetto is the focus of Wirth's study. He contends that within the ghetto's invisible walls, Jews "received that appreciation and sympathetic understanding which the larger world could not offer."[42] And he adds that "in [the Jew's] own community, which was based upon solidarity of the families that composed it, he was a person with status."[43] A more thorough analysis on the formation of the Jewish ghettoes in the city of Chicago is provided in Wirth's book *The Ghetto*. Starting as early as the early-to-mid-nineteenth century, Jewish immigrants, mostly from Eastern Europe, settled in Chicago. According to Wirth, Jewish immigrants settled in the "Loop, in the vicinity of the markets and the light manufacturing district."[44] An anecdote given by Wirth conveys how this section of the city was regarded by Chicago residents:

> One of these newcomers tells of arriving in Chicago and asking a stranger where the Jews lived: He was directed west, where he was told the "greenhorns" were to be found. . . . He tells us: "Chicago, especially the West Side, then was a place of filth, infested with the worst element any city could produce. Crime was rampant. No one was safe. Jews were treated in the streets in the most abhorrent and shameful manner, stones being thrown at them and their beards being pulled by thugs.[45]

This community of Jewish immigrants fueled the growth of the ghetto on the West Side of Chicago. And it continued to grow until the beginning of the twentieth century, most evident as the population of Russian Jews became the majority of Jewish residents, numbering about 50,000. Eventually, the tide of Jewish immigrants settling in the West Side would abate, and ghetto residents spread throughout the city—for example, in Hyde Park, Humboldt Park, and Columbus Park, all of which were "high-grade residential neighborhoods on the outskirts of [Chicago]."[46]

A new group of immigrants from the American South would arrive in Chicago and metropolises throughout the North, and the ghetto would now be their home. Wirth states that "the Negro, like the [Jewish] immigrant, is segregated in the city into a racial colony; economic factors, race prejudice, and cultural differences combine to set him apart."[47] Moreover, Wirth comments that "the Negro has drifted to the abandoned sections of the ghetto for precisely the same reasons that the Jews . . . came there."[48] Of course, differences between the experiences of Jews and African Americans in the ghetto are manifold. But Wirth identifies a similarity that is worth mentioning. The ghetto must be examined as a sociopsychological phenomenon, "for it is not merely a physical fact, but also a state of mind."[49] The challenges of the ghetto as a mind-set, a way of viewing the world, is vital to understanding why many ghetto residents remain imprisoned within its walls.

THE SPECTER OF THE GHETTO

In their insightful essay "Creating the Black Ghetto: Black Residential Patterns before and during the Great Migration," sociologists John R. Logan and associates contend that the characteristics of ghettoization were in place as early as the late-nineteenth century but were intensified by the large influx of Black residents in urban areas during the early twentieth century.[50] The authors point out, for instance, that as early as 1880 there was a high level of residential segregation for Blacks in the city of Chicago, which is much earlier than the time period suggested by other studies.[51] Their research suggests that what occurred over the next several decades, peaking around 1940, is an expansion and solidification of a "zone of black settlement."[52] Similar patterns of Black ghettoization were found in other cities throughout North America.

For instance, in his study *The Origins of the Urban Crisis*, historian Thomas J. Sugrue examines the rise of the racialized ghetto in Detroit, Michigan. He argues that the city's ghetto "had emerged in the midst of the World War I–era Great Migration of blacks from the South to the Urban North."[53] In response, Detroit's white residents began to create a series of boundaries to keep Black residents restricted within certain spaces, such as "establishing restrictive covenants to assure the homogeneity of neighborhoods." A similar story emerges from historian Gilbert Osofsky's research on how Manhattan's Black residents were concentrated into an urban slum, Harlem. New York City's Black population remained small throughout the nineteenth century, never exceeding more than one percent of the city's population, about 9,000 to 15,000 residents.[54] "By 1910," states Osofsky, "there were 91,709 Negroes in the metropolis, the majority southern born."[55] But a radical change occurred that created a concentration of poor Blacks in Harlem. Osofsky writes that the areas of the city that housed Russian Jews and Italians were being "depopulated; and Negro Harlem, within the space of ten years, became the most 'incredible slum' in the entire city."[56] Most of this was driven by a massive increase in the Black population, about 115 per cent, between 1920 and 1930. During the 1920s, "Harlem was transformed from a potentially ideal community to a neighborhood with manifold social and economic problems."[57]

In their influential text *Black Metropolis*, sociologists St. Clair Drake and Horace Cayton focus on the development of the Black ghetto in Chicago, particularly the Bronzeville neighborhood. The authors analyze the "formal and informal social controls used to isolate [Black residents] . . . within congested all Negro neighborhoods," referred to as the Black Belt.[58] They report that these areas suffer "from a type of social disorganization which is reflected in high illegitimacy and juvenile delinquency rates and a high incidence of insanity."[59] Restrictive covenants ensured that Chicago's ghetto residents remained within the most impoverished areas of the city, making it difficult for ghetto residents to live elsewhere. Drake and Cayton state that "three-fourths of all the residential property in the city was bound by restrictive covenants."[60] Sociologist Mitchell Duneier remarks that for the authors of *Black Metropolis* "such aspects of black life, which contributed to pathological behavior such as juvenile delinquency and teenage pregnancy, were attributable directly to the restrictive covenant."[61] The living conditions brought on by restrictive covenants created the behaviors that the city's white population found threatening. Therefore, Drake and Cayton contend,

> These Negroes, upon whom the city depends for much of its unskilled and semi-skilled labor and for a large part of its domestic service, continue to pile up upon one another within these congested areas. As they do so, morbidity and mortality rates rise out of all proportion to those in the rest of the city. Crime and juvenile delinquency rates, too, indicate that serious maladjustments are present in the Black Belt. Black Metropolis acquires the reputation of being a "slum area," and the bare statistical record and surface impressions seem convincing evidence that Negroes make undesirable neighbors. . . . Rumor and

chance impressions further confirm the reputation of Black Metropolis as a "rough" neighborhood.[62]

Similar to restrictive covenants, the stigma of the ghetto soon became something from which its residents—and also those who never resided in the ghetto—could not escape. Elijah Anderson, a sociologist whose work focuses on inner-city youth, provides a telling personal account of his struggles to overcome the judgment that equates *all* Black life with the ghetto. Anderson shares that he was vacationing with his family in Wellfleet, Massachusetts, a town that attracts mostly upper-middle-class white vacationers. Anderson notes that during his family's two-week stay, he seldom encountered another Black person. That mattered little to Anderson, though, as his attention was focused instead on the serenity of Wellfleet's majestic natural environment. Anderson felt so at home in the town that he decides to go for a jog one morning. Everything is going well, and he says, "It seemed I had *this world* all to myself."[63] Then something happens. Anderson is jolted out of the reverie of the moment when a red pick-up truck appears in the middle of the road. After rolling down the driver's side window, a middle-aged white man begins to yell, but because of the distance between himself and the truck, Anderson has difficulty making out what the man is saying. He moves closer, cups his ear, and hears the white man yelling, "Go home! . . . Go home! . . . Go home!"[64] His peaceful morning jog was over. Anderson quickly understood that the white man he encountered that morning wanted him to know that Wellfleet was not the Black man's home. His hostile command—Go home!—conveyed his conviction that Black people come from and should forever remain in their true home, the ghetto. Anderson confesses that this encounter troubled him greatly:

> This incident not only spoiled my morning jog but nagged me for the rest of the day. Days afterward, I shared it with friends, black and white. Many of the blacks recounted their own similar tales. But who was this man? What was his problem? Was the incident merely a fluke? Did many other white people here feel similarly? And exactly what did he mean by "go home"? Did he assume, because of my black skin, that I was from the ghetto? These questions remained with me, and over the years have inspired my thinking about what I have come to call the iconic ghetto.[65]

No matter their efforts, even if they ascend to the upper regions of the economic and educational scale, the iconic ghetto is regarded as the home for Black people. But is the ghetto truly a home? According to Anderson, the ghetto is not only a place marked by its physical distinction from the surrounding society but also one consumed by a "tangle of pathology" that "produces a cycle or culture of poverty through generations of men who fail as providers, women who bear children 'out of wedlock,' and youths who grow up without discipline."[66] The image of the iconic ghetto also conveys that its inhabitants are overwhelmed by failed relationships. Anthropologist Tony L. Whitehead comments that the severe isolation ghetto residents experience is due to their "lack of participation in significant ethnic, family and kinship organizations, voluntary associations such as work or fraternal organizations, and informal networks of friends and acquaintances."[67] On Whitehead's account, these support systems, which were essential to community survival during slavery and later periods of racial oppression, have deteriorated in the "racialized urban ghetto,"[68] leaving many inhabitants isolated.

In *Economy and Society*, sociologist Max Weber maintains that persons isolated in this manner suffer from "closed relationships."[69] "A relationship will . . . be 'closed' against outsiders so far as . . . participation of certain persons is excluded, limited, or subjected to conditions."[70] Weber adds that the closed relationship will be opened only on the condition that the excluded can improve the situation of the dominant party. Simply stated, the relationship itself must be deemed valuable to those with the power to close the relationship. Therefore, sociologist Loic Wacquant argues that the ghetto is an "instrument of exclusionary closure" that ensures that its inhabitants remain separated from the more esteemed segments of society.[71] Another relevant point is that these closed relationships are also found among the inhabitants of the ghetto themselves, especially within the familial environment. Weber, who was a keen observer of city life in modern Western Europe, argues that the city "is a closed settlement . . . which forms a colony so extensive that the reciprocal personal acquaintance of the inhabitants, elsewhere characteristic of a neighborhood, is lacking."[72]

The focus of Weber's study was on the economic development of the city—for instance, the rise of the urban economy—but he was also concerned with how life in the city strained communal bonds. For example, he remarks that "the group of neighbors may take on different forms depending on the type of settlement: scattered farms, a village, a city street or slum; neighborly social action may have different degrees of intensity and, *especially in the modern city* [italics mine], it may be almost non-existent."[73] Contrary to an ecological view of community that focuses on how neighborliness is formed by residence in a common location, Weber postulates that an authentically relational community is formed through social actions that evince shared social power. Without the shared meaning that creates social action, there is no social power and thus no community. Weber defines communal social relations as follows:

It is by no means true that the existence of common qualities, a common situation, or common modes of behavior imply the existence of a communal social relationship. Thus, for instance, the possession of a common biological inheritance by virtue of which persons are classified as belonging to the same "race" naturally implies no sort of communal social relationship between them. By restrictions of social intercourse and on marriage persons may find themselves in a similar situation, *a situation of isolation from the environment which imposes these distinctions*. But even if they all react to this situation in the same way, this does not constitute a communal relationship. The latter does not even exist if they have a common "feeling" about this situation and its consequences. It is only when this feeling leads to a mutual orientation of their behavior to each other that a social relationship arises between them rather than of each to the environment. Furthermore, it is only so far as this relationship involves *feelings of belonging together* [italics mine] that it is a "communal relationship."[74]

For Weber, neither sharing a common language nor participation in a "market," though encouraging a certain level of association, are enough to guarantee the establishment of social relationships.

Sociologist Gertrud Neuwirth points out that "much of Weber's work is concerned with the impact of power (in its various economic, political, and social forms) on the emergence and structure of social relationships."[75] Using Weber's theory of social power, Neuwirth contends that the Black residents of the American ghetto lack the social power to create their own communal life and, by extension, have great difficulty in forming communal relationships. Most of this, according to Neuwirth, is due to the fact that ghetto residents lack the ethnic honor (or social self-esteem) to define themselves and have "no positive system of identification."[76] Rather, the system of identification they adhere to, which promotes their negative social status, has been created by the dominant culture that upholds Western bourgeoise values as the norm, particularly as it relates to the patriarchal family structure. Neuwirth states that the lack of self-esteem is especially problematic for Black men in the ghetto, wherein the family's disorganized structure "perpetuates the denial of social esteem to the Negro male, even in his own family and community setting."[77] Hence, even in the ghetto, Black men maintain a low social status. Elijah Anderson notes that, because of his low social status, it is not uncommon for a Black man to find that "people—black as well as white—necessarily avoid him, and through their avoidance behavior teach him that he is an outsider in his own society."[78] If Anderson's observation is accurate, then, unfortunately, not even the ghetto is the Black man's home.

NO PLACE TO GROW A MAN

In *Black Rage*, psychologists William H. Grier and Price M. Cobbs share the story of a twelve-year-old boy named Jimmy, who is experiencing the challenges of coming of age, of growing up, in the ghetto. His main problem is that he "had trouble seeing anything in his life as definite, with any form or shape."[79] Though he was uncertain about much, Jimmy was clear about one thing: "He saw his father as weak and powerless."[80] Jimmy did not form this opinion due to his father's diminutive stature or any other physical characteristic. Instead, it was his father's broken and inequitable relationships with others that led to Jimmy's awareness that "his father could never 'stand up.'"[81] Simply put, in Jimmy's eyes, his father could never be a man. But it is not Jimmy's problem alone. Grier and Cobbs explain:

> Jimmy is beginning to realize that he has no power and, like his father, will not get it. At his age the concepts are misty, but he realizes that his father and fathers of his friends are lacking something. He has had few, if any, traumatic incidents with whites. There have been no overt acts of discrimination. The family has lived in a ghetto, and all their socialization has been within that framework. But Jimmy is part of a historical legacy that spans more than three hundred years. He lives in a large city but he shares his insight with every black child in every city in this country. He must devise individual ways to meet group problems. . . . In time he comes to see that society has locked arms against him, that rather than help he can expect opposition to his development, and that he lives not in a benign community but in a society that *views his growth with hostility* [italics mine].[82]

Grier and Cobbs's psychological analysis of Jimmy's dim prospects for growing into manhood was echoed by certain influential policymakers in the U.S. government during the 1960s. No other study during that time was more consequential than *The Negro Family: The Case for National Action*, now referred to as the "Moynihan Report." Led by Daniel Patrick Moynihan, then assistant secretary of labor for Lyndon Johnson's "Great Society" program, the report focused on the deterioration of the African American family. When examining the report closely, however, one can see that Moynihan is concerned with the failure of Black men to assert their male authority in the home. For Moynihan, assertion of male authority was the only way to uplift the race and change the conditions of the ghetto. In July 1965, a few months after the report was released, Moynihan sent a memo to White House aide Harry McPherson declaring that "*above all things the down-and-out Negro boy needs to be inducted into the male American society*."[83] The report highlights the impediments that make this assimilation "into the male American society" so difficult, particularly the Black family's matriarchal structure. By doing so, the Moynihan Report joined a chorus of observers, such as Kenneth Clark, Nathan Glazer, E. Franklin Frazier, and Gunnar Myrdal, each of whom argued that the Black family's disorganization, most notably in the ghetto, was creating antisocial behaviors in Black males. Historian Darryl M. Scott remarks that an emerging theme in these studies was that "white men were not the dominant force in emasculating black men; black women were."[84]

The central thesis of the Moynihan Report is that stable families create a stable society. According to the report, "the white family has achieved a high degree of stability and is maintaining that stability,"[85] in contrast to the "highly unstable" family structure of African American families in the ghetto.[86] The report does not, however, ignore the lingering effects that slavery has had on the Black family. Following the arguments made in E. Franklin Frazier's *The Negro Family in the United States*, the report traces the origins of family disorganization to the trauma of plantation life. Frazier notes not only the breakdown of kinship bonds, but, even more relevant to the report's central claim, he states that "under all conditions of slavery, the Negro mother remained the most dependable and important figure in the family."[87] The report argues that in conjunction with the rise of the Black matriarchy was the equally damaging rise of hostilities toward Black men in the larger society, summed up as an effort to keep "the Negro in his place."[88] Black men were therefore undergoing a double emasculation. The report declares,

> Unquestionably, these events worked against the emergence of a strong father figure. The very essence of the male animal, from the bantam rooster to the four-star general, is to strut. Indeed, in 19th century America, a particular type of exaggerated male boastfulness became almost a national style. Not for the Negro male. The "sassy nigger" was lynched.[89]

The transition to city life, which, as discussed earlier, occurred during the early decades of the twentieth century, worsened the problem of familial disorganization. In *Dark Ghetto*, a study of Black urban life, psychologist Kenneth Clark discusses how a loss of power has lingering effects on urban Black men. Clark begins by providing a quote by a Harlem resident who protests, "A lot of times, when I'm working, I become as despondent as hell and I feel like crying. I'm not a man, none of us are men! I don't own anything. I'm not a man enough to own a store; none of us are."[90] Similar to Moynihan, Clark identifies a lack of power as the reason for the Black family's disorganization.[91] In the section of *Dark Ghetto* titled "The Psychology of the Ghetto," Clark argues that because the Black male is not able to "support his normal desire for dominance," due to various structural issues, he must assert his self-esteem and status in "ways that seem either antisocial, escapist, [or] socially irresponsible."[92] The lack of socially approved power within the ghetto damages the self-esteem of its residents to such an extent that they isolate themselves from the larger society and fellow ghetto residents. "A most cruel and psychologically oppressive aspect and consequence of enforced segregation," Clark says, "is that its victims can be made to accommodate to their victimized status and under certain circumstances to state that it is their desire to be set apart, or to agree that subjugation is not really detrimental but beneficial."[93] Mitchell Duneier observes that there are a number of differences between *Dark Ghetto* and similar studies but that it still "generally adopts a male perspective and even blames women for certain of the ghetto's problems."[94] Recent sociological studies still purport the message that the ghetto's pathologies have a damaging effect on Black men, specifically. Many of these young men do not have a healthy image of what it means to grow up in the ghetto.

In *More than Just Race: Being Black and Poor in the Inner City*, William Julius Wilson contends that the findings of the Moynihan report were "prophetic," particularly as the issues raised in the report are placed in "current perspective."[95] According to Wilson, a number of trends noted in the Moynihan Report are still present and, in some instances, have worsened. For example, Wilson states that "in 1965 a single woman headed 25 percent of all nonwhite families; by 1996, however, the proportion of all black families headed by a single women had swelled to 47 percent, dropping slightly to 45 percent in 2006."[96] Following Moynihan and Clark, Wilson underscores the disadvantages of single-parent households; he states, for example, that "single-parent households tend to exert less control over the behavior of their adolescent children."[97] The absence of adequate role models, most specifically Black-male role models, also contributes to the behavioral challenges of inner-city youth. Mitchell Duneier explains that, according to Wilson's research, isolation in the ghetto means that "not only did [residents] have limited access to networks of people who could help them . . . but they also had few role models."[98]

The lack of adequate role models for young Black males in the inner city is a central theme of sociologist Elijah Anderson's research. In *Code of the Street*, Anderson observes the *intra*communal interactions in a Philadelphia inner-city neighborhood. The insecure social status of young Black males is central to the text. Anderson remarks that "for many young men, the operating assumption is that a man, especially a 'real' man, knows what other men know—the code of the street,"[99] defined by Anderson as a "set of informal rules governing interpersonal public behavior, particularly violence."[100] For outsiders, these codes reflect the distorted values of the inner city, an alternative culture, but for those within the ghetto's walls, adhering to these codes makes the difference between a person's staying alive or being destroyed by the streets. Anderson remarks that these informal rules allow "those who are inclined to aggression to precipitate violent encounters in an approved way."[101] Therefore, verbal and physical altercations, unfortunately, are the common ways ghetto residents seek to attain respect, the most precious commodity in the inner city, particularly among young Black men.

Anderson's analysis differs from that of, say, William Julius Wilson's or Kenneth Clark's in that he argues that there is a hypersegregated community within the ghetto that is not only separated from the larger society but is alienated within the ghetto itself. Whereas some ghetto residents cautiously use the "code of the street" as a tool for survival, picking it up and putting it down when needed, other residents embrace it as a permanent way of life. Anderson says that "people in this class are profound casualties of the social and economic system, and they tend to embrace the street code wholeheartedly."[102] These are not the "decent" ghetto families who still attempt, as best as possible, to attain a middle-class lifestyle. Oftentimes due to the absence of the "man of the house," street-oriented women, as Anderson calls them, are left to raise children on their own, and often do so only "sporadically."[103] In such an environment, children are forced to learn early on the hard lessons of the street: "You cannot take survival itself, let alone respect, for granted; you have to fight for your place in the world."[104] However, even if they possess the interminable grit to make something of themselves, these children of the street, especially young Black males, will have to fight the stigma of growing up in the ghetto.

AN ALTERNATIVE VIEW OF THE GHETTO

According to Loïc Wacquant, the space inhabited by the ghetto underclass is perceived as a modern wilderness, an "opaque and evil territory to be avoided," where people "live like animals."[105] Furthermore, being identified with these urban wildernesses "carries an automatic presumption of social unworthiness and moral inferiority."[106] To illustrate, Wacquant provides the following testimonial, given by a high school student from the South Side of Chicago: "People really look down on you because of where you come from and who you are. People don't want to have anything to do with you."[107] Those who reside in the urban wilderness are cut off from the rest of society, but is their isolation even worse than that? Is there a more profound isolation that cannot be captured by sociological analysis? How do we better understand that the loss of inner sources leaves countless Black men in the ghetto feeling utterly hopeless—as if they were abandoned by God? Some might even ask, *"Where is God in the ghetto?"*

In "Suicide Patterns among Black Males," Sean Joe, a scholar of social development, notes that African Americans "attribute negative life events to internal causes, even in the context of extreme disadvantages and challenging developmental experiences, and this attribution increases the risk of psychological distress and suicide."[108] When Black males do not possess the resiliency that enables them to attribute their plight to external factors, they find fault within themselves. The situation is worsened, notes Joe, by a pattern of hypermasculinity that discourages help seeking and increases vulnerability, leaving many Black males abandoned in their despair. Philosopher and social critic Cornel West identifies this sense of loss as a "pervasive spiritual impoverishment" that causes a "collapse of meaning in life—the eclipse of hope and absence of love of self and others, the breakdown of family and neighborhood bonds—[which] leads to a social deracination and cultural denudement of urban dwellers, especially children."[109] Rhetorical flourishes aside, West's observation makes it clear that this is a spiritual problem.

The decades of research provided by sociologists make a damning claim: young Black men in the ghetto are destined for a life of failure, loneliness, constant conflict, and early death. The sociological perspective is limited, however, in that it focuses on the individual and society. According to sociologist C. Wright Mills, sociology, at its best, helps us to answer three questions: 1) "What is the structure of this particular society as a whole?"; 2) "Where does this society stand in human history?"; and 3) "What varieties of men and women now prevail in this society and in this period?"[110] By answering these questions, the sociologist can identify the structural changes in society—such as high unemployment, low marriage rates, and so on—that are impacting the lives of individuals. Mills was aware that data provided by sociologists can often become "facts of milieu" that are used as the final word about what is occurring in a person's world.[111] Needless to say, when sociologists describe the ghetto as disorganized and pathological, they also, knowingly or not, are making statements perceived as the truth, the facts, about ghetto *residents*. The aim of sociology, however, is not to provide an alternative discourse on the present order of things. Rather, this is religion's task.

Sociologist David Martin, a scholar of the sociology of religion, argues that "religion introduces into human language an alternative discourse based on non-violence, universalism, self-sacrifice, service, repentance and reconciliation."[112] Religion rejects "the fundamental dynamics of the social order."[113] The symbols provided by religion underscore the inescapable tension between the trauma of social reality and the hope for a better world. In short, Martin views theology as the means by which we come to understand the signs and symbols of religion. Theology brings into focus "angles of transcendence and degrees of tension with the world that in the course of the last three thousand years have generated contrast between the way of faith and the ways of the world."[114] Martin also states that the symbolic logic of theology entails a "*double entendre* created by an angle of transcendence between the givens of existence, the raw data . . . of the human condition, and the visionary transformation of revelation."[115] That is to say, reality is held in dialectical tension with the transcendent, or "condensed signs like the city and desert are overheard in two registers, physical and spiritual."[116]

Within the African American religious tradition, the symbolic has been pivotal in the struggle against oppression, and the Bible is the primary source for religious symbolism that inspires counternarratives to oppose the hardships of reality. Theologian Frederick L. Ware states that there "is a pervasiveness of biblical motifs, metaphors drawn from the Christian language . . . in African American communities."[117] Citing the scholarship of theologian Charles H. Long, Ware suggests that there are "deep symbols," such as *God*, *race*, *Africa*, and *freedom*, that are "words of power that constrain, guide, and become a focus of thought and action."[118] But there are other symbols that African Americans use to perceive their daily experiences in the light of Scripture. Albert J. Raboteau, scholar of African American religion, argues that during slavery these symbols, such as freedom, created within the slaves an "inner world" wherein the "primary value and fixed point was the will of God," which was opposed to the prevailing order of the slaveholders.[119] For example, the story of Israel's liberation from Egypt was incorporated into the slaves' own story of enslavement so as to keep them from being overwhelmed by despair. Slaves could hold on to hope because, as Raboteau remarks, "Was there not precedent in God's emancipation of Israel from Egypt?"[120] Raboteau says,

> The Christian slaves applied the Exodus story, whose end they knew, to their own experience of slavery, which had not ended. In identifying with the Exodus story, they created meaning and purpose out of the chaotic and senseless experience of slavery. Exodus functioned as an archetypal event for the slaves. The sacred history of God's liberation of his people would be or was being repeated in the American South. . . . The story of Israel's exodus from Egypt helped make it possible for the slaves to project a future radically different from their present.[121]

The precedent of God's deliverance was not instructive during the era of slave religion alone. In *Conjuring Culture*, scholar of African American religion Theophus H. Smith argues that African Americans have made "incantatory use of biblical figures like Exodus and Promised Land" throughout their history.[122] For Smith, this entails a theological reading through which "biblical figures are employed in synergy with a Deity who cooperates in the concrete historical realization of such figures." But Smith warns that this "incantatory use of biblical figures"—or figural-theological reading—is not a given. It is a communal practice that, if not cherished and preserved, can be lost.

> We have seen that in African American theological perspective, for example, Exodus becomes historical in the emancipation of the slaves in the 1860s, and in the civil rights movement of the 1960s, under the historical supervision of a provident God. It remains to be seen, however, whether this tradition of figural-theological reading and synergetic reenactment will continue to flourish in Black America. It remains to be seen, that is, whether the culture will continue to let the biblical text absorb the world, "rather than the world the text."[123]

Smith is not proposing that African Americans embrace a literalist approach to the Bible, one tied to the past, but rather one that encounters the text creatively, with the goal of transforming the community's current reality. Are there biblical symbols that could "absorb the world" of Black men in the ghetto, here and now? Similar to Raboteau's question, one must ask "What are the precedents in Scripture that can speak to the experience of life in the ghetto?" "Who are the figures in the Bible who were considered outcasts in Scripture, cut off from society, but still, somehow, remained in relationship with God?" "And what did God provide to these outcasts that allowed them not only to survive but, in many instances, to flourish in dangerous environments?" What does the Bible say to those who must grow in the ghetto?

4

The Wilderness

Where Our Gift Grows

And I say, "O that I had wings like a dove!
  I would fly away and be at rest;
truly, I would flee far away;
  I would lodge in the wilderness;
                    Selah
I would hurry to find a shelter for myself
  from the raging wind and tempest."

—*Psalm 55:6–8*

THE WILDERNESS REMOVED AND RECOVERED

Who wants to go to the wilderness? To us moderns, the wilderness is an enigma. Geographically, especially for Westerners, it is challenging to locate the wilderness as an actual space. The rapid rise of global urbanization over the past centuries has made it difficult to find ourselves residing near any place officially designated as wilderness. Besides this, however, there is also the loss of the word *wilderness* in our everyday discourse, where it seldom occurs to describe a specific location. Philosopher Max Oelschlaeger suggests that a reason for this opinion regarding the wilderness in the United States is that "relatively little of its land remains unhumanized."[1] Therefore, as a result of our humanizing (or civilizing) the once-untamed landscape, we have developed a negative attitude toward any wilderness that remains, along with its residents. In an article published in 1930 titled "The Problem of the Wilderness," wilderness activist Robert Marshall attempted to define the wilderness in the North American context. Marshall states that the wilderness "has no permanent inhabitants, [and] possesses no possibility of conveyance"; and its primary characteristics are "that it requires anyone who exists in it to depend exclusively on his own efforts for survival; and . . . it preserves as nearly as possible the primitive environment."[2] Isolated, unreachable, primitive; for Marshall, these characteristics define the wilderness.

"The philosophy that progress is proportional to the amount of alteration imposed on nature never seemed to have occurred to the Indians,"[3] writes Marshall. Native Americans, including the Incas, Aztecs, and the pueblo peoples, made only minor changes to the land in which they lived.[4] Marshall was not an advocate of the total conversion of the wilderness, however. To the contrary, he insisted that the wilderness had benefits that helped fight off, as he put it, "the coddling of civilization."[5] The primary benefits were physical, mental, and aesthetic. Physically, the wilderness builds independence; in the wilderness only the truly strong can survive. Mentally, the wilderness fortifies independent thinking, especially as its intense isolation provides the optimal environment for the formation and nurturing of original ideas. Finally, the aesthetic value of the wilderness is that its beauty is untouched "from all temporal relationship."[6] Marshall was in awe of the wilderness's dynamic beauty, viewing it as more alive than a "Beethoven symphony or a Shakespearean drama."[7] The advantages of the wilderness, however, are counterbalanced with several disadvantages. Atop Marshall's concerns are the lack of fire protection, economic loss, and the civilized population's lack of affection for the wilderness. Despite the negative opinion of the masses, Marshall held firm that the wilderness, at least in a few preserved locations, was essential to maintaining the American character of rugged individualism and conquest. He protested that "immediate steps should be taken to establish enough tracts to insure everyone who hungers for it a generous opportunity of enjoying wilderness isolation."[8] Without the wilderness, our society would be in great danger, as Marshall argues,

> Then it will be a few years until the last escape from society will be barricaded. If that day arrives there will be countless souls born to live in strangulation, countless human beings who will be crushed under the artificial edifice raised by man. There is just one hope of repulsing the tyrannical ambition of civilization to conquer every niche of the whole earth. That hope is the organization of a spirited people who will fight for the freedom of the wilderness.[9]

Almost a century since Marshall voiced his fear that the wilderness would be lost, it is obvious that his warnings were ignored. The benefits of the wilderness, its unique ability to build and nourish the American character, have been overshadowed by its negative characteristics. Why would anyone want to enter the wilderness, willfully? To many modern observers, particularly in the urbanized West, the wilderness is a wild place, overrun by wild plants and animals, and most frightening of all, wild people. Wilderness, as a place and a symbol, represents all that the civilized world is to avoid and, when needed, conquer.

Oelschlaeger has it that the wilderness was not always viewed with apprehension. For instance, our Paleolithic ancestors, hunters and gatherers, "lived comfortably in the wilderness," making no distinction between themselves and untamed nature.[10] Contrary to popular belief, such communities as the Inuit of the Artic regions or the Kalahari Bushmen of southern Africa did not find themselves starving in the wilderness. According to Oelschlaeger, "Paleolithic people *were not* [italics mine] constantly living on the margin of survival."[11] Scholars agree that poverty did not arise until later in history, as an elite group created various mechanisms to exploit nature and the underclass. Up to that point, however, an outlook prevailed in which "harmony with rather than exploitation of the natural world was a guiding principle."[12] A radical shift occurred when Hebrew and early Christian thought, fused with Greek rationalism, introduced profound anthropocentrism. This change altered the way humankind interacted with nature, "for *nature was conceived as valueless until humanized*."[13] Within the Hebrew Bible, however, the wilderness is not viewed in a one-sided manner. Oelschlaeger states that "the Hebrew Bible . . . is no one thing; even with its most ancient sacred document competing ideas of wilderness are presented."[14] Uncovering the diverse meanings of the wilderness in the Hebrew Bible is not the focus of Oelschlaeger's study. Instead, he explores the changes in thought on the wilderness from Neolithic to modern times, while also offering analysis of the attitudes toward wilderness amongst North American figures, including but not limited to Henry David Thoreau, John Muir, Aldo Leopold, and Gary Snyder. Therefore, though Oelschlaeger's research provides insights regarding humanity's relationship with the wilderness through the ages, questions remain about the idea of the wilderness in Old Testament theology.

THE WORD ON THE WILDERNESS

The theology of the wilderness is related to the theology of land in the Hebrew Bible. In *The Land*, Walter Brueggemann notes that "the Bible itself is primarily concerned with the issue of being displaced and yearning for a place."[15] On the one hand, land is a designated space, a location that can be pinpointed on a map; on the other hand, land is also a place that has a symbolic sense, filled with cultural meanings, such as the claim "this is *our* land." Land, for Israel, was not just about a specific location (i.e., the promised land) but rather "*a place with Yahweh*, a place well filled with memories of life with him and promise from him and vows to him."[16] The land represents

Yahweh's promise. Conversely, there is the wilderness tradition that depicts Israel's frustrations over wandering without adequate resources for survival. This is different from the experience of the chosen sojourner, such as Abraham, depicted in the book of Genesis as one who is on the way somewhere. The wanderer in the wilderness, according to Brueggemann, "is destined to die the long death of the desert, on the way to nowhere."[17]

After the exodus, Israel was so surprised and dismayed by the wilderness experience, its no-land status, that it began to utter complaints against Yahweh. Brueggemann's description of the wilderness demonstrates that Israel's grumblings were warranted:

> Wilderness is formless and therefore lifeless. To be placed in the wilderness is to be cast into the land of the enemy—cosmic, natural, historical—without any of the props or resources that give life order and meaning. To be in the wilderness is landlessness par excellence, being only a resident alien, as were the fathers, but in a context hostile and destructive. . . . Such a land is not only not sown, that is, beyond cultivation, but it is seedless. *Not only is nothing growing, but nothing can grow* [italics mine]. It is land without promise, without hope, where no newness can come. . . . This is Israel's dominant memory of landlessness: to be at the disposal of an environment totally without life supports and without any visible hint that there is an opening to the future.[18]

As an utterly hopeless landscape, the wilderness could not sustain human life, or any life for that matter. Nothing grows in the wilderness. In "The Desert Motif in the Bible and in Qumran Literature," Shemaryahu Talmon, a Hebrew Bible scholar, observes that "wilderness is a place of utter desolation: a vast void or parched earth with no streams or rivers to provide sustenance for plants and wildlife."[19] Talmon adds that the Israelites loathed the desert, and that this was the "attitude of the city-dweller, the farmer, the semi-sedentary shepherd" who would never, under any conditions, enter the wilderness voluntarily. In his study of the theology of wilderness in the Bible, literary scholar Robert Barry Leal argues that Israel's negative view of the wilderness was not formed on its own but was greatly influenced by the cultural context of the ancient world. At its core, the wilderness "encapsulates the attitude of a society to the unknown."[20] The wilderness was the abode of the Other. *Midbar* is the word most used for wilderness in the Hebrew Bible, but there is no specific place or type of landscape that it designates. Grazing land or steppe, vast region or limited space, adjacent to the city or beyond the outskirts of settlements—all of these are classified as *midbar*, the wilderness. Though the characteristics of the actual place might differ, a reoccurring theme of "desolation" or "laid waste" is associated in the "Hebrew mind with wilderness."[21]

Laura Feldt, a historian of Hebrew religion, states that the wilderness is often viewed negatively by scholars of the Hebrew Bible because "prime attention is focused on the alimentary area."[22] Therefore, "when *midbar* and related words are used, it is the lack of water that is stressed."[23] Nothing in the wilderness supports life, any form of life. Feldt's research is unique in that her focus is on more than just the wilderness as a negative space, its nonhuman characteristics, but also on its central role in Israel's religious identity formation. Moving beyond the materiality of the wilderness allows Feldt to uplift the positive aspects of the wilderness, particularly its theological function in the Hebrew Bible. A notable instance of this is the narrative of Israel's being fed with manna in the wilderness (Exod. 16:14–15):

> When the layer of dew lifted, there on the surface of the wilderness was a fine flakey substance, as fine as frost on the ground. When the Israelites saw it, they said to one another, "What is it?" For they did not know what it was. Moses said to them, "It is the bread that the LORD has given you to eat."

Manna was supernatural. In fact, according to Feldt, the manna the Israelites received "represents a systematic inversion of what constitutes ordinary food according to the Hebrew Bible: manna is an imaginary, fantastic type of bread raining from the sky."[24] The significance of manna in the wilderness is not just about natural versus supernatural nourishment, however. Rather it represents a "systematic inversion of the normal in the Hebrew Bible,"[25] which is integral to understanding the theological function of the wilderness. The wilderness is a place of refuge and of divine revelation, certainly. But most of all, it is "a space of nearness to the deity, a time of great intimacy" when Yahweh provides much-needed "parental care" to outcasts.[26]

Israel's religious identity formation is established through its relationship with Yahweh. Feldt notes that in the wilderness "Yahweh and Israel renew and redefine their relationship."[27] Because it is cut off from the influence of the civilized world, the wilderness is a space that allows Israel to learn of and live out God's unique purpose for them as a nation. For Feldt, a central feature of Israel's identity formation is that it is always in tension. Israel is always in the process of maturation, transformation; as Feldt puts it, "These texts suggest . . . a discrepancy between what Israel is and what Israel ought to be."[28] Feldt suggests the following four aspects of the religious significance of the wilderness:

1. It is where intimate meetings with Yahweh occur, "a place of personal and communal religious transformation."

2. The wilderness narratives are opposed to the ways of "city life and large institutions."
3. In the wilderness we learn that religious identity is always in process, that it is "a continual work of self-creation."
4. The wilderness narratives instructed readers that provisions in the wilderness were dependent on religious transformation.[29]

Walter Brueggemann's *The Land* comes close to Feldt's study in recognizing the ambiguity of the wilderness in the Hebrew Bible. As noted earlier, Brueggemann neither overlooks nor minimizes the negative aspects of the wilderness, stating that it represented "a sentence to death," a place where "faith is not easy."[30] Again, the wilderness's barrenness is its primary characteristic. Aside from the depiction of the wilderness as a deadly environment, however, Brueggemann notes that it is the place where unexpected nourishment occurs.[31] Brueggemann explains:

> [Yahweh's] glory is known, his presence is discerned, and his sovereignty acknowledged in his capacity to transform the situation from emptiness to satiation, from death to life, from hunger to bread and meat. He acted decisively to make for landless Israel an environment as rich and nourishing as any landed people had ever known. Yahweh is the transformer of situations. The surprise is that landlessness can become nourishing.[32]

The very site of death, the wilderness, is the place where Yahweh declares to Israel, "No lack!"[33] It is an inversion of the norm. Not only is Yahweh providing for Israel's well-being in the wilderness but doing so to such an extent that this barren land, somehow, is as nourishing as any fertile land. No lack!

Similar to Feldt, Brueggemann cites Exodus 16 as an example of Israel's struggling with the nourishment provided by Yahweh in the wilderness. Wilderness bread, according to Brueggemann, is outside of the established order of things, and it could not be understood or appreciated with the "land mentality," a mentality that was developed while Israel was enslaved in Egypt.[34] Israel's desire for managed land—land that adhered to the established order of earthly potentates—lessened its ability to appreciate the imaginative (unorthodox) ways Yahweh was meeting its needs in the wilderness. Brueggemann notes that imagination is a central feature of Old Testament theology. Imagination, he says, is the "capacity to generate, evoke, and articulate alternative images of reality, images that counter what hegemonic power and knowledge have declared to be impossible."[35] Whereas Feldt describes this as an inversion, Brueggemann uses the term "counter-version" (or *subversion*) to describe how hearers of these narratives are invited to "recharacterize what is given or taken as real."[36] Of course, this inversion or counterversion is necessary for those persons or communities who must survive in the wilderness. The normative view is that the wilderness is an accursed place, but Brueggemann, in his reading of the wilderness narratives, declares, instead, that it is "gifted land."[37]

Exodus 16 explicitly describes the wilderness as a "place of surprising expectations and unexpected resources."[38] It also addresses another major concern in Old Testament theology: the crisis of Yahweh's presence. The wilderness represents the biblical N. G. I. (No God Involved) land. Israel's focus is on the wilderness bread, but Brueggemann contends that Yahweh "transforms the question so that bread-talk has the dimension of God-talk concerned with fidelity and power."[39] Israel cannot ignore the fact that their miraculous survival in the wilderness is because of Yahweh's presence. Put another way, God is involved *with* them in the wilderness. The struggle to survive the wilderness is torment enough. "Being there alone, abandoned is unbearable," writes Brueggemann.[40] But Israel is not alone. Yahweh "enters in the desolation with his people. He subjects himself to the same circumstances as Israel."[41] It is Yahweh's presence that transforms the wilderness from a place of death into a place of life. Brueggemann sums it up by stating,

> Israel's reflection on that forty-year landlessness leads to a remarkable affirmation. Wilderness should have been a place of death, but life is given. Wilderness should have been a place of weariness, sickness, poverty, and disease, but Israel is sustained and kept well. Israel has no tattered clothes, no sore feet. It is subjected to the worst thinkable conditions and is kept well. The place of all lack, because Yahweh is present, is where nothing is lacking.[42]

No lack! No lack! No lack! Such is the experience of the sojourner, the wanderer, the landless, the wilderness people, of the Hebrew Bible.

Unfortunately, Brueggemann does not mention that the first instance of this counterversion (subversion) of the negative perspective of the wilderness did not occur with Israel's wandering in the wilderness. That honor belongs to Hagar, the Egyptian slave. Not only in *The Land* but also in his commentary to the book of Genesis, Brueggemann doesn't mention Hagar's foundational role in subverting the dominant theology of the wilderness.[43] Other scholars have not overlooked Hagar's role, however. Robert Barry Leal points out that "Hagar's encounter with God in the wilderness on two occasions in Genesis makes her the first person in the Pentateuch to highlight wilderness as a place of divine encounter and call."[44] He adds that "to this extent, she pioneers the biblical tradition of critical encounter in the wilderness."[45] Part of the reason Hagar is overlooked is that neither she nor her son, Ishmael, is part of the Abrahamic covenant. They are not promised the gift of land. Instead, they are forced to contend with the desolate prospect of founding a great nation in the wilderness. Somehow, the wilderness must become their home.

HAGAR, UNSEEN BY ABRAHAM AND SEEN BY GOD

Old Testament scholar Claus Westermann begins his commentary on Genesis 12–36 with an important distinction: "The primeval story [Genesis 1–11] speaks about the basic elements of the world and humanity, the patriarchal story of the basic elements of human community."[46] Various relationships of importance exist within the patriarchal story, but for Westermann, the parent-child relationship is essential to the Abrahamic narrative. The Abrahamic family is where the story of Israel as a nation begins, and it therefore serves as the paradigm of communal relations. Westermann adds,

> The whole arrangement shows that at the time when a people was coming into being and a state was being formed, the perspective was based on the memory of origin from families and ancestors. Thus is expressed the basic meaning of family for all further forms of community, and thus is acknowledged that whatever happens in these more developed communities and their spheres of endeavor, be it in politics, economics, civilization, education, art, and religion, goes back to what has happened in the family. No other form of community can ever completely replace the family.[47]

Moreover, the family stories have a theological function, that is, "they cannot be spoken of without at the same time speaking of God."[48] God is actively involved in the life of the families depicted in the patriarchal stories, as "the family relationships as such are based on God's action and preserved by it."[49] The covenant, the sign of God's ongoing relationship with the elect, is of primary importance in securing the succession of generations.

Joseph Blenkinsopp, a biblical scholar, remarks that the story of Abraham would have been important during times of immense social challenges. For instance, after the Babylonian conquest in 586 BC the Abraham story was relevant to the experience of those Israelites who survived the conquest. One aspect that Blenkinsopp highlights is that the Abraham story provides an assurance of blessing, which "reversed the situation in the postdeluge world, the world of Nimrod and Babel, mythic counterpart to the postdisaster world of Judah under the imperial world of Babylon."[50] The story of Abraham served to inspire listeners to be confident in God's benevolence in the context of Babylonian oppression, all due to God's covenant with Abraham. The fatherhood of Abraham is also significant to the patriarchal stories. Fatherhood, says Westermann, "refers to a type of relationship of occurrences that stretches from the second part of Genesis into the New Testament."[51] In the Jewish tradition Abraham is referred to as "Our Father Abraham." Hebrew scholar Jon D. Levenson states that "as the father of the Jewish people, he is not simply their biological progenitor . . . he is the founder of Judaism itself— the first Jew" and therefore is the model of faith for his descendants "who are to walk in the trails he blazed."[52]

Levenson underscores the fundamental problem in the Abrahamic family conflict: who will inherit the patriarchal promise? "Is the son Ishmael or Isaac?" asks Levenson. Part of the promise is the heir's inheriting Abraham's wealth. In Genesis 12:16, Abraham received from the Pharoah of Egypt "sheep, oxen, male donkeys, male and female slaves, female donkeys, and camels." The family conflict in the Abraham narrative is mostly about securing Abraham's wealth because the other parts of the promise are not fulfilled until well after Abraham's death.[53] Levenson argues that Abraham and Sarah's frustrations, especially given their advanced age, at not seeing God's promise of descendants coming to fruition resulted in their taking matters into their own hands. Blenkinsopp refers to these acts of self-reliance as "expedients."[54] But they, too, bring about greater frustration. After Abraham impregnates the Egyptian slave Hagar, the family conflict ensues as "the slave (and foreigner) Hagar, unlikely to find a husband, has now become a wife, and to a very rich man."[55] Hagar is now a co-wife with Sarah, but does it change her status? Will she be viewed as Sarah's equal? Not at all. The birth of Ishmael secures her neither a higher status in the house of Abraham nor an equal share of Abraham's blessing, that is, the covenant, for her son. Hagar and Ishmael will remain the non-elect. And, moreover, in the house of Abraham, Hagar, because of her status, remains unseen.

Joel S. Kaminsky, scholar of Jewish studies, explores the role of God's election in the Hebrew Bible's family conflicts and notes a pattern whereby great importance is placed on the "elect child coming from a chosen wife."[56] In the Abrahamic narrative the center of the family tension "is the possible strain between the two sons, yet the major tension in the story is between the two women and the husband they share."[57] According to Kaminsky, a number of elements suggest that Hagar, not Sarah, is indeed the chosen wife; for example, she is the first person to receive a divine oracle announcing the birth of a child. A similar claim can be made about Ishmael, who, even though it is affirmed that he is not the chosen child, is still circumcised, the primary mark of election (Gen. 17:25). But none of this changes his status. He remains designated as non-elect. However, Kaminsky maintains that "all of these facts indicate that while Ishmael is ultimately excluded from God's covenant and thereby is non-elect, his case is the least clear-cut instance of dis-election in the Hebrew Bible, and even after his non-elect status is confirmed, he still inherits those portions of the promise made to Abraham that deal with progeny, nationhood, prosperity (Gen. 17:20), and divine presence (Gen. 21:20)."[58] Careful not to classify the status on non-election too negatively, Kaminsky states that non-elect does not mean anti-elect, that is, the non-elect are not necessarily enemies of God. He also attests that biblical election is not a sign of ethnic superiority.

Unfortunately, what is often communicated in the discourse of non-election, if not ethnic superiority, is certainly superiority of some kind. How did this influence how these stories were shared and heard? If, as Westermann claims, the family is the basis for every human community, then how non-election has been interpreted in the family conflict in the patriarchal stories influenced how the non-elect were treated in the wider community, particularly during times of religious and/or sociopolitical insecurity. What about personal insecurity? In most stories of Father Abraham we don't often hear about his struggles with insecurity; as seen previously, however, Levenson discusses Abraham's frustrations at being a foreigner (e.g., Gen. 12) and then later, worst of all, of not seeing the fulfillment of all of God's promises, most notably the gift of the land. Even those promises that he did live to see, such as progeny, did not come easy and were themselves rather insecure (e.g., the binding of Isaac in Gen. 22).

Feminist biblical scholar J. Cheryl Exum speaks to Abraham's vulnerability when she states that throughout the patriarchal stories, he is attempting to secure an identity for himself and the nation he is to father. Furthermore, the nation of Israel itself, much like its progenitor, is a subject in process (*sujet en proces*),[59] a "subject on trial, never able but zealously striving to create stable boundaries between itself and the world around it."[60] The expulsion of Hagar, according to Exum, is an (over-)reaction by Abraham and Sarah to the threat the Egyptian slave and her son posed to their insecure identities. "As one of the first in a series of abjections, or separations, in Genesis, the dismissal of Hagar and Ishmael is one of the most forceful because . . . the greater the challenge the self perceives to its boundaries, the stronger the reaction," writes Exum.[61] There are scholars who support Exum's view that the expulsion into the wilderness was an excessive move to reenforce Hagar's non-elect status.

Old Testament scholar Victor P. Hamilton's commentary on Genesis suggests that when Sarah finds Ishmael playing with Isaac, the episode that causes the expulsion, she is perturbed by "the impropriety of her child associating with a child from a lower social class."[62] Hamilton's analysis puts this episode into a wider context, however. Ishmael is playing on the day of Isaac's weaning ceremony,[63] a pivotal rite of passage marking his incorporation into the community. Gerhard von Rad, an Old Testament scholar and theologian, adds that "the picture of the two boys playing with each other on an equal footing is quite sufficient to bring the jealous mother to a firm conclusion: Ishmael must go!"[64] This was to be the day that Isaac's identity is secured: "You are one of us!" Hamilton notes that Sarah is offended that Ishmael, who will never partake of this rite of passage, would dare be found "doing something to make himself like Isaac, setting his sights on a familial position equal to that of Isaac."[65] Ishmael, too, as the non-elect, is to remain unseen. As subjects in process, Abraham and Sarah, along with the just-weaned Isaac, had to establish the boundaries between the elect and non-elect, the seen and the unseen, so the slave woman and her son were cast out into the wilderness. According to Hamilton, the verb used for the expulsion (*garas*: drive out) is also used to describe the banishment of Adam in Genesis 3:24 and Cain in Genesis 4:14. The difference in the Hagar story, however, is that her greatest sin was her status. She was seen as a slave; that's all. Therefore, Sarah declares, "The son of the *slave woman* [italics mine] shall not be heir with my son Isaac" (Gen. 21:10). In other words, Sarah declares, "He will never be seen as one of us!" Feminist and, even more so, Black feminist and womanist interpreters of the Hebrew Bible have not overlooked the excessively harsh treatment of Hagar and Ishmael by Abraham, Sarah, and God. These scholars interpret Hagar's story to find ways of reimagining God-talk in such a way that the non-elect are seen by God. However, this was part of a larger effort by feminist scholars to change how women are seen in the world of the Bible and, in the current context, in biblical scholarship.

Alice Ogden Bellis, a scholar of Old Testament literature and language, discusses the many shifts that occurred as feminist interpretations of the Bible became more prominent during the second half of the twentieth century. It was necessary to combat the tendency in biblical scholarship to present women in the Hebrew Scriptures as secondary figures who lacked the complexity of their male counterparts. Bellis quotes feminist biblical scholar Esther Fuchs, who says, "The patriarchal framework of the biblical story prevents the mother figure from becoming a full-fledged *human* role model, while its androcentric perspective confines her to a limited literary role, largely subordinated to the biblical male protagonists."[66] Oftentimes, the women of the Bible are depicted in a way that only highlights a deficiency that later becomes the defining element of their characterization. Eve made Adam sin. Sarah is barren. Hagar is a slave. Rahab is a harlot. Jezebel is just wrong. Therefore, even if the narrator portrays these women sympathetically, "interpreters . . . have often assessed the characters of these women in negative terms."[67] Bellis contends that the Hagar narrative is a story of a servant and her mistress, of a struggle for status, and of abuse and exile.[68] In surveying some of the biblical scholarship on Hagar's story, Bellis demonstrates that there remain different, and at times opposing, views among scholars who approach the text from a subversive hermeneutical framework.

A crucial issue for Black feminist and womanist scholars is whether the Hagar story can be interpreted in the light of current racial dynamics in America. Much of the debate has to do with the blackness of Hagar, particularly for womanist scholars. Bellis believes it would be wrong to read racial tensions into the text. "It is not the story of a black woman oppressed by a white one," writes Bellis. In *Reimagining Hagar*, biblical scholar Nyasha Junior points out that even though Hagar's ethnicity (i.e., the Egyptian woman) is mentioned in the Scriptures and other nonbiblical religious texts, she is not racialized.[69] Within the African American cultural context itself, a distinction must be made between the biblical Hagar and Aunt Hagar. The latter is a figure who served as a literary "trope that involves abandonment, racial or ethnic ambiguity, and sexual expression."[70] Junior argues that womanist biblical scholars have not always been clear in making that distinction.

In her study *Texts of Terror*, feminist biblical scholar Phyllis Trible sees in the stories of Hagar, Tamar, the Unnamed Woman (Judg. 19:1–30), and the daughter of Jephthah "four portraits of suffering in ancient Israel."[71] But their suffering is not the end of their stories. Trible does not want to minimize the suffering of these women by conjuring happy endings. Rather, her focus is on how these stories may lead to repentance and therefore "yield new beginnings."[72] Walter Brueggemann calls Trible "the most effective interpreter of the Old Testament" because she "continues to pay close attention to the text itself" and "her work evidences no heavy ideological theory."[73] Be that as it may, Trible herself understands that there are biblical scholars, because of how they are viewed within the larger sociopolitical structure, who need to bring ideological issues, such as race, class, and gender oppression, to the fore in the interpretive task. In commenting on the Hagar story, Trible attests that "it yields an abundance of hermeneutical reflections."[74] Trible explains:

> As a symbol of the oppressed, Hagar becomes many things to many people. Most especially, all sorts of rejected women find their stories in her. She is the faithful maid exploited, the black woman used by the male and abused by the female of the ruling class, the surrogate mother, the resident alien without legal recourse, the other woman, the runaway youth, the religious fleeing from affliction, the pregnant young woman alone, the expelled wife, the divorced mother with child, the shopping bag lady carrying bread and water, the homeless woman, the indigent relying on handouts from the power structures, the welfare mother, and the self-effacing female whose own identity shrinks in service to others.[75]

Hagar's story is similar to that of the communities of persons unseen in today's society. Trible recognizes that women who identify with Hagar do so not solely based on race but because of their own experiences of oppression, which lead them to feel a sense of community with her as a fellow sufferer. Trible hopes that recognizing the terror in Hagar's story leads to repentance not only for the abuses committed against her but for those committed against the women who identify with her story. Womanist interpreters of the Hagar story have endeavored to discover how it not only resonates with their experiences of terror but also provides instructions for reimagined God-talk and subversive survival practices. They not only read the Hagar story to see how God changed the circumstances of this slave woman and her son but also with the hope of discovering how God can do the same for them—here and now.

A SISTER, AND HER GIFT, IN THE WILDERNESS

Womanist biblical scholar Renita Weems comments that the story of Hagar is all too familiar to Black women. Similar to Bellis and Trible, Weems does not want to interpret Hagar's story as one focused on racial and ethnic differences alone. "It would not be totally fair," writes Weems, "to make the Old Testament story of Hagar and Sarai carry all the weight of the history of race relationships in the modern world."[76] Though there is evidence that could suggest this kind of interpretation, she observes that the issues of racial and ethnic prejudice must be viewed in tandem with the presence of economic and sexual exploitation. Weems contends that the class difference between Hagar and Sarah caused their inequitable relationship. Sarah's disregard for Hagar's status caused the terror that Hagar experiences in the story. Hagar is not without blame, however. Though Weems commends Hagar for initiating her freedom by fleeing from Sarah in Genesis 16, she is found lacking courage for returning to Abraham and Sarah, indicating, to Weems, that Hagar was still willing to define herself according to their standards. "What Sarai thought of Hagar had become what Hagar thought of herself," writes Weems.[77] Above all, the exploitation of one woman over another, in an ongoing struggle to secure status, or to be seen, is what Weems finds so troubling about the story. Sarah could have helped Hagar but failed to do so on several occasions. For Weems, Hagar's story resonates with the current experience of Black women who are looking to create alliances—mutually edifying relationships—with white women in power but instead find themselves exploited and rejected by these women of higher status.

Weems also reflects on the significance of broken human relationships in her essay "Reading *Her Way* through the Struggle: African American Woman and the Bible." Weems argues that the Bible remains meaningful for African American women because of the ways it portrays "how human beings relate to one another."[78] African American women read the Bible in such a way that those elements that contribute to further oppression are not taken as valid (e.g., Howard Thurman's grandmother's rejecting Pauline portions of the Bible promoting the obedience of slaves). However, Weems contends that those narratives in the Bible deemed relevant to the reader fulfill two pressing needs: "First, the Bible, or portions of it, is believed to provide existential insight into the dilemmas that grip African American women's existence. Second, it reflects values and advocates a way of life to which African American female readers genuinely aspire."[79] Reading the Bible this way is in itself subversive because it requires an intentional act to recover the voice not only of the reader but also of the oppressed characters in the biblical text. Hagar's story, Weems confirms, is instructive to the current plight of African American women. "Here the status, ethnicity, gender, and circumstances of a biblical character have been seen as unmistakably analogous to those of the African American reader," writes Weems.[80] The terror within the text is honored as Weems documents the many ways that Hagar's oppression "coincides in some crucial ways with African American women's experience of reality."[81] Yet in the midst of the terror are "minimal positive strategies for survival."[82] African American women can see that single motherhood, slavery, poverty, and abandonment are not all of Hagar's story and not all of their story, either. Though Weems does not document the "minimal positive strategies for survival" in the Hagar story, we should not assume that such strategies are insignificant.

Womanist theologian Delores S. Williams's *Sisters in the Wilderness* underscores that Hagar's survival strategies are integral to the African American women's interpretation of the text because they see "God responding to the African slave Hagar and her child in terms of survival strategies."[83] These strategies are needed today to survive what Williams terms the *wilderness experiences*, "a symbolic term used to represent a near-destruction situation in which God gives personal direction to the believer and thereby helps her make a way out of what she thought was no way."[84] Williams challenges readers to view the Hagar-in-the-wilderness story as providing survival strategies for the Black community as a whole, not just Black women. Hagar's story can therefore be used to teach Black men how to survive in the environment that most resembles the biblical wilderness: the American ghetto. Williams provides some answers to the critical question "How did Hagar survive in the wilderness?"

Williams begins *Sisters in the Wilderness* by confessing that, as a Black woman, she sees herself in Hagar's story. She recalls her own wilderness experiences that have taught her to "see the miraculous in everyday life: the miracle of ordinary black women resisting and rising above evil forces in society, where forces work to destroy and subvert the creative power and energy my mother and grandmother taught me God gave black women."[85] Her story and the story of the Black women that influenced her describe God's helping her to live her life, creatively, even in the face of dire circumstances. This framework informs her faith, a "faith seeking understanding" that doesn't ignore "the necessity of political and spiritual 'works'—affirming these for the salvation of one's self and for the salvation of the black family . . . of the young black people lost in the drug culture in North America."[86] To discover these necessary resources, Williams went on a search to discover a tradition of African American biblical interpretation that focused on the ways in which women in the Bible formulated their own unique theology (or God-talk). According to Williams, there is a long-standing tradition of using Hagar's story in African American culture.[87] In reviewing not only the cultural memory of Hagar but the biblical story itself, Williams discovered that "there were striking similarities between Hagar's story and the story of African American women."[88] The experiences of terror are similar—the brutality of slave owners and employers, single-parenthood, and lack of resources to care for loved ones, to name a few. But there is also the noticeable similarity between Hagar and Black women of finding ways to resist their oppression. In spite of it all, Williams says, "[Hagar] has serious personal and salvific encounters with God—encounters which aided Hagar in the survival struggle of herself and her son. Over and over again, black women in the churches have testified about their serious personal and salvific encounters with God, encounters that helped them and their families survive."[89] Williams employs this survival motif to formulate a "survival/quality of life tradition of African American biblical appropriation."[90] There are two pivotal events in Hagar's story wherein Williams finds God actively participating in the survival of Hagar and her son in the wilderness. As discussed earlier, the first is caused by *escape* (Gen. 16) whereas the second is caused by *expulsion*.

While fleeing into the wilderness, Hagar has her first encounter with the angel of the Lord, who tells her to resume her slave status under Sarah. After telling Hagar to return (Gen. 16:9), the angel of the Lord makes Hagar a promise in Genesis 16:11–12:

> "Now, you have conceived and will bear a son;
>   you shall name him Ishmael,
>   for the LORD has given heed to your affliction.
> He shall be a wild ass of a man, with his hand against everyone,
>   and everyone's hand against him."

These words could have been received as a curse rather than a blessing. Her son, Ishmael, will be different, radically different from everyone else—e.g., a wild ass of man, his hand against every man. Negative interpretations abound regarding Ishmael's character; in fact, some interpreters have hypothesized that he simply took on the character of his mother Hagar. Such is the opinion of biblical scholar Hermann Gunkel, who remarks, "This intractable Ishmael is an unruly son of his stubborn mother, who did not want to submit to the yoke."[91] In the essay "The Wild Man in the Bible and the Ancient Near East," Hebrew Bible scholar Gregory Mobley shares that the wild man tradition in Mesopotamia has three categories: 1) the hairy man; 2) uncivilized barbarians or "wild races"; and 3) the warrior who transforms into the wild man when in a state of rage.[92] An Old Babylonian literary figure named Enkidu is the oldest representation of the wild man.[93] As for the depiction of Ishmael as a wild man, Mobley comments that he is "the feral double of the patriarch Isaac."[94] The other part of the wild man's legend is his equally wild abode, the wilderness. God's promise to Hagar makes no assurance that her son will ever be like Isaac nor that their lifestyle will be similar to their experience in the house of Abraham. However, Williams doesn't view God's promise to Hagar as a curse. The "survival/quality of life" mode of biblical interpretation leads Williams to perceive that "the promise assures survival, and the birth announcement forecasts the strategy that will be necessary for survival and for obtaining a quality of life in the wilderness. . . .[Ishmael] will be able to help create and protect the quality of life he and his mother, Hagar, will later develop in the desert."[95]

The other significant event that occurs during Hagar's escape into the wilderness is that she names God. Opinions differ on the exact meaning of Hagar's name for God, El Roi, but, for Williams, the most important aspect of the name is that "this deity is not associated with Hagar's oppressors, the patriarchal family."[96] Thomas Booij, a scholar of Hebrew literature, suggests that the narrator of the text wants to focus attention on the "notion of seeing."[97] Booij raises several interesting points regarding this act of seeing. To begin, the words used in Genesis 16:13 suggest an act of searching, that is, "just as one may pursue someone, or have someone pursued, to somewhere."[98] The wording indicates that Hagar's escape was also due to her active search for a god while alone in the wilderness. Booij also suggests that Hagar's naming God El Roi speaks to the mutual act of recognition between Hagar and God—"man's searching for God, the Living One . . . and God's looking after [Hagar]."[99] Booij offers the following summary:

> The meaning of Hagar's words in v. 13b is: "Would I have gone here indeed searching for him that watches me?" If, in conformity with the

Hebrew, we want to express the repeated "seeing" or "looking," we may render: "Would I have gone here indeed looking for him that looks after me?"[100]

Bible scholar Yael Avrahami states that sight is an important theme in the book of Genesis and is "a central tool for acquiring knowledge and passing it on (memory)."[101] Seeing provided firsthand knowledge that validated one's experience. For instance, when discussing the verification of divine action, miracles and the like, Avrahami says, "To see is structurally parallel to know, and . . . seeing the wonders implies a strong response on behalf of the viewer."[102] Delores Williams emphasizes the value of seeing for Hagar and asks, "Was Hagar's naming God an act of defiance and resistance as well as an expression of awe?"[103] Though she is instructed to return to the house of Abraham, Hagar returns knowing, because of what she has seen in the wilderness, a number of things that she did not—and was not allowed to—know before: First, her God, El Roi, is looking after her; second, she has a promise that she will bear a unique son; third, if she must escape once again, it is possible to survive in the wilderness.

It is unclear how much time expires between the *escape* (Gen. 16) and *expulsion* (Gen. 21) episodes of the Hagar story. Nevertheless, biblical scholars agree that by the time of the expulsion Ishmael was a teenager. Thus for more than a decade, at minimum, Ishmael was raised in and, by extension, influenced by the social and religious views of Abraham. Though Hagar had received the promise and had named God El Roi, all of those events transpired in the wilderness. In Abraham's house, he was the father—*paterfamilias*—designated by God and man as the sole authority figure in the household. Westermann notes that patriarchal society in ancient times was prepolitical, and there are notable differences in how the family functioned in a prepolitical society. According to Westermann, "the decisive difference is that the prepolitical family is self-sufficient."[104] The family in this context was totally reliant on its own resources because there was no larger political, economic, or religious institution available to provide assistance. All conflict was resolved within the family. Therefore, "it is thrown back on its own resources to protect it from without and to order it from within."[105] This is the case with the religious life of the family as well, for there was not yet an official religious community that gathered, say, for weekly worship or various religious rituals. In the patriarchal family, the father alone was responsible for religious instruction. The father's God was the God of the household. Any communication with God had to go through the father, as the "father exercises the priestly function."[106] Therefore, it is reasonable to hypothesize that, even though Hagar had seen God in the wilderness, she was, upon returning to Abraham's house, never able to communicate much of her knowledge about El Roi to her son, Ishmael. Such an act was forbidden in the patriarchal form of society. Ishmael would not be allowed to know El Roi. Westermann points out that a number of characteristics regarding the religion of the patriarchs, such as the designation "the God of my Father" is associated with the family narratives in Genesis, which also contributes to the notion that "the personal relationship with God" was a central religious theme as well.[107] In other words, it was understood that God is with the father, the patriarch. Abraham was the source not only of economic security but of the household's spiritual well-being as well. As Abraham's son, even though not the one who would be heir to the covenant, Ishmael was well aware of this.

Circumstances soon change, however, when Hagar and Ishmael are thrown out of Abraham's house and into the wilderness. They are no longer under the protection of Abraham's patriarchal authority, which included the protection of his God. Victor P. Hamilton notes that, because of the expulsion, "Abraham transfers Ishmael from his guardianship to Hagar's."[108] Hagar is now returning to the wilderness, but this time with the heavy burden of caring for a son who knows there is no one to care for him and his mother. Without Abraham—homeless, poor, and disconnected from "the God of my Father"—life in the wilderness is an utterly hopeless situation. Will Hagar ever see "the gift of numerous progeny" God promised her?

Williams notes the severe economic crises Hagar and Ishmael encounter during their expulsion. The limited resources supplied by Abraham—bread and a skin of water (Gen. 21:14)—are certain to run out fast, which they did. A more terrifying issue arises for Hagar during the expulsion, however, which differs from her escape in Genesis 16. Scholar of Hebrew literature Ed Noort contends that the reason Hagar was willing and prepared to escape the first time was that "she knows where to go; knows the way to the springs in the desert and survives there on the way to Egypt."[109] A clue that leads Noort to this conclusion is that "the spring on the way to Shur" (Gen. 16:7) indicates her destination was a place 'on the north-eastern border of Egypt."[110] Hagar had a destination and knew how to get there. According to Noort, "She was not helpless, she did not have any difficulty finding springs and water on the desert road to Egypt. . . . She was desert savvy."[111] The expulsion is a different experience, totally. Now she is lost. She is not able to see her way around *this* wilderness. Victor P. Hamilton states that the verb for Hagar's hopeless wandering in the wilderness is used in other places in the Hebrew Bible to describe "straying animals . . . persons who are lost . . . drunkenness."[112] This unknown wilderness, where she is without resources and unprotected, soon becomes too much for Hagar. She sees no way of survival for herself nor for Ishmael. What she does see is that Ishmael is deteriorating fast, near death, which Hagar believes leaves her no other choice but to abandon her child under a bush (Gen, 21:15–16).

Some interpreters of the story view this abandonment as the intentional separation between a mother and her son. I want to offer a different interpretation by claiming that Ishmael was not simply Hagar's son but *her gift*. A gift in this context points to something more than how the word is commonly understood, such as, according to *Merriam-Webster*, "a notable capacity, talent, or endowment."[113] When viewed in this light, the gift is limited to interpersonal exchanges that have been explored by, for example, sociologist Marcel Mauss and philosopher Jacques Derrida. The gift in Hagar's story is about her relationship with God being affirmed through her son, Ishmael—a relationship that was established on the promise that God would "'so greatly multiply [her] offspring that they cannot be counted for multitude'" (Gen. 16:10). It was stated earlier that Delores Williams refers to this as "the *gift* of numerous progeny," but the firstfruits of this gift, the sign that the promise is indeed true, is her son Ishmael. By separating herself from Ishmael, Hagar is, in essence, terminating the relationship with her gift and, therefore, terminating God's promise.

Hagar needs a miracle. What can save Ishmael, her gift? Her cries of despair are echoed by her son, now a "distance of a bowshot" away (Gen. 21:15). Ishmael is now voicing his own anguish, not only his physical pain but the psychological torment of abandonment. With nothing left, she offers what Victor Hamilton calls one of the first prayers in the Bible: "'Do not let me look on the death of the child'" (Gen. 21:16). Put another way, Hagar is asking that she not see the death of God's promise, her gift. God's response to Hagar's plea is telling. God hears the cries of Ishmael. Some may view this as God's ignoring Hagar's suffering, but following Williams's survival/quality-of-life model, I read this as God's instructing Hagar to see that there is only *one* way she will survive in the wilderness: she must reconnect with and take care of her gift. "'Come, lift up the boy and hold him fast with your hand, for I will make a great nation of him'" (Gen. 21:18), God commands Hagar. Williams argues that this command indicates that "tender loving care is in order."[114] Once Hagar reestablishes her relationship with Ishmael, the gift, she immediately begins to see things differently. Miraculously, resources begin to appear. God opens her eyes to see a well so that Ishmael can drink. Her gift will not die but live. God also makes sure that Ishmael will grow in the wilderness, for "God was *with* the boy, and he grew up" (Gen. 21:20). God's caring presence—or God's involvement—with Ishmael is what allows him to grow. God is with the gift.

Gerhard Von Rad's view of the expulsion is that Hagar and Ishmael had lost so much because they were no longer in the house of Abraham.

According to Von Rad, "this way of life [in the wilderness] became different from that of the patriarchs."[115] Unlike the covenantal promise made to Abraham, "the promise of land and the call into special relationship with God are here missing."[116] That is not true! An alternative interpretation of the text negates such a claim. According to Walter Brueggemann's observation in *The Land*, the central characteristic of the wilderness is that "not only is nothing growing, but nothing can grow. It is a land without promise, without hope, where no newness can come."[117] But Brueggemann calls the wilderness gifted land. It provides life but not life according to managed land or, in the case of Hagar's story, life according to Abraham's house. The wilderness can be a place where things grow, but only if God's presence is there. "Like manna," says Brueggemann, "his wilderness presence is always enough on which to survive . . . as Yahweh's presence transforms wilderness."[118] The wilderness can become a gift as God's presence transforms it from a place of barrenness into a place where miraculous growth occurs. So too did God's presence *with* Ishmael transform him from a burden that was left for dead into a gift that would grow to create a life for himself and Hagar in the wilderness. God is with the gift.

Ishmael's story in the wilderness differs from that of Hagar's. He must grow up to become a man in the wilderness. That is, there is much he will have to learn about himself and the world in the wilderness. Whereas Delores Williams interprets Hagar's story as being instructive to Black women suffering from various forms of oppression, I see Ishmael's story as a helpful resource for young Black men who are forced to grow in the modern wilderness environment of the American ghetto. For one, Ishmael's growth was unique. He had to find an alternative way to gain not only survival skills but an indomitable identity that could withstand the challenges he would face in the wilderness, the abode of the outsider. Elijah Anderson notes that, due to his oppositional nature and status, the young Black male in the ghetto is viewed as mysterious, dangerous, and fearsome. He is, like Ishmael, deemed a wild ass of a man. But there are advantages to this oppositional style that are often overlooked. In fact, given Ishmael's experience in the wilderness, this radical difference can be the source of one's growth in the ghetto.

5

Talking about Our Gifts

"Son, you've got to be a big man now," his mother said. . . . "Right here in Harlem, son."

—*Richard Wright, Rite of Passage*[1]

BEEP-BEEP: DO YOU HAVE A DIAGNOSIS?

Several years ago, I participated in a conference call convened by the White House's Office of Faith-Based and Neighborhood Partnerships to discuss the challenges facing young men of color. Led by Melissa Rogers, director of the agency, this conversation included various persons (e.g., public-policy officials, NGO leaders, clergypersons, etc.) from around the country. The participants were chosen because they had some knowledge of the issues that were to be addressed by then-president Obama's "My Brother's Keeper Alliance" initiative.

The conference call started with a brief presentation by the director and other representatives from the agency, each of whom made it clear that the initiative's goal was to help young men of color reach their full potential. For some of these young men, "My Brother's Keeper" would serve as their initiation into manhood. After the introductory remarks, we were informed that the phone lines would be opened so that participants could ask questions and, if inspired to do so, offer suggestions. Then we were instructed to wait for a loud beep, signaling that it was time to enter a code so that we would be placed in a queue to join the conversation. On being chosen, we would hear two loud beeps—BEEP-BEEP—to signal that it was now our turn to speak. I never learned how many participants were on the call that day. Dozens? Hundreds? Thousands? Who knows? But I'm sure that most, if not all, of us quickly entered the code to join the queue. I, for one, immediately entered the code to join the anxious line of commentators, hoping that my quick fingers had secured me an early spot. I then reclined in my office chair, took in a few deep breaths, and listened patiently as the first few respondents shared their diagnoses concerning the lives of young men of color in the United States.

The first person to respond was a gentleman from Chicago, Illinois—the South Side—who headed a community organization that worked with young Black males. Though I recall neither the name of the organization nor the name of the respondent, his poignant diagnosis remains fixed in my mind. There was noticeable sorrow in his voice as he talked about how he saw, first-hand, the damaging effects of rampant fatherlessness that left many young Black males without, among many things, a sense of protection. He added to this diagnosis that Chicago's frightening epidemic of gun violence, which had claimed the lives of more than four hundred people in 2014, several of whom were Black men he had known personally, has its source in the anger and hopelessness young Black men are experiencing. Next, a school official from Los Angeles, California, was chosen to speak, and he was a bit more poetic with his comments. With keen insight, he looked underneath the manifest content of fatherlessness, poor education, and high incarceration to offer the diagnosis that young men of color are suffering from what he termed "hidden wounds." His diagnosis focused on the manner in which this inner turmoil is an unspoken yet deeply painful trauma that finds expression in various break-downs in communal relationships. As these two respondents and a few other participants shared their specific diagnoses of the causes of distress among young men of color, I noticed a primary theme emerging.

Though the conversation about the "My Brother's Keeper Alliance" initiative was focused on young men of color, the conversation continually returned to the plight of young Black men. For the most part, it was this spe-cific group of young men of color that was identified as not *one of* but rather as *the* problem the initiative should address. Time and time again, I heard state-ments about the lack of hope in young Black men, the lack of jobs for young Black men, the high rates of fatherlessness among young Black men, the rage of young Black men, the untreated depression of young Black men. What immediately came to mind while I was on the conference call, however, was W. E. B. Du Bois's well-known question "How does it feel to be a problem?" Du Bois goes on to say that it is not in adulthood that his question arises but rather in the "early days of rollicking boyhood that the revelation bursts upon one."[2] For a young Black man, therefore, the trauma is not that he *has* a num-ber of problems that are diminishing his opportunities for fulfillment but that as a Black male—due to the color line—he *is* the problem.

While listening to numerous callers offer diagnoses of the young Black male problematic, I began to grow anxious and uncertain regarding the topic at hand. I began to think, "Do I really have anything unique to offer about this issue?" If given the opportunity to speak, would I simply restate, with some rhetorical flourishes perhaps, data on fatherlessness, low education, and high incarceration? Maybe I could provide a psychoanalytic diagnosis that would sound astute to some participants but could, conversely, be interpreted by others as being too pedantic. It seemed out of place to go into a summary of how the Oedipus complex creates rivalry between fathers and sons or, possibly, how the paranoid-schizoid position leads to aggression. What if I just put my own spin on the "hidden wounds" motif, thereby highlighting the unknown inner pain that afflicts so many young Black men? Unfortunately, when it came to matters concerning the more, dare I say, spiritual aspects of lives of young Black men, I struggled to formulate a diagnosis from my own field of expertise. It is reasonable to hypothesize that besides the numerous identified social issues plaguing young Black men in America's ghettoes, there are several unseen problems that are never discussed.

After thirty minutes or so, the participants were informed that the conference call was coming to an end. Though I patiently waited for my turn, I never heard those two beeps—BEEP-BEEP—but now that I think about it, I've heard that signal for a diagnosis whenever I'm confronted with the crisis of young Black men. I hear BEEP-BEEP when I read stories about unarmed young Black men being shot by police officers. I hear BEEP-BEEP in the classroom when students from across the racial spectrum, males and females, sometimes with tears in their eyes, ask me to say something about the devaluing of young Black men in America's ghettoes. I hear BEEP-BEEP at home, unfortunately, when I see my two young Black sons and, quite honestly, don't know when I should tell them that some people don't have enough faith to believe that these two persons so full of promise are more than just a problem. Yes, I must admit, it is at these times that I am overwhelmed by the tyranny of the cliché and wish I had something unique to say.

MISSING THE MAN TALK

Providing any kind of diagnosis within the African American context is fraught with challenges, particularly when it comes to matters that resist readily available categorization. For instance, Earlise Ward and Maigenete Mengesha, scholars of African American mental health, note that information on the mental health of African American men is scant. According to their study, "only 19 empirical studies focusing on depression among African American men were identified in a 25-year time span."[3] Though not a text devoted to empirical research, *Standing in the Shadows: Understanding and Overcoming Depression in Black Men*, written by journalist John Head, is a valuable reflection on the silent epidemic of depression among Black men. Head ties the prevalence of depression to the ways in which Black males are taught "an idea of manhood that requires a silence about feelings, a withholding of emotion, an ability to bear burdens alone, and a refusal to appear weak."[4] What makes Head's commentary so captivating is that he places his argument within his own story of struggling with depression. From the outside looking in, a casual observer would find it difficult to categorize Head as a depressed Black man because, ostensibly, he has the characteristics of a successful, self-made American man. Even he admits that "good fortune has followed [him]"[5] He went from growing up in a single-parent household in Jackson, Georgia, to becoming an accomplished columnist for such noted newspapers as the *Detroit Free Press*, *Atlanta Journal-Constitution*, and *USA Today*. Nevertheless, even with his accomplishments, Head viewed this impressive journey negatively. He explains:

> In my mind, however, there was one thread running through all the good things in my life: I didn't deserve them. I thought of myself as a phony, an imposter who was certain to be found out in the end. Any praise directed at me was a generous lie. I was destined for spectacular failure but mere fate for some reason kept preventing it from happening. I believed in my heart that eventually I would fall and get what I really deserved.[6]

Head contends that racism was the pivotal—not the only—contributor to his depression. "I feared the fulfillment of the prophecies of doom made by those who hate me because of the color of my skin," writes Head.[7] The diagnosis for Head is simple: he is a Black man and is therefore a problem. His battle with depression was the answer to Du Bois's haunting question, "How does it feel to be a problem?"

Head's text offers an exceptional survey of the effects that the dangerous admixture of racism and depression has on Black men. But again, Head's own story is what makes the work truly compelling. During an especially dark period in his life, Head began to self-isolate, keeping himself away from his family, especially his two young sons. His dark mood was creating an unpleasant atmosphere in his household, and he feared that "his sons' minds would hold long-running movies of [him] as a sullen, resentful, and angry man who did not show them the love they craved."[8] Head held the same image of his own father. Head's parents divorced when he was four years old, leaving his mother to raise him and his four siblings on her own. Her efforts to provide for the overall well-being of her children were so effective that Head doesn't "ever recall feeling deprived of a father."[9] Believing that his mother's care had inoculated him to father-hunger, Head never realized how much the loss of a relationship with his father was causing intergenerational trauma. He wouldn't follow his father's path entirely, as he was committed to remaining in their lives; but, still, he "didn't want to be the constant negative force [he] had become for them."[10] In doing so, however, Head was willingly passing on the inheritance of broken father-son relationships, giftlessness, to his sons.

It took some time, but Head did find a therapist whom he credits with listening to aspects of his selfhood that, since childhood, were silent. Though Head did not recant his claim that he had never felt deprived of a father due to his mother's sufficient care, he now admitted, "I knew deep down that my father was a presence in my life even in his absence."[11] But he never shared this with his therapist. Why? Head readily admits that minimizing his father's importance is a "coping device [he] and other African American men use to deal with a fundamental trauma in [their] lives: the absence of a father."[12] I find Head's story instructive not just because it entails how the therapeutic conversation creates an environment in which hidden parts of our stories come to the surface but also how, even in this safe space, there is much we choose not to share. Some talks remain off limits. Oftentimes, these are the most intense, most shameful, most personal losses that, for whatever reason, leave us too vulnerable, undone. They make a grown man feel as though he hasn't grown at all but remains just a boy, unprotected and alone. Giftless.

The following excerpt is the story that Head chose not to share with his therapist. He was to meet his father after not seeing him for several years. Head was now in college, with his feet firmly planted in the initial years of his flowering manhood. His mother told him that his father, who was a mechanic, agreed to help him fix a used car that Head recently purchased. Here's what he said happened:

> A few days later, Mom called me and said she had arranged for my father to get the car towed to his shop in Atlanta's Southside. He wanted me to come over so he could show me the work that needed to be done; he would call to set up a meeting. When the call came, the voice was mine, only with the country accent diluted. He would pick me up the following Saturday. I gave him directions to the campus and said I would meet him on a corner near my dorm.
>
> Saturday came and I was on the corner at the appointed hour. There was no sign of my father. I waited. After about half an hour, I went back to the dorm and stood by the pay phone for a while. It didn't ring. I was about to go back to the corner again when I realized something: I had no idea what my father looked like. He could drive by, and I wouldn't recognize him. I had no reason to believe he would recognize me.
>
> I had this image of myself standing on the street corner, stopping passing strangers and asking, "Are you my father?" I didn't go back to the corner.[13]

The pain of Head's recognizing the lack of physical recognition between him and his father is understandable, but I suggest there is much more going on in this story. If all went as planned, his father would have, at minimum, had to discuss the car's mechanical problem with his son. Would this have started a talk about other things as well? Because Head was in college at the time, they could've talked about what he was studying—his major, favorite courses, and the like. Head's father might have asked him why he had taken an interest in that specific subject. As his father was talking to him about the needed car repairs, Head could ask him questions about, say, how he learned to fix cars. "How did you get good at being a mechanic?" is another possible question.

Now let me offer the *ideal* scenario. As Head's father is showing him what is wrong with the car, he offers not just to make the repairs but, even better, to teach his son how to make the repairs himself. This would facilitate the kind of talk that serves to form a creative relational bond between a father and son. A man-to-man talk, one that is not reserved solely for discussing matters of sexuality, has a pivotal role in initiating the son into his manhood. But Head never had the talk—or any talk—with his father. Far too many Black men have an experience like John Head where they are eager to have the kind of man-to-man, ideally father-to-son, talk that provides them a sense of their transitioning into manhood. The talk is a ritual of initiation. It helps a son form his identity. Unfortunately, some end up like Head: abandoned, cast down, and deciding, ultimately, never to pursue this man talk again.

Novelist and scholar of African American studies Daniel Black observes that this lack of initiation into manhood is a recurring theme in African American literature. By using an "Afrocentric analysis," which privileges the community over the individual, Black makes the connection that this loss leads to spiritual deprivation, for it disconnects the son not only from his father but from his spiritual heritage.[14] "The lack of such self-knowledge usually results in one's inability to determine his own self-worth and, consequently, the power of spirit within," writes Black. Black uses the main fictional characters in Ernest Gaines's *In My Father's House* and John Edgar Wideman's *The Lynchers* as examples of deficient spirituality. Due to their inability to connect with their fathers, "they are troubled, pain-stricken, spiritually lost souls desperate for their father to affirm their existence and to authenticate their sense of self—the ingredients of their manhood."[15] Black offers a captivating portrayal of just how spiritually deprived these young Black men are when he states, "these boys roam the world as Bigger Thomases, full of anger and rage that a spiritual connection to their fathers could have alleviated."[16] What Black is speaking of is a sense of loss that is similar to life in the wilderness. It is an experience that Hagar's son, Ishmael, knew all too well. He desired to talk with Abraham about survival in the wilderness, but Ishmael also needed to know his identity. Without a connection to Abraham, Ishmael didn't know who he was. Was he more than just a "wild ass of a man" in the wilderness—a biblical Bigger? Ishmael needed to know, but whom could he trust to be with him during this process of self-discovery?

BUILDING (BASIC) TRUST IN THE WILDERNESS

Ishmael, like many Black men, was destined to be a problem. The prophecy of Genesis 16:12—"'He shall be a wild ass of a man, with his hand against everyone, and everyone's hand against him'"—condemns him to the life of an outsider. Ed Noort claims that the portrayal of Ishmael in Genesis 16:12 cannot be separated from the worldview of the biblical text's author. According to Noort, the evidence suggests that the writer was "somebody with a settled way of life . . . someone looking at nomadic life in complete amazement and astonishment."[17] Noort explains:

> Nomads and nomadic life are strange and dangerous. They are fighters, solitaries, at home nowhere. They live over a widespread area. They are a threat. It is no accident that in the biblical texts Amalekites, Midianites and Ishmaelites are sometimes interchangeable. The image chosen for Ishmael is perfect. In all the prophetic . . . and poetic . . . texts in which the wild ass is portrayed, its freedom from humans and civilization is stressed.[18]

Theologian John T. Noble also sees Ishmael as an outsider, but an outsider with significant theological status. His research suggests that Ishmael "figures into P's [i.e., the Priestly tradition] larger theological outlook as a special representative of those whom God favors, even outside of the direct line of the Abrahamic covenant."[19] Before proceeding, a brief digression is in order to discuss the Priestly tradition.

The P (Priestly) source was the last significant narrative source to be put together, and Hebrew Bible scholars attest that it was intended to supplement what the E (Elohist) and J (Yahwist) sources state about the history of Israel, specifically as it relates to worship, observance of the covenant, and social structures within the community. Gerhard von Rad avers that the Priestly narrative is recognizable, even for untrained scholars, because of its unique form and content. The most impressive feature of the P source is its sacrifice of literary ornamentation—none of J's good storytelling is present—for an intense "concentration on what is revealed by God."[20] "Thus it describes a course of history only with respect to God's revealed judgments and regulations, with respect to divine regulations which with increasing number establish and assure the salvation of God's people," writes von Rad.[21] Noble remarks that for some biblical scholars, such as scholar of Hebrew literature

James Kugel, the Priestly writer's depiction of God is "the most chilling conception of the deity."[22] P's God is distant and impersonal, one "for whom prayers are unnecessary and festive hymns without practical effect."[23] In contrast, Noble sees P endeavoring to portray a God who is in intimate relationship not only with Israel but with all of humanity, even the non-chosen. That is, there is a universal focus in P's theology in which outcasts are the benefactors of God's favor.

For example, Walter Brueggemann argues that a list of foreigners in Deuteronomy 23:1 was created in order to "maintain the purity of Israelite worship and Israelite community by rigorously excluding those who are disqualified."[24] The designation as a foreigner includes anything from having a physical flaw (e.g., eunuchs) to simply being a person who is not part of the community, an outsider. Brueggemann notes that Yahweh's stance against the foreigner changes in Isaiah 56:

> In Isaiah 56 the post-exilic community is in dispute concerning who qualifies as a member. Against rigorous exclusivism, seemingly sanctioned by Deut 23:1–7, the oracle of Yahweh in Isa 56:3–8 insists that eunuchs (*sris*) and "a foreigner" can indeed be admitted to the community by "hold[ing] fast my covenant." That is, the prohibition and the exclusionary rule of Deut 23:1–7 are not here operative. *The same Yahweh who uttered the old command, we are to believe, issued the present oracular invitation* [italics mine]. [25]

Also, for Brueggemann, there is a "tradition of presence" in the Priestly tradition that attests that humanity can, in fact, be in communion with God.[26]

It is worth repeating that Noble wants to use the story of Ismael as a case study of God's establishing an intimate relationship with an outsider. Therefore, whereas other sources focus on Ishmael's rejected status, there are "many indications of Ishmael's favor" in the Genesis narrative, such as his circumcision.[27] According to Hebrew Bible scholar Thomas B. Dozeman, Ishmael's positive status is evident in that he served as a "model of how Israel must live in the wilderness."[28] Not rejected, Ishmael demonstrates "an expansion of election beyond the boundaries of Israel."[29] Furthermore, the Priestly tradition rejects the violent connotations associated with Ishmael's "wild ass" moniker. The tension between him and his neighbors, as prophesied in Genesis 16:12 (i.e., "'his hand [will be] against everyone'") is not the result of his violent nature but instead "his fierce independence from surrounding culture."[30] His hand is against every man because he must establish his own way of life, grounded in a peculiar identity, in the wilderness. But he must grow up, and do so fast, as "the place of Ishmael's exile became his domicile"[31] Let us now return to Ishmael's initiation.

"God was with the boy, and he grew up; he lived in the wilderness, and became an expert with the bow" (Gen. 21:20). What is the significance of Ishmael's becoming a bowman in the wilderness? Nowhere in the promises made to Hagar in Genesis 16 is it mentioned that her son would become a bowman, an expert bowman no less. A wild ass of a man, yes, but not a bowman. Victor P. Hamilton remarks that in the wilderness "one could survive *only* [italics mine] by developing skills with a bow, and thus Ishmael adapted to that environment and became a *bowman*."[32] Of further interest is Claus Westermann's observation that "this is the first and virtually the last time that there is mention of a weapon in the patriarchal story."[33] Scholar of religion Hugh C. White suggests that Ishmael's growth is not about his skills as a bowman but are instead indicators of his initiation into manhood.[34] White suggests that the Genesis narratives depicting Ishmael's development in the wilderness comprise a genre that he terms an "initiation legend," which is grounded in tribal forms of initiation that mark a boy's transition into manhood. In *Manhood in the Making*, anthropologist David D. Gilmore states that every society distinguishes between male and female according to a range of normative rules and roles. There is, it appears, a structure that regulates these roles across cultural boundaries. For Gilmore, however, "there is a constantly recurring notion that real manhood is different from simple anatomical maleness, that it is not a natural condition that comes about spontaneously through biological maturation but rather is a precarious and artificial state that boys must win against powerful odds."[35] Initiation rituals facilitate this transition into manhood among the simplest hunters and fishermen, among peasants and sophisticated urbanized peoples; it is found in all conditions and environments."[36] Without question, initiation is important in our modern (civilized) society, and it was pivotal within the communities of the Hebrew Bible as well.

In the previous chapter, it was mentioned that Victor Hamilton's commentary makes an insightful distinction regarding Isaac's weaning ceremony, a form of tribal initiation, that was taking place prior to the expulsion of Hagar and Ishmael. Hamilton states that Sarah was angered by Ishmael's playing on the same day of Isaac's weaning. "Perhaps," Hamilton says, "she sees Ishmael doing something to make himself like Isaac, setting his sights on a familial position equal to that of Isaac."[37] A definition of the term *wean* offered by *Merriam-Webster* is to "detach from a source of dependence."[38] Whereas Isaac underwent this ceremony to mark his transition from boyhood dependency to independent manhood, Ishmael was left as an envious onlooker. Ishmael, who was older than Isaac, knew that because he never participated in this initiation, he would always be seen as an immature, dependent boy in Abraham's house. The language of Genesis 21 even conveys that Ishmael was immature. On this solemn day of initiation, Ishmael is found "playing" with Isaac, that is, he is acting childish with the chosen one, Isaac, who is about to become a man.

Moreover, not only is Ishmael deprived of initiation; his expulsion all but ensures that his transition to manhood will never occur. As discussed in the previous chapter, the expulsion into the wilderness signaled that Hagar was now fully responsible for Ishmael's entire well-being. Was she supposed to supervise Ishmael's initiation into manhood? As a practical matter, how could she support an initiation process that (over-)valued separation from the mother when Hagar and Ishmael needed each other to survive in the wilderness? Independence from each other in the wilderness would only hasten their death. Is this not the reason that, when Hagar sought to abandon Ishmael after all their resources were spent, God commanded her, "'Come, lift up the boy and hold him fast with your hand'" (Gen. 21:18)? If Ishmael were to undergo his initiation in the wilderness, it would have to be a different, uncommon transition into manhood. He would have to be weaned from his dependence on the ways of Abraham's house and forget about Isaac's weaning ceremony and the form(s) of manhood it approved. Ishmael's manhood would be different. It has to be so in the wilderness. He would also have to trust that this initiation could take place without Abraham. Someone else would have to see him through his initiation into manhood. But whom could he trust to be with him, all the way, through this process?

With all that he had experienced, Ishmael had every reason not to trust anyone. Abraham and Sarah, with God's approval, had cast him and his mother into the wilderness. Soon after, his mother attempts to abandon him when she is overwhelmed by conditions in the wilderness. But even before the expulsion, there is nothing to indicate that Hagar and Ishmael had a particularly close relationship. Claus Westermann observes that in the patriarchal form of society the father was responsible for the family's material and cultural well-being. Ishmael's overall well-being was Abraham's responsibility. Also, according to Hamilton, Abraham's apprehension regarding Sarah's call for expulsion evinces his "emotional tie with his son," Ishmael.[39] But Abraham still abandons him. What about God? The God of Abraham was the reason, ultimately, for their expulsion into the wilderness. Again, Westermann's commentary is instructive as he underscores that in the patriarchal society the family is religiously self-sufficient. The God of Abraham is the God of the household. Ishmael would not have learned about the God Hagar encountered in her escape into the wilderness (Gen. 16). It is certainly reasonable to consider that Ishmael never heard the name of Hagar's God, El Roi. Who could Ishmael trust in the wilderness?

Psychoanalyst Erik Erikson's theory of psychosocial development begins with basic trust versus basic mistrust. "The general state of trust," Erikson notes, "implies not only that one has learned to rely on sameness and continuity of the outer providers, but also that one may trust oneself and the capacity of one's own organs to cope with urges; and that one is able to consider oneself trustworthy enough so that the providers will not need to be on guard lest they be nipped."[40] Basic trust is therefore inherently relational. Ideally, it is formed in the mother's presence during the first year of the infant's life. Joseph M. Kramp, psychology of religion scholar, contends that Erikson was aware of the connection between basic trust and religious belief. According to Kramp, "Erikson describes the child's interactions with the mother as ritualized and the infant's first experience of a numinous presence. The infant has, thus, a need to be seen, to see and respond, and then to be responded to."[41] When basic trust is established, the first life cycle virtue is achieved: hope. There is no guarantee, however, that things will turn out well. The absence of basic trust is seen in adults who suffer from various forms of social withdrawal or manifest "schizoid and depressive states." Erikson thought that such maladies could be treated by the reestablishment of basic trust in a psychotherapeutic relationship.

Erikson reflects on basic trust again in *Identity: Youth and Crisis* when he writes,

> In adults a radical impairment of basic trust and a prevalence of *basic mistrust* is expressed in a particular form of severe estrangement which characterizes individuals who withdraw into themselves when at odds with themselves and with others. . . . What is most radically missing in them can be seen from the fact that as we attempt to assist them with psychotherapy, we must try to "reach" them with the specific intent of convincing them that they can trust us to trust them and that they can trust themselves.[42]

To prevent this failure, however, Erikson puts a great deal of emphasis on the caring environment created by the mother during infancy. Erikson observes,

> But let it be said here that the amount of trust derived from earliest infantile experience does not seem to depend on absolute quantities of food or demonstrations of love, but rather on the quality of the maternal relationship. Mothers create a sense of trust in their children by that kind of administration which in its quality combines sensitive care of the baby's individual needs and a firm sense of personal trustworthiness within the trusted framework of their culture's lifestyle. This forms the basis in the child for a sense of identity which will later combine a sense of being "all right," of being oneself, and later of becoming what other people trust one will become.[43]

Erikson goes on to make the connection to religion, commenting,

Trust born of care is, in fact, the touchstone of the actuality of a given religion. All religions have in common the periodical childlike surrender to a Provider or providers who dispense earthly fortune as well as spiritual health.[44]

In *The Birth of the Living God*, psychoanalyst Ana-Maria Rizzuto analyzes how we form God representations throughout the life cycle. Her main thesis is that representations of significant others, along with our sociocultural environment, influence a person's representations of God. When discussing the religious dimensions of Erikson's basic trust, she states that this trust is grounded in God's silent presence. Though silent, this presence, for Rizzuto, is a trusted "personal companion."[45] She goes on to hypothesize, speaking from an object relations point of view, that God as a transitional-object representation[46] is used by children "to modulate the unavoidable failures of their parents."[47] This representation is not static, however. Throughout life, as the objects and our self-awareness change, so too does our God representation, thereby influencing our belief and unbelief.[48]

The trauma of the wilderness certainly shaped how Ishmael developed his representation of God. The dominant interpretation of the story suggests that Hagar failed to provide an environment wherein basic trust could be established. Although her abandonment of Ishmael in the wilderness provides enough evidence to make such a claim, J. Gerald Janzen and John T. Noble provide a different perspective. They argue that Hagar's plea in Genesis 21:16—"'Do not let me look on the death of the child'"—is "a prayer that Ishmael's life may be spared."[49] The authors do not ignore the fact of abandonment, noting that Hagar did indeed seek to relinquish her caregiving role by "entrusting [Ishmael's] care, without recourse, to the kindness of strangers and the mercy of God."[50] But in response to her prayer God instructs her to "perform the caring office that she had moments earlier abandoned into some other hand—in effect, to reclaim her maternal relation to Ishmael."[51] Hagar is given a second chance to care for her gift, Ishmael. This time, however, she is not doing so alone. God is with the boy and would help her care for Ishmael. As his relationship with his mother was being repaired, Ishmael would have to learn to trust God, too.

THE INITIATION OF THE BOWMAN, THE BIRTH OF THE GIFT

Ishmael's initiation includes a common theme found in initiation myths: "the separation of the mother and/or child from the father and the exposure of the mother and/or child to some kind of hazard."[52] The earliest examples are found in the birth stories of gods and heroes in Greek mythology. Left exposed in a hostile environment, such as on a mountain side or in a cave, the child is miraculously rescued and nourished. Hugh C. White points out that this represents the child's being incorporated into the cosmic order. This return to the cosmic order also indicates that the child is no longer the mother's responsibility alone. White sees this motif operating in the story of Ishmael when, in abandoning her son, Hagar places the care of her child in the hands of God. According to White, "if the child is to be saved it must be by divine intervention."[53] It is now time for Ishmael to meet Hagar's God, El Roi. White notes that through "miraculous sight" Hagar sees a well that will allow her to restore her son's health. She now knows that their dreadful situation has improved, but if they are to survive the wilderness, the well will not be sufficient. Both she and Ishmael must learn to *see* other ways of survival. *This is when God steps in to begin Ishmael's initiation.*

White states that the "original wilderness episode now preserved in [Genesis 21:15–21] bears the most striking marks of the ritual initiation."[54] Similar to the god and hero initiation myths in Greek mythology, Ishmael is abandoned in a hostile environment, the wilderness, in which he is expected to die. Also, as mentioned earlier, this event is juxtaposed with Isaac's weaning ceremony that was to mark his passage into independent manhood. Ishmael was also at the age, around sixteen or so, when his initiation rite would have occurred. Now it's Ishmael's turn. According to White, "That this episode has indeed been a rite of passage from childhood to adulthood for Ishmael is finally made explicitly clear in 21:20–21 where the reference is to his acquisition of the skills of manhood ('he became an expert with the bow')."[55] Though White's analysis of the initiation of Ishmael offers a number of helpful insights, he overemphasizes Ishmael's acquisition of manhood at the expense of appreciating his growth as a bowman. "The significant point," White attests, "is that the narrative culminates with the chief character fully a man."[56] I see the significant point of the story, instead, as Ishmael's coming into a fuller awareness of himself as a gift by trusting that God was with him. I contend that being only "fully" a man wouldn't help Ishmael and his mother in the wilderness. He needed to be a *gifted* man. Manhood, even full manhood, without a gift is dangerous, for it only seeks to dominate. Manhood without a gift is too isolated and doesn't trust. It lacks generativity and has no identity. Without a gift, a man seeks the presence of other powerful men rather than the presence of God and sees only wilderness, never what God wants him to see.

There is no clear indication as to the duration of Ishmael's initiation. White argues that it was a sudden transition,[57] but that would not be sufficient time to establish basic trust with Ishmael. It takes time to learn to trust again. Also, a significant duration would be needed to teach Ishmael the skills of an expert bowman. Moreover, Ishmael would need to learn to trust himself as a bowman. Ryan P. Bonfiglio, a scholar of the Old Testament, notes that in Zechariah 9, archer imagery is associated with royal authority; the text includes "figurative language surrounding Yahweh as [a] Divine Warrior" who "takes on the form of an archer."[58] Bonfiglio adds that "Yahweh's arrows become a source of protection . . . and deliverance for a people against their enemies."[59] Usually in the Hebrew Bible the bow is a weapon used by Israel's enemies, but in Zechariah 9 it is used by God for Israel's protection and restoration. In the image of the archer in Achaemenid art, created in fifth to third century BCE Persia, the themes of divine authority are present, for "the Achaemenid king, rendered with divine visual connotations, is a legitimate, divinely authorized ruler."[60]

Egyptologist Richard H. Wilkinson notes that the bow was also used as a weapon for hunting and warfare "from very early times in Egypt and the ancient Near East."[61] Symbolically, moreover, the bow was "an important symbol of monarchial power . . . in Egypt, [and] . . . was used as a symbol of royal strength."[62] Similar to the representation of the bow in Achaemenid iconography, there is in Egyptian art "a close symbolic connection between the bow and the institution of kingship among gods and men."[63] I suggest that Hagar, as an Egyptian, would have been aware of the symbolic authority of the bowman. Seeing her son develop not only skills but also, according to Genesis 21:20, *expertise* with the bow served to prove that the prophecy she received in Genesis 16 was coming to fruition. Her son was growing into someone with royal authority, the leader of a nation. Ishmael was growing in other ways as well. His creativity was growing and, therefore, he was becoming more alive.

ALIVE IN THE WILDERNESS

In his essay "The Place Where We Live," psychoanalyst and pediatrician Donald Woods Winnicott explores the place that is in between the exterior and interior, a place "we shall find that we spend most of our time neither in behavior nor in contemplation, but somewhere else."[64] This somewhere else, or third way of living, is what Winnicott terms "a potential space." To make his point, Winnicott uses an example of the relationship between a baby and its mother. The mother who is able to provide an environment where trust and reliability is established creates a potential space. This space between mother and child is "an infinite area of separation, which the baby, child, adolescent, adult may creatively fill with playing, which in time becomes the enjoyment of the cultural heritage."[65]

Margaret Clark, a scholar who focuses on the psychology of human relationships, argues that for Winnicott, "this intermediate area is the proper place for non-pathological illusion."[66] Clark identifies this capacity for illusion as spirituality. In defining spirituality, Clark is careful to distinguish it from religion, which, for her, is "a particular formulation of a spiritual quest which includes a focus on 'God.'"[67] Spirituality "is closely linked to imagination, and manifests frequently in images, as well as in a wide range of emotional experiences . . . and in intellectual formulations, which we call theology of philosophy."[68] According to Clark, Winnicott's potential space allows for spirituality because it facilitates "our capacity and the opportunity for learning how to create/find, understand, and use symbols, and so to enter the freedom and expansiveness of our imagination."[69] There is a definite link, then, between creativity and spirituality.

In his essay "Living Creatively," Winnicott says, "Creativity, then, is the retention throughout life of something that belongs properly to infant experience: the ability to create the world."[70] Creativity in the infant and throughout life is needed to contend with what Winnicott terms the "insult" of the reality principle. Put simply, the reality principle is a psychoanalytic term that describes the "recognition of the real environment by a child, the growing awareness of its demands and the need to accommodate to them."[71] The reality principle is not just our lived environment but the ways in which our given culture teaches us how to interact with our surroundings. Winnicott warns that the reality principle is an insult because it can define all that one is, leaving little room for the imaginative life, that is, the ability to see things differently. He writes,

> In creative living you or I find that everything we do strengthens the feeling that we are alive, that we are ourselves. One can look at a tree (not necessarily at a picture) and look creatively. . . . Although allied to create living, the active creations of letter writers, writers, poets, artists, sculptors, architects, musicians, are different. You will agree that if someone is engaged in artistic creation, we hope he or she can call on some special talent. But for creative living we need no special talent. This is a universal need, and a universal experience, and even the bedridden, withdrawn schizophrenic may be living creatively in a secret mental activity, and therefore in a sense [be] happy. Unhappy is a you or a me who, over a phase, is conscious of the lack of what is essential to the human being, much more important than eating or than physical survival.[72]

Winnicott contends that this capacity for creative living is universal, not something reserved for those deemed talented in artistic creations. "However poor the individual's equipment," Winnicott attests, "experience can be creative and can be felt to be exciting in the sense that there is always something new and unexpected in the air."[73] This has significance in our spiritual lives as well. Clark suggests that creativity takes place within the transitional space and is where we "can create (or find) our own image and experience of God."[74]

In a 1962 lecture given at the University of London Institute of Education titled "Morals and Education," Winnicott explores the idea of "belief in God" or "belief in."[75] Clark interprets Winnicott's remarks as meaning that the child can have this "belief in" "only if he has had the experience of his own creative activity being seen as good in the transitional space between himself and his mother."[76] This creativity, not what the creativity produces [e.g., an object] but the creativity itself, is then "placed up in the sky" and referred to as God. The God of the moral educator, Winnicott says, must be relatable to the God the child has encountered in its experiences of creative living. Therefore, if the moral educator instructs the child that God is a distant deity who demands the child's submission to the rules of the environment, that will contribute neither to the health of the transitional space nor the child's formation of a healthy God image. Throughout our development, but during childhood especially, we need a God representation that is not rigid. More to the point, we need a God who can play *with* us. Play is essential to life and the search for identity because "it is in playing, and perhaps only in playing, that the child or adult is free to be creative."[77] Again, creativity is not necessarily found in one's ability to create an object. Rather, there is a sense of rest while playing because the person trusts that the environment is not forcing one to create order out of the seemingly chaotic activity that is taking place. Winnicott notes that there must be an opportunity "for formless experience, and for creative impulses, motor or sensory, which are the stuff of playing" and essential to creativity.[78] He also mentions that this play occurs in the place where we live, the transitional space, there "in the exciting interweave of subjective and objective observation, and in an area that is intermediate between the inner reality of the individual and the shared reality of the world that is external to individuals."[79]

Pastoral theologian and psychology of religion scholar Jaco Hamman makes a helpful connection between Winnicott's theory of playing and the experiences of men. He argues that men "play to be true to themselves, even to their wild, irrational thoughts."[80] This, of course, is related to the "formless experience" Winnicott believes is an essential part of playing. Through play, the true self emerges, which, for Hamman, is the self that "seeks aliveness, authenticity, spontaneity, creativity, and freedom."[81] Hamman adds that men use their toys (such as sports, motorcycles, tools, and so on) to recover this stage of playing and reconnect with the creative self. "Here we discover self and others anew as relationships strengthen, we find deeper personal integration and restoration, we learn how to engage reality differently, and we experience feeling alive," writes Hamman.[82] Playing in this way, though, is looked upon unfavorably in many environments. Far too often, the rush to reestablish order quickly ends one's much-needed forays into the reverie of creativity discovered in playing. And the reign of the reality principle soon compels one to conform. Remember, Ishmael's playing is what caused both himself and his mother to be thrown into the wilderness: "But Sarah saw the son of Hagar the Egyptian, whom she had borne to Abraham, *playing* [italics mine] with her son Isaac" (Gen. 21:9). Maybe Ishmael was being true to his "wild ass of a man" nature and acting freely with Isaac; who knows? Was he playing to escape conforming to the dominant order (the reality principle) of Abraham's house? Did Sarah fear that he would influence Isaac to play in the same way? What cannot be contested is that this experience must have instilled a great deal of doubt within Ishmael regarding his ability not only to play but to be creative, leaving him with negative feelings about his true identity. He would have to learn to play again in order to live—be alive—in the wilderness.

Dozeman states that the wilderness in Genesis 21 is "as a location outside civilization, where entire nations can live at risk with God."[83] The wilderness itself has the characteristics of a transitional space as it is "drift or borderland between civilization and chaos."[84] Ishmael's self-awareness as a gift could grow in the wilderness because he was free to explore creatively various aspects of his self without fear of being chastised for his playing. It has already been discussed that the development of his expertise as a bowman was the chief means by which he engaged in the kind of playing that nurtured his creative self. Also, this playing is what helped him form an identity of his own. He was a wild ass of a man, but a wild ass of a man *with* God. The common interpretation of Ishmael's character is that his wild-man status is due to his violent nature, which is the only reason "his hand is against everyone" (Gen. 16:12). John T. Noble observes that the "description is enigmatic, to be sure, but whatever else it might convey, it is clear that Ishmael will be no one's slave."[85] In a footnote, Noble quotes Hebrew Bible scholar Jon D. Levenson who states that Ishmael had a "fierce independence."[86] Part of Ishmael's freedom in the wilderness is due to his expertise as a bowman, a weapon of self-defense to be sure, but his experience also entails a growing trust in himself that he could see resources in the wilderness that others couldn't see. His time playing in the wilderness with God allowed him to create a world of his own, a place to live, in a place where others, due to their civilized perspective, saw only death. The initiation was complete.

There are two pivotal elements that verify Ishmael's initiation as a gift. The first is that Hagar was so impressed by Ishmael's growth that she believed he was mature enough to have a relationship with others outside of their community. Ishmael had grown into a gift that could be shared with others, but they needed to appreciate Ishmael not just as a bowman but as a gift. They would therefore not attempt to have him conform to a way of life that would compromise his unique identity. "He lived in the wilderness of Paran; and his mother got a wife for him from the land of Egypt" (Gen. 21:21). As an Egyptian, his wife would be aware of his bowman status. The other mark of Ishmael's initiation as a gift is his peaceful return to the house of Abraham in Genesis 25:7–11 after Abraham's death. Ishmael's time in the wilderness growing with God was so restorative—had created so much hope—that he could return to the family that hurt both him and his mother and not seek revenge. He doesn't desire anything that belongs to Abraham or Isaac, nor does he request to be made a full heir of the Abrahamic covenant. He doesn't confront Isaac about the injustice of his receiving an inheritance as the second-born son. Westermann states that the "two brothers bury [Abraham] in harmony and peace."[87] Whether or not Ishmael was in harmony with Isaac is debatable,[88] but what is certain is that this "'wild ass of a man, with his hand against everyone'" (Gen. 16:12) demonstrated that he was too gifted to do harm to those who had cast him into the wilderness, leaving him for dead. He did not use what his gift had produced—the bow and arrow—nor his expertise as a bowman to hurt Isaac. I also want to offer a nonbiblical indicator of the initiation of Ishmael's gift. Ishmael could talk about his experience of growing in the wilderness without shame. That is, his life in the wilderness was not a curse but a gift to be shared with others facing a wilderness experience of their own. I want to explore the value of this idea as it relates to Black men in the ghetto. A talk about our gifts growing in the ghetto is needed.

6

Warning

God Don't Like Ugly

GO IN THE WILDERNESS

Can a gift grow in the ghetto? As stated earlier, Delores Williams's *Sisters in the Wilderness* interrogates the Bible's responses to the current experiences of African American women. A central question for her is "What was God's response to Hagar's predicament? Were her pain and God's response to it congruent with African American women's predicament and their under-standing of God's response to black women's suffering?"[1] The similarities of predicament were clear, for African American women, like Hagar in the biblical narrative, must contend with "poverty, sexual and economic exploi-tation, surrogacy, domestic violence, homelessness, rape, motherhood, single-parenting, ethnicity and meetings with God."[2] Can the same similar-ities of predicament be found between the story of Ishmael in the wilderness and that of young Black men in the modern American ghetto? Reading the account of Ishmael in Genesis 16 and 21 provides evidence that his predica-ment was violence, fatherlessness, abandonment, poverty, segregation, iso-lation, hopelessness, single-parenting, homelessness, non-initiation, and a lack of a wholesome identity. All of these things form a sense of inescapable vulnerability not only in the biblical wilderness but also for young Black men in the ghetto.

Sociologist Raymond Gunn suggests that we must understand "how easy it is for young black males in poor inner-city communities to go from being full of promise to hypervulnerable."[3] Doubtless there is congruity between Ishmael's predicament and that of many Black men in the ghetto, as Ish-mael, full of promise (Gen. 16), was indeed made hypervulnerable, left for dead in fact, after he and Hagar were thrown into the wilderness and, once again, afterwards, when he was abandoned in Hagar's moment of despair. The modern ghetto resembles the biblical wilderness in the myriad ways they both foment hypervulnerability; however, they are also both places of divine encounter where God makes certain that, no matter the challenging circumstances, one's promise is fulfilled. Common knowledge supposes that neither the wilderness nor the ghetto is viewed as a place where anything—particularly not a gift—grows. Ishmael's story proves that such a limited perspective does not capture the overlooked possibilities for growth with God, especially for outcasts who must make the wilderness or the ghetto their home.

In chapter 4 of this study, we saw that Walter Brueggemann identified the wilderness as bad land that is "seedless . . . formless and therefore lifeless . . . hostile and destructive" where "not only is nothing growing, but nothing can grow."[4] The same is often said of the American ghetto. Richard Wright's *12 Million Black Voices* provides a vivid portrayal of the deadly conditions he encountered in the urban ghetto. He views the kitchenette, a staple of tenement housing in early-twentieth-century inner cities, as symbolic of the conditions of the ghetto: "The kitchenette, with its filth and foul air, with its one toilet for thirty or more tenants, kills our black babies so fast that in many cities twice as many of them die as white babies."[5] The kitchenette is the source not only of numerous medical maladies (scarlet fever, dysentery, typhoid, tuberculosis, etc.) but also of interrelational problems, most specifically among family members:

> The kitchenette, with its crowded rooms and incessant bedlam, provides an enticing place for crimes of all sort—crimes against women and children or any stranger who happens to stray into its dark hallways. The noise of our living, boxed in stone and steel, is so loud that even a pistol shot is smothered.
>
> The kitchenette throws desperate and unhappy people into an unbearable closeness of association, thereby increasing latent friction, giving birth to never ending quarrels of recrimination, accusation, and vindictiveness, producing warped personalities.
>
> The kitchenette injects pressure and tension into our individual personalities, making many of us give up the struggle, walk off and leave wives, husbands, and even children behind to shift as best they can.[6]

The following describes the kitchenette's and, by extension, the ghetto's most devastating and long-lasting effect:

> The kitchenette blights the personalities of our growing children, disorganizes them, blinds them to hope, creates problems whose effects can be traced in the characters of its child victims for years afterwards.[7]

Wright's haunting analysis identifies the ghetto, like the wilderness, as a place where growth, literally and metaphorically, is a challenge for those trapped within its walls. But is there a different way—a subversive view—to see the ghetto? As discussed previously, the wilderness is also gifted land, a place of refuge for outcasts, a place where we are allowed to live a life in contrast to the established order's sustenance, a place where we encounter the God who causes us to see the wilderness and ourselves anew. The wilderness is a place where our gifts can grow. This alternative perspective of the wilderness is found in the African American religious experience. Delores Williams contends that "nothing links the two women [Hagar and an African American woman] more securely than the religious experiences in the wilderness."[8] In the slave songs, for example, there is a clear message declaring that the wilderness is not to be avoided but rather is to be embraced as a place where God is encountered; this, for Williams, demonstrates that the "slaves had a positive concept of the wilderness."[9]

Erik Nielson, a scholar of African American literature, states that the "central message of 'Go in the Wilderness'—that the Lord can be found in the wilderness (rather than a church)—places the song squarely within the tradition of spirituals that link religious worship and conversion with forests, rivers, swamps, and hidden valleys common throughout the rural south."[10] According to Nielson, the slaves' experiences in rural places outside the restrictions of the plantation allowed them to see the wilderness differently. He says, "In 'Go in the Wilderness' and the many other songs that locate spiritual revival in the slave's rural landscape, we see a profound shift, one that rejects typical formulations of the wilderness, instead associating the rural landscape with the privacy and autonomy needed for religious conversion."[11] Not to be overlooked is the fact that an alternative view of the wilderness is also present in the literary work of several African American male authors who saw value, most notably the opportunity for self-discovery, in the wilderness experience.

THE FANTASY OF THE GOODIE GOODIES

In *Ride Out the Wilderness*, Melvin Dixon, a scholar of African American literature, writes that "Afro-American writers, often considered homeless, alienated from mainstream culture, and segregated in negative environments, have used language to create alternative landscapes where black culture and identity can flourish apart from any marginal, prescribed 'place.'"[12] The symbolism of the wilderness is seen in such "alternative landscapes" as the "sewer, cellar, or subway settings in the fictions of [Richard] Wright, [Ralph] Ellison, [LeRoi] Jones."[13] These are places where all forms of ugliness flourish. According to

Dixon, Richard Wright's *The Man Who Lived Underground* compels readers to consider that alienation in a wilderness space is a "precondition for self-creation."[14] Fred Daniels, the novella's main character, discovers a new level of freedom while underground and emerges "a different man, beyond the authority of home, church, and state."[15] Certainly, as Dixon observes, "upon discovering in the underground cave that he can give new meaning to objects and new significance to the subterranean space, he embraces a new, self-chosen identity."[16] The underground *qua* wilderness forces Daniels to create beauty in a place of utter desolation, thereby showing his ability "to handle old objects anew."[17] Daniels had accomplished this amazing feat of self-creation—but at what cost? Unlike the wilderness tradition discussed earlier in Delores Williams's text and Erik Nielson's essay, Wright's *The Man Who Lived Underground* depicts survival in the wilderness without the religious experience. God is not involved, anywhere, in the life of Daniels.

Dixon states that "in the lion's den of the urban slum and sewer (signs of deterioration and waste), Wright envisions Daniels as a different everyman—one more like himself, whom the Lord neither redeemed nor delivered."[18] Wright's wilderness offers a self-transformation caused by and reliant on the self alone. A telling scene in the story is when, upon hearing a church choir singing, Daniels, who is still moving about underground, condemns the choir members for their misplaced faith. His experience in the underground has convinced him that seeking a relationship with the divine is unnecessary, and even foolish.

> When he had sung and prayed with his brothers and sisters in the church, he had always felt the way they felt; but here in the underground, distantly sundered from them, he saw a defenseless nakedness in their lives that made him disown them. A physical distance had come between them and had conferred upon him a terrifying knowledge. He felt that these people should stand silent, unrepentant, with simple manly pride, and yield no quarter in whimpering.[19]

Daniels, it would appear, wants those persons singing in the church to embrace a "manly pride" that would enable them to deal with the wilderness by their might and power alone. But this is not how wilderness experiences have been endured throughout African American history. And "manly pride" alone cannot help Black men survive the ghetto. Something more is needed. The example of Bigger Thomas helps to prove the point.

Novelist James Baldwin, in his collection of essays titled *Notes of a Native Son*, critiques Bigger Thomas's lack of relationships—with community, with self, and with God—as depicted in Richard Wright's novel *Native Son*. Baldwin's revelatory essay "Many Thousands Gone" reflects his own search for identity in the ghetto of Harlem, New York. Baldwin says that "Bigger has no discernable relationship to himself, to his own life, to his own people, not to any other people—in this respect, perhaps, he is most American."[20] Baldwin critiques Wright for making Bigger's isolated—and all-too-material—existence emblematic of the ways Black people survive the ghetto. "What this means for the novel," Baldwin argues, " is that a necessary dimension has been cut away; this dimension being the relationship that Negroes bear to one another, that depth of involvement and unspoken recognition of shared experience which creates a way of life."[21] What we have in the character of Bigger, instead, "is the isolation of the Negro within his own group and the resulting fury of impatient scorn."[22] But Baldwin's criticism was not of *Native Son* alone but rather of the entire genre of the Negro protest novel. The protest novel, in his view, overlooked the many ways Black people in America had creatively overcome oppression; these ways were born "out of the battle waged to maintain their integrity or, to put it more simply, out of their struggle to survive."[23] Unfortunately, on Baldwin's telling, those like Bigger had "arrived [at] no sensibility sufficiently profound and tough to make this tradition articulate."[24] Could an awareness of this tradition have changed Bigger Thomas? Could this tradition have opened his eyes to the ways in which he himself could seek not only to survive but also to create a new way of life in the ghetto? Furthermore, in what ways would this tradition inform him that God was with him even in the ghetto? Through his experience of growing with God, would Bigger have increased his awareness of himself not as the "Nigger!"; "Rapist!"; and "Murderer!" that his environment called him, but, instead, perceived himself as a gift growing with God in the ghetto. It's time for Bigger, and the countless others like him in America's ghettoes, to learn about and from the story of Ishmael in the wilderness.

As we saw in chapter 5, Ishmael was to be "'a wild ass of a man'" (Gen. 16:12). Unfortunately, in the eyes of some, a relationship with God is often associated with a person's being tame and, in many instances, silent—that is to say, redeemed from any "wild ass" characteristics. In fact, when all else has failed, God is often regarded as the supreme antidote for persons or maligned groups who resemble the wild ass of a man. Ishmael's relationship with God in the wilderness demonstrates that not only is God involved with him but even more so that God is responsible for his full development, his very growth as a wild ass of a man. Nowhere in the story is there any indication that God attempts to change Ishmael's identity. Instead, Ishmael is to remain uncompromisingly unique, that is, "'with his hand against everyone'" (Gen. 16:12). I want to suggest that the gift of Ishmael's radical difference is the source of his wild-ass-of-a-man status. Theologian Victor Anderson notes that the grotesque— something that departs from the natural, the expected, or the normal—is an essential feature of the African American religious experience. Anderson writes,

> The unresolved ambiguities of African American experience leave interpreters open to the creative interplay of an undifferentiated unity of experience that comes into focus only by the activity of squeezing the eye one way or another. It sees African American experience as being open to the *feel* of unresolved joys and laughter; open to the experiencing of the comedic and tragic in experience; open to the interplay of sameness and difference. Ambiguity is *the feel of experience* before it is captured, frozen, domesticated by our clear, distinct racial descriptions and our totalized frames of reference for understanding and interpreting African American religious experience.[25]

For Anderson, God is not absent from the grotesqueness of our experience but is totally involved in and expands our vision of reality within the ambiguity of our experience. Therefore, one is not entrapped into a closed-in view of what experience is supposed to be, particularly for those whose experience has been framed, for the most part, by the dominant culture. He adds,

> I realized early in my college and seminary years that I could not be a black liberation theologian if it meant bracketing the grotesqueries, the unresolved ambiguities, of black life for a picture of black experience defined by the blackness that whiteness created. I could not suppress the worlds of difference that keep African American experience open to more than struggle, more than survival, more than resistance, and more than suffering.[26]

The grotesqueries are what moves Anderson to seek for and attest to broader definitions of the African American experience. In like manner, given the biblical account of Ishmael in the wilderness, I too seek ways of creating a picture of Black men in the ghetto that cannot be captured by current descriptors. Ishmael was a wild ass of a man. He was fatherless. His hand was against everyone. His home was in the wilderness. In many ways, he was grotesque, that is, someone whose very way of being departed from the expected or the typical. But he was so much more. He was a wild ass of a man with purpose. He could see the wilderness in new ways. He was a wild ass of a man with an identity (i.e., a bowman), and he was a man with God. He was a man who was a gift.

"God was with the boy" (Gen. 21:20), the wild ass of a man. Far too often, Black men in the ghetto are made to believe that God is not involved with them because of their purported fallen status. They are too poor, too uneducated, too immoral, and too ghetto to be loved by God. Renowned hip-hop artist Biggie Smalls, née Christopher Wallace, gives voice to his spiritual pain in his song "Suicidal Thoughts." Smalls confesses,

When I die, fuck it, I wanna go to hell
'Cause I'm a piece of shit, it ain't hard to fuckin' tell . . .
It don't make no sense, goin' to heaven with the goodie-goodies.[27]

He earnestly believes that he has been rejected by God because, in his own eyes, everyone has always put him at the bottom of the pile. He talks too wild (e.g., the continuous profanity). He dresses too wild (e.g., black Timbs and black hoodies). He lives in a wild place (e.g., Clinton Hills in Brooklyn, NY). It's all too grotesque. God doesn't want anything to do with Smalls, nor anyone else like him, due to the fact that God is too involved with the goodie-goodies. It is a dangerous fantasy.

Who created this distorted picture of the Black religious experience? Who has convinced many of us that God is absent from the lives of Black men in the ghetto? How have they been depicted as a grotesquerie that must be bracketed out of the Black religious experience? Is it because we within the Black community have decided that these men cannot be saved, at least not according to our traditional views of salvation? How have we ourselves further ghettoized these Black men by casting them from our homes, our churches, and our hearts back onto the streets of the inner city? Can't God also be with the wild ass of a man, with his black Timbs and hoodies, in the ghetto? Remember that, according to Daniel B. Schwartz, the word *ghetto* is "derived from the Venetian verb *gettare*, meaning to throw or to cast."[28] Ghetto is therefore not simply a place but a constant activity, a verb, a repeated act of discarding the unwanted, the grotesque, or the wild ass of a man into a desolate place. This is done whenever we declare that God is not involved with a person we deem too grotesque to be redeemed. "All my life I been considered as the worst"[29] is how ghettoized young Black males view themselves. But I ask, how can we cast away God's gift? Even worse, how do we cut down God's gift before it grows?

Toni Morrison's novel *Bluest Eye* provides some guidance when searching for an answer to such questions. According to Morrison, the story is about "beauty, miracles, and self-images, about the way in which people can hurt each other, about whether or not one is beautiful."[30] The story is centered around the life of a Black girl named Pecola Breedlove who is brutally traumatized—verbally, physically, and otherwise—by her community and family due to her ugliness. She is a gift to no one, or so it seems. As the novel nears its conclusion, a character named Claudia MacTeer, who grew up with Pecola in Lorain, Ohio, considers the reasons Pecola was cast away, treated so badly, by her own community:

> The birdlike gestures are worn away to a mere picking and pluck-
> ing her way between the tire rims and the sunflowers, between Coke

bottles and milkweed, among all the waste and beauty of the world—
which is what she herself was. All of our waste which we dumped on
her and which she absorbed. And all of our beauty, which was hers
first and which she gave to us. All of us—all who knew her—felt so
wholesome after we cleaned ourselves on her. We were so beautiful
when we stood astride her ugliness. Her simplicity decorated us, her
guilt sanctified us, her pain made us glow with health, her awkward-
ness made us think we had a sense of humor. Her inarticulateness
made us believe we were eloquent. Her poverty kept us generous.
Even her walking dreams we used—to silence our own nightmares.
And she let us, and thereby deserved our contempt. We honed our
egos on her, padded our characters with her frailty, and yawned in the
fantasy of our strength.

    And fantasy it was, for we were not strong, only aggressive; we
were not free, merely licensed; we were not compassionate, we were
polite; not good, but well behaved. We courted death in order to call
ourselves brave, and hid like thieves from life. We substituted good
grammar for intellect; we switched habits to simulate maturity; we
rearranged lies and called it truth, seeing in the new pattern of an old
idea the Revelation and the Word. . . . *There is no gift for the beloved*
[italics mine].[31]

Claudia offers this analysis in her adult years as she laments what all of this
has done to Pecola, who now, also in her adult years, has become a wild ass
of a woman, all alone in a desolate place, spending her days "walking up and
down, up and down, her head jerking to the beat of a drummer so distant only
she could hear."[32] Pecola has "stepped over into madness."[33] But would the
ones who used her to maintain their fantasy of sanctification—the goodie-
goodies—ever be judged "for the thing [they] assassinated?"[34] The goodie-
goodies made sure Pecola was dead before she ever had a chance to grow.

    What happened to Pecola occurs every day to young Black men in the
ghetto. In "How Bigger Was Born," Wright mentions the numerous Bigger
Thomases he encountered throughout his life.[35] One of them, Bigger No. 4
as he calls him, was eventually sent to the asylum for the insane. There are
far more, however, that walk the streets every day, burdened by what others
have cast or thrown on them. This is the process of *gettare* that is rife throughout America's inner cities. Young Black men not only live in the ghetto but
become a ghetto themselves that holds the despair of others. Our desire to rid
ourselves of the grotesque, the wild ass of a man, the ghetto that lies within
our very being— which is an inescapable part of our humanity—means that,
just as Pecola's community needed her ugliness to make themselves feel beautiful, so too do we use the young Black man's fallenness and godlessness (and,
by extension, giftlessness) to maintain a fantasy of our own righteousness.
Unfortunately, it is a redemption without growth. The goodie-goodies don't

possess spiritual vitality. They are giftless. Although we often say the ghetto is the problem—and there is certainly some truth to that—a more harmful issue is that we don't have faith that God is with the wild ass of a man, those young Black men who adorn themselves in the royal garbs of the ghetto: black Timbs and a black hoodie. Therefore, the young Black male is ignored, rejected, abused, incarcerated, and killed; he is not accepted as a gift that must be allowed to grow with God.

MY GHETTO, MY GOD, AND MY GIFT

I was born and raised in the ghetto. East Orange, New Jersey, is the place. The 1980s and 1990s were the times. There is much that I remember about my younger days, but it seems that there is far more, I hate to admit, that I have tried to forget. I suppose I'd rather not bring back those feelings of fear, confusion, and loss that overwhelmed me during those years. I do remember, though, that nothing troubled me more than an unrelenting sense of emptiness. Mind you, I'm not speaking of hunger, as I do not recall ever going to bed without having a decent meal, but rather of something far more invasive, something reaching into my soul. While eating away at me internally, this emptiness began to have an effect on me externally as well. I was angry at everyone and everything. I didn't want to love because I didn't feel loved. I feared intimacy because I thought that, eventually, if allowed too much access, someone was certain to discover my secret: the emptiness. The most troubling thing was that this experience allowed me to form a bond with other young Black men in the ghetto. Elijah Anderson writes that "the black youth sees others similarly situated and naturally identifies with them . . . this limited experience and perspective forms his orientation and outlook on life, its possibilities and limitations."[36] The emptiness is what drew us together. It was like a badge of honor. But we never talked about it. No-no-no, not ever. It was to remain hidden, locked away, which meant that we never made any attempt to discover what this emptiness was and what, if anything, could be done to fill it.

It would do me great joy to report that I was able to address this dilemma, finally, when I went to counseling. But that is not *my* story. I can recall going to a counselor, a pastoral counselor in fact, at a time when the emptiness was intense, and the first thing she did was construct a genogram. I remember thinking, "Lady, I don't need a *fucking* genogram. . . . I'm hurting." At its best, pastoral counseling is supposed to address, says James Dittes, "this sense of self-depletion and insufficiency, this sense of being a misfit and wrong."[37] I appreciate the way Dittes focuses on the ontological nature of the problem.

It is, in truth, a matter of one's beingness. He makes it clear that the issue at hand has to do with the self. What my pastoral counselor, who I am sure meant no harm, failed to recognize that day was that it was not just my experiences of growing up in the ghetto that perturbed me so but that I myself (or my self) had become a ghetto. *What does that mean?* The ghetto, for me, was not simply a geographical location where, as discussed earlier, marginalized people are isolated from the dominant culture. Rather, I had introjected the ghetto to such an extent that the self, as it were, was treated as a place void of value to the external world. In this condition, where was I to go for help? Is there anything, I ask you, in the current training of caregiving professionals, whether pastors, psychotherapists, social workers, or others, that equips them to deal with the ghetto when it—and all its ugliness—walks into their offices?

I have learned that when diagnosing this kind of spiritual dilemma, one needs to begin by assessing the person's awareness of the gift that lies within. It should not be identified simply as one's talent or even as a God-given ability. Rather, it is that part of one's self that God takes an active role in developing so that we can find a sense of home even in a desolate place. I hope that what has been offered in this book helps to address the spiritual needs of young Black men. Though not all encompassing, perhaps this reimagined perspective can alleviate some of the torment of not just living in but believing oneself to be the ghetto. As for me, I have peace knowing that I am a gift that is still growing with God.

Notes

Introduction

1. James Baldwin, *The Fire Next Time* (New York: Vintage International, 1993), 7.
2. Sylvia Wynter, "No Humans Involved: An Open Letter to My Colleagues," in "Knowledge on Trial," special issue, *Forum NHI* 1 (Fall 1994): 42.
3. Wynter, "No Humans Involved," 42.
4. Wynter, "No Humans Involved," 42.
5. Zygmunt Bauman, *Wasted Lives: Modernity and its Outcasts* (Cambridge: Polity Press, 2004), 82.
6. Wynter, "No Humans Involved," 43.
7. Wynter, "No Humans Involved," 43.
8. Wynter, "No Humans Involved," 43.
9. Wynter, "No Humans Involved," 43.
10. Wynter, "No Humans Involved," 55.
11. Carter G. Woodson, *The Mis-Education of the Negro* (1933; repr., New York: Tribeca Press, 2011), 7.
12. Woodson, *Mis-education of the Negro*, 8.
13. Woodson, *Mis-education of the Negro*, 8.
14. Erik H. Erikson, *Dimensions of a New Identity: The 1973 Jefferson Lectures in the Humanities* (New York: W. W. Norton & Co., 1974), 115.
15. Wynter, "No Humans Involved," 69.
16. William A. Jones Jr., *God in the Ghetto* (Elgin, IL: Progressive Baptist Publishing House, 1979), 50.
17. Jones, *God in the Ghetto*, 51.
18. Willie James Jennings, *The Christian Imagination: Theology and the Origins of Race* (New Haven, CT: Yale University Press, 2011), 3.
19. Jennings, *Christian Imagination*, 3.
20. Jennings, *Christian Imagination*, 3.
21. St. Clair Drake and Horace R. Cayton, *Black Metropolis: A Study of Negro Life in a Northern City* (New York: Harcourt, Brace, & Co.), 611.
22. Drake and Cayton, *Black Metropolis*, 615.
23. Drake and Cayton, *Black Metropolis*, 625.
24. Drake and Cayton, *Black Metropolis*, 612.
25. James Baldwin, "The Fire Next Time," in *Baldwin: Collected Essays*, ed. Toni Morrison (New York: Library of America, 1998), 299.
26. Gilbert Osofsky, *Harlem: The Making of a Ghetto 1890–1930*, 2nd ed. (Chicago: Elephant Paperback, 1996), 144.

27. Omar M. McRoberts, *Streets of Glory: Church and Community in a Black Urban Neighborhood* (Chicago: University of Chicago Press, 2005), 85.
28. R. Drew Smith, "Churches and the Urban Poor: Interaction and Social Distance," *Sociology of Religion* 62 (Autumn 2001): 302.
29. Smith, "Churches and the Urban Poor," 312.
30. Smith, "Churches and the Urban Poor," 312.
31. W. E. B. Du Bois, *The Souls of Black Folk* (1903; repr., New York: Barnes & Noble Classics, 2003), 7.
32. Margaret Walker, *Richard Wright: Daemonic Genius: A Portrait of the Man, A Critical Look at His Work* (New York: Warner Books, 1988), 238.
33. Richard Wright, "How Bigger Was Born," in *Native Son* (1940; repr., New York: Harper Perennial Modern Classics, 2005), 437.
34. Wright, "How Bigger Was Born," 436.
35. Wright, "How Bigger Was Born," 436.
36. Wright, "How Bigger Was Born," 436.
37. Wright, "How Bigger Was Born," 436.
38. Wright, *Native Son* (1940; repr., New York: Harper Perennial Modern Classics, 2005), 16.
39. Wright, *Native Son*, 19.
40. Wright, "How Bigger Was Born," 440.
41. Wright, "How Bigger Was Born," 452.
42. Wright, "How Bigger Was Born," 439.
43. Wright, "How Bigger Was Born," 446.
44. Wright, *Native Son*, 16.
45. Wright, "How Bigger Was Born," 437.
46. Wynter, "No Humans Involved," 43.
47. *Merriam-Webster*, s.v. "spirituality," https://www.merriam-webster.com/dictionary/spirituality.
48. Kenneth I. Pargament, *The Psychology of Religion and Coping: Theory, Research, Practice* (New York: Guilford Press, 1997), 38.
49. E. G. Hinson, "Spirituality (Protestant Tradition)," in *Dictionary of Pastoral Care and Counseling*, ed. Rodney J. Hunter (Nashville: Abingdon Press, 2005), 1223.
50. Hinson, "Spirituality," 1223.
51. Peter J. Paris, *The Spirituality of African Peoples: The Search for a Common Moral Discourse* (Minneapolis: Fortress Press, 1995), 22.
52. Paris, *Spirituality of African Peoples*, 110–11.
53. Dwight N. Hopkins, *Shoes That Fit Our Feet: Sources for a Constructive Black Theology* (Maryknoll, NY: Orbis Books, 1994), 63–64. Hopkins discusses the positive and negative aspects of African American women's connectedness to community. Eva Peace in Morrison's novel *Sula* has "a spirituality of dynamic relatedness to her blood ties, [and] she also defined her immediate family to include parentless children in her neighborhood" (p. 64). Conversely, according to Hopkins's interpretation, Hagar in Morrison's novel *Song of Solomon* "lacked an intricate system of women bonding as women" and because of this "she became addicted to a blind love for a black male character" (p. 65).
54. Archie Smith Jr., "Reaching Back and Pushing Forward: A Perspective on African American Spirituality," *Theology Today* 56 (April 1999): 45.
55. Smith, "Reaching Back," 45.
56. Smith, "Reaching Back," 45.

57. Archie Smith Jr., *Navigating the Deep River: Spirituality in African American Families* (Cleveland: United Church Press, 1997), 35.

58. Smith, *Navigating the Deep River*, 37.

59. Edward P. Wimberly, *Relational Refugees: Alienation and Reincorporation in African American Churches and Communities* (Nashville: Abingdon Press, 2000), 22.

60. Marcel Mauss, *The Gift: The Form and Reason for Exchange in Archaic Societies*, trans. W. D. Halls (New York: W. W. Norton & Co., 1990), 5.

61. Mauss, *The Gift*, 13.

62. Jacques Derrida, *Given Time: 1. Counterfeit Money*, trans. Peggy Kamuf (Chicago: University of Chicago Press, 1992), 12.

63. Alain Caillé and Jacques T. Godbout, *The World of the Gift*, trans. Donald Winkler (London: McGill-Queen's University Press, 2000), 15.

64. Caillé and Godbout, *World of the Gift*, 15.

65. Caillé and Godbout, *World of the Gift*, 146.

66. Thomas R. Blanton, *A Spiritual Economy: Gift Exchange in the Letters of Paul of Tarsus* (New Haven, CT: Yale University Press, 2017).

67. Wayne Meeks, *The First Urban Christians: The Social World of the Apostle Paul* (New Haven, CT: Yale University Press, 1983), 54.

68. Pheme Perkins, *Reading the New Testament: An Introduction*, rev. ed. (1978; repr., New York: Paulist Press, 1988), 177.

69. Blanton, *Spiritual Economy*, 116.

70. Blanton, *Spiritual Economy*, 123.

71. Blanton, *Spiritual Economy*, 132.

72. Loic Wacquant, *Urban Outcasts: A Comparative Sociology of Advanced Marginality* (Malden, MA: Polity Press, 2008), 49.

73. Shemaryahu Talmon, "The Desert Motif in the Bible and in Qumran Literature," in *Literary Studies in the Bible: Form and Content, Collected Studies* (Jerusalem: Magness Press, 1993), 229.

74. Elijah Anderson, "Against the Wall: Poor, Young, Black, and Male," in *Against the Wall: Poor, Young, Black, and Male*, ed. Elijah Anderson (Philadelphia: University of Pennsylvania Press, 2008), 3.

75. Anderson, "Against the Wall," 6.

76. Gregory Mobley, "The Wild Man in the Bible and the Ancient Near East," *Journal of Biblical Literature* 116 (Summer 1997): 226.

77. James H. Evans Jr., *Spiritual Empowerment in Afro-American Literature: Frederick Douglass, Rebecca Jackson, Booker T. Washington, Richard Wright, and Toni Morrison* (Lewiston, NY: Edwin Mellen Press, 1987), 111.

78. Evans Jr., *Spiritual Empowerment*, 112.

79. Frederick L. Ware, *African American Theology: An Introduction* (Louisville, KY: Westminster John Knox Press, 2016), 58.

80. Ware, *African American Theology*, 58–59.

81. Paul Tillich, *Systematic Theology*, vol. 1., *Reason and Revelation, Being and God* (1951; repr., Chicago: University of Chicago Press, 2006), 60. Theologian David Tracey rejects Tillich's notion of mutual interdependence by arguing that Tillich seeks answers from only the Christian faith. A truly correlational method would allow for the Christian faith to be altered by the answers given by nontheological fields of inquiry (see David Tracy, *Blessed Rage for Order: The New Pluralism in Theology* (New York: Seabury Press, 1975).

82. James E. Dittes, *Driven by Hope: Men and Meaning* (Louisville, KY: Westminster John Knox Press, 1996), 4.

83. Richard Wright, *The Man Who Lived Underground*: *A Novel* (1942; repr., New York: Literary Classics of the United States, 2021).

Chapter 1: "I WAS A MAN NOW"

1. Epigraph taken from Erving Goffman, *Stigma: Notes on the Management of Spoiled Identity* (New York: Simon & Schuster, 1963), 128.
2. Karl Barth, *Church Dogmatics*, II/1, *The Doctrine of God* (Edinburgh: T. & T. Clark, 1957), 322.
3. Barth, *Church Dogmatics*, II/1, 323.
4. Karl Barth, *Church Dogmatics*, IV/1, *The Doctrine of Reconciliation* (1956; repr., Edinburgh: T. & T. Clark, 1990), 422.
5. Reinhold Niebuhr, *The Nature and Destiny of Man: A Christian Interpretation*, vol. 2, *Human Destiny* (Louisville, KY: Westminster John Knox Press, 1964), 164.
6. Niebuhr, *Nature and Destiny*, 2:164.
7. Niebuhr, *Nature and Destiny*, 2:171.
8. Paul Tillich, *Systematic Theology*, vol. 3, *Life and the Spirit, History and the Kingdom of God* (Chicago: University of Chicago Press, 1963), 230.
9. Tillich, *Systematic Theology*, 3:241.
10. Tillich, *Systematic Theology*, 3:36.
11. David Tracy, *Blessed Rage for Order: The New Pluralism in Theology* (New York: Seabury Press, 1975), 27.
12. Tracy, *Blessed Rage for Order*, 30.
13. Sylvia Wynter, "Unsettling the Coloniality of Being/Power/Truth/Freedom: Towards the Human, After Man, Its Overrepresentation—An Argument," *CR: The New Centennial Review* 3 (Fall 2003): 264.
14. Jerome J. Pollitt, *Art and Experience in Classical Greece* (Cambridge: University of Cambridge Press, 1972), 106.
15. Pollitt, *Art and Experience*, 108.
16. Pollitt, *Art and Experience*, 107.
17. Immanuel Kant, *Critique of Judgement* (1790), trans. J. H. Barnard (Minneola, NY: Dover Publications, 2005), 52.
18. Kant, *Critique of Judgement*, 53.
19. Kant, *Critique of Judgement*, 53.
20. Immanuel Kant, "On the Different Races of Man," in *Race and Enlightenment: A Reader*, ed. Emmanuel Chukwudi Eze (Oxford: Blackwell Publishers, 1998), 41.
21. Emmanuel Chukwudi Eze, *Achieving Our Humanity: The Idea of a Postracial Future* (New York: Routledge, 2001), 80.
22. Kant, "Different Races of Man," 46.
23. Kant, "Different Races of Man," 46.
24. Eze, *Achieving Our Humanity*, 81.
25. Kant, "Different Races of Man," 46.
26. Kant, "Different Races of Man," 46.
27. Erving Goffman, *Stigma: Notes on the Management of Spoiled Identity* (New York: Simon & Schuster, 1963), 1.
28. Goffman, *Stigma*, 4.
29. Goffman, *Stigma*, 5.
30. Goffman, *Stigma*, 129.
31. William H. Turner, "Myths and Stereotypes: The African Man in America," in *The Black Male in America: Perspectives on His Status in Contemporary Society*, ed. Doris Y. Wilkinson and Ronald L. Taylor (Chicago: Nelson-Hall, 1977), 122.

32. Turner, "Myth and Stereotypes," 122.

33. Patricia A. Turner, "Sambo," in *The Oxford Companion to African American Literature*, ed., William L. Andrews, Frances Smith Foster, and Trudier Harris (New York: Oxford University Press, 1997), 642.

34. Joseph Boskin, *Sambo: The Rise & Demise of an American Jester* (New York: Oxford University Press, 1986), 8.

35. Boskin, *Sambo*, 45.

36. Boskin, *Sambo*, 46.

37. Sterling Stuckey, *Slave Culture: Nationalist Theory and the Foundations of Black America*, rev. ed. (1987; repr., New York: Oxford University Press, 2013), 71.

38. Stuckey, *Slave Culture*, 72.

39. Stuckey, *Slave Culture*, 81.

40. Kenneth M. Stampp, *The Peculiar Institution: Slavery in the Ante-Bellum South* (1956; repr., New York: Vintage Books, 1989), 143.

41. Edwin Adams Davis, ed., *Plantation Life in the Florida Parishes of Louisiana, 1836–1846, as Reflected in the Diary of Bennet H. Barrow* (New York: AMS Press, 1943), 406–7.

42. Davis, *Plantation Life*, 407.

43. Stampp, *Peculiar Institution*, 146.

44. Frederick Douglass, *My Bondage and My Freedom*, (1855; repr., New York: Penguin Books, 2003), 97.

45. Sylvia Wynter, "Sambos and Minstrels," *Social Text* 1 (Winter 1979): 151.

46. Boskin, *Sambo*, 75.

47. Wynter, "Sambos and Minstrels," 155.

48. Wynter, "Sambos and Minstrels," 155.

49. Stanley M. Elkins, *Slavery: A Problem in Institutional and Intellectual Life*, 2nd ed. (Chicago: University of Chicago Press, 1968), 82.

50. Elkins, *Slavery*, 86.

51. Elkins, *Slavery*, 112.

52. Bruno A. Bettleheim, "Individual and Mass Behavior in Extreme Situations," *Journal of Abnormal Psychology*, (October 1942) quoted in Elkins, *Slavery*, 112.

53. Elie Cohen, *Human Behavior in the Concentration Camp* (New York: Norton, 1953) quoted in Elkins, *Slavery*, 113.

54. Elkins, *Slavery*, 113.

55. Elkins, *Slavery*, 113.

56. John W. Blassingame, *Slave Community: Plantation Life in the Antebellum South*, rev. ed. (1972; repr., New York: Oxford University Press, 1979), 304.

57. Wynter, "Sambos and Minstrels," 154.

58. Charles Regan Wilson states that "the Sambo image included such specific types as Uncle Tom, Coon, Mulatto, Mammy, and Buck" ("Sambo," in *Encyclopedia of Southern Culture*, 1141). Boskin suggests that "The Uncle Tom" show became a widely accepted version of the minstrel show in the South and West. Particularly among pious viewers, Uncle Tom provided a less sinful version of the Sambo stereotype. Boskin reports that "by the mid-1920s there were more than a dozen Toms operating in small towns and cities" (*Sambo*, 86).

59. Jason Richards, *Imitation Nation: Red, White, and Blackface in Early and Antebellum Literature* (Charlottesville: University of Virginia Press, 2017), 116.

60. Patricia A. Turner, "Uncle Tom," in *Companion to African American Literature* (New York: Oxford University Press, 1997), 741.

61. Wilson Jeremiah Moses, *Black Messiahs and Uncle Toms: Social and Literary Manipulations of a Religious Myth*, rev. ed. (1982; repr., University Park: Pennsylvania State University Press, 1993), 49.
62. Moses, *Black Messiahs*, 52.
63. Harriet Beecher Stowe, *Uncle Tom's Cabin: Or Negro Life in the United States* (1852; repr., London: Wordsworth, 1995), 331.
64. Harriet Beecher Stowe, *A Key to Uncle Tom's Cabin: Facts and Documents upon Which the Story Is Founded* (1852; repr., Bedford, MA: Applewood Books, 1970), 39.
65. Stowe, *Key to Uncle Tom's Cabin*, 39.
66. Stowe, *Key to Uncle Tom's Cabin*, 40.
67. Stowe, *Uncle Tom's Cabin*, 353.
68. Stowe, *Uncle Tom's Cabin*, 320.
69. Blassingame, *Slave Community*, 259.
70. Stowe, *Uncle Tom's Cabin*, 384.
71. Blassingame, *Slave Community*, 225.
72. Nat Turner, *The Confessions of Nat Tuner: The Leader of the Late Insurrection in Southampton, VA* (Windham, NH: Windham Press, 2014).
73. William L. Andrews, "Nat Turner," in *The Oxford Companion to African American Literature*, ed. William L. Andrews, Frances Smith Foster, and Trudier Harris (New York: Oxford University Press, 1997), 739.
74. Andrews, "Nat Turner," 739.
75. Moses, *Black Messiahs*, 65.
76. James H. Moorhead, "Millennialism," in *Encyclopedia of Religion in the South* (Macon, GA: Mercer University Press, 2005), 510.
77. Lawrence W. Levine, *Black Culture and Black Consciousness: Afro-American Folk Thought from Slavery to Freedom* (New York: Oxford University Press, 2007), 400.
78. Moses, *Black Messiahs*, 1.
79. Moses, *Black Messiahs*, 4.
80. Peter Schäfer, *Two Gods in Heaven: Jewish Concepts of God in Antiquity* (Princeton, NJ: Princeton University Press, 2020), 55.
81. Schäfer, *Two Gods in Heaven*, 57.
82. Schäfer, *Two Gods in Heaven*, 57.
83. Albert J. Cleage, "The Black Messiah," in *Black Theology: A Documentary History, vol. 1, 1966–1979*, ed. James H. Cone and Gayraud S. Wilmore (Maryknoll, NY: Orbis Books, 1993), 103.
84. Richard A. Long, "New Negro, The," in Andrews, Foster, and Harris, eds. *Oxford Companion*, 536.
85. Alaine Locke, "The New Negro," in *The New Negro Voices of the Harlem Renaissance*, ed. Alaine Locke (1925; repr., New York: Atheneum, 1992), 4.
86. Locke, "New Negro," 4.
87. Locke, "New Negro," 5.
88. Locke, "New Negro," 5.
89. Leslie Pinckney Hill quoted in August Meier, *Negro Thought in America 1880–1915: Racial Ideologies in the Age of Booker T. Washington* (Ann Arbor: University of Michigan Press, 1963), 258.
90. Leon F. Litwack, *Trouble in Mind: Black Southerners in the Age of Jim Crow* (New York: Vintage Books, 1998), 197.
91. Litwack, *Trouble in Mind*, 198.
92. Gunnar Myrdal, in Ronald Walters and Robert C. Smith, *African American Leadership* (Albany: State University of New York Press, 1999), 21.

93. Walters and Smith, *African American Leadership*, 18–19.
94. Walters and Smith, *African American Leadership*, 20.
95. Peter J. Paris, *Black Religious Leaders: Conflict in Unity* (Louisville, KY: Westminster John Knox Press, 1991), 17.
96. Paris, *Black Religious Leaders*, 17.
97. Walters and Smith, *African American Leadership*, 110.
98. Walters and Smith, *African American Leadership*, 110.
99. Frederick Douglass, 1846, quoted in *Frederick Douglass: Selected Speeches and Writings*, ed. Philip S. Foner (Chicago: Lawrence Hill Books, 1999), 22.
100. Douglass, 1846, quoted in Foner, ed., *Frederick Douglass*, 22–23.
101. Frederick Douglass, *My Bondage and My Freedom*, ed. John David Smith (1855; repr., New York: Penguin Books, 2003), 181.
102. Douglass, *My Bondage*, 181.
103. Douglass, *My Bondage*, 180.
104. Douglass, *My Bondage*, 122.
105. Douglass, *My Bondage*, 122.
106. John David Smith, "Introduction," in Douglass, *My Bondage*, xxxiii.
107. William F. McFeely, *Frederick Douglass* (New York: W. W. Norton & Co., 1991), 48.
108. Max Weber, *Economy and Society: An Outline of Interpretive Sociology*, vol. 1 (Berkeley: University of California Press, 1978), 241.
109. Weber, *Economy and Society*, 1:241.
110. Weber, *Economy and Society*, 1:242.
111. Weber, *Economy and Society*, 1:242.
112. Weber (*Economy and Society*, 1, 241–46) posits three types of legitimate domination: charismatic domination, traditional domination, and rational-legal domination.
113. Erica R. Edwards, *Charisma and the Fictions of Black Leadership* (Minneapolis: University of Minnesota Press, 2012), xv.
114. Edwards, *Fictions of Black Leadership*, xv.
115. Edwards, *Fictions of Black Leadership*, 129.
116. Na'im Akbar, *Visions for Black Men* (Tallahassee, FL: Mind Productions, 1991), 65.
117. Akbar, *Visions for Black Men*, 65.
118. Akbar, *Visions for Black Men*, 66–81.
119. Ossie Davis, "On Malcolm X," in *The Autobiography of Malcolm X*, ed. Alex Haley (New York: Ballantine Books, 1965), 527.
120. Ossie Davis, quoted in Steve Estes, *I Am a Man: Race, Manhood and the Civil Rights Movement* (Durham: University of North Carolina Press, 2005), 87.
121. Sanchez interview in Hampton, Frasier, and Flynn, *Voices of Freedom: An Oral History of the Civil Rights Movement from the 1950s through the 1980s*, quoted in Estes, *I Am a Man*, 105.
122. Goffman, *Stigma*, 128.
123. Robert C. Smith, *We Have No Leaders: African Americans in the Post-Civil Rights Era* (Albany: State University of New York Press, 1996), 3.
124. Smith, *We Have No Leaders*, 6.
125. Joel E. Spingarn, quoted in David Levering Lewis, *W. E. B. Du Bois: Biography of Race 1868–1919* (New York: Henry Holt & Co., 1993), 552.
126. Lewis, *Du Bois*, 556.
127. W. E. B. Du Bois, "The Color Line Belts the World," in *W. E. B. DuBois: A Reader*, ed. David Levering Lewis (New York: Henry Holt and Co., 1995), 42.

128. Du Bois, "The Color Line," 42.
129. Hubert Harrison, "The Descent of Dr. Du Bois," in *A Hubert Harrison Reader*, ed. Jeffrey B. Perry (Middletown, CT: Wesleyan University Press, 2001), 174.
130. Harrison, "The Descent," 174.
131. August Meier, "On the Role of Martin Luther King," in *The Making of Black America: Essays in Negro Life and History*, vol. 1, ed. August Meier and Elliot Rudwick (New York: Atheneum, 1969), 356.
132. Meier, "Martin Luther King," 357.
133. Rudolph P. Byrd, "The Tradition of John: A Mode of Black Masculinity," in *Traps: African American Men on Gender and Sexuality*, ed. Rudolph P. Byrd and Beverly Guy-Sheftall (Bloomington: Indiana University Press, 2001), 3.
134. Zora Neal Hurston, "High John De Conqueror," *The Sanctified Church: The Folklore Writings of Zora Neal Hurston* quoted in Byrd, "Tradition of John," 5.
135. Hurston, quoted in Byrd, "Tradition of John," 6.
136. Hurston, quoted in Byrd, "Tradition of John," 7.
137. Byrd, "Tradition of John," 7.
138. Byrd, "Tradition of John," 22.

Chapter 2: The Hero's Sorrow

1. Sigmund Freud, *Moses and Monotheism*, trans. Katherine Jones (1939; repr., New York: Vintage Books, 1967), 9.
2. Karlheinz Stockhausen, *Stockhausen on Music: Lectures & Interviews* (London: Marion Boyars Publishers, 2000), 19.
3. Stockhausen, *Stockhausen on Music*, 19.
4. Stockhausen, *Stockhausen on Music*, 23.
5. Stockhausen, *Stockhausen on Music*, 23.
6. Franz Kafka "Letter to His Father" in *Franz Kafka: The Sons* (New York: Schocken Books, 1989), 144.
7. Kafka, "Letter to His Father," 144.
8. Melvin R. Lansky, *Fathers Who Fail: Shame and Psychopathology in the Family System* (Hillsdale, NJ: Analytic Press, 1992), 4.
9. Lansky, *Fathers Who Fail*, 4.
10. James E. Dittes, *Driven by Hope: Men and Meaning* (Louisville, KY: Westminster John Knox Press, 1996), ix.
11. Dittes, *Driven by Hope*, 123.
12. Dittes, *Driven by Hope*, 123.
13. Dittes, *Driven by Hope*, 34.
14. Lansky, *Fathers Who Fail*, 5.
15. Lansky, *Fathers Who Fail*, 7.
16. Dittes, *Driven by Hope*, 4.
17. Peter Gay, *Freud: A Life for Our Time* (New York: W. W. Norton & Co., 2006), 544.
18. Gay, *Freud*, 544.
19. Sigmund Freud, *The Future of an Illusion* (New York: W. W. Norton & Co., 1989).
20. Sigmund Freud, "A Disturbance of Memory on the Acropolis," in *Sigmund Freud: Collected Papers*, vol. 5, *Miscellaneous Papers, 1888–1939*, ed. James Strachey (New York: Basic Books, 1959), 302.
21. Freud, "Disturbance of Memory," 302.
22. Freud, "Disturbance of Memory," 302.
23. Freud, "Disturbance of Memory," 302.

24. Max Schur, *Freud: Living and Dying* (New York: International Universities Press, 1972), 225.

25. Sigmund Freud, *The Interpretation of Dreams*, trans. Joyce Crick (New York: Oxford University Press, 1999), 314.

26. Carl E. Schorske, *Fin-De-Siecle Vienna: Politics and Culture* (New York: Vintage Books, 1981), 182.

27. Schorske, *Fin-De-Siecle Vienna*, 182.

28. Freud, *Interpretation of Dreams*, 108.

29. Gay, *Freud*, 56.

30. Gay, *Freud*, 56.

31. Sigmund Freud, 1890, in *The Complete Letters of Sigmund Freud to Wilhelm Fliess 1887–1904*, trans. and ed. Jeffrey Moussaieff Masson (Cambridge, MA: Belknap Press, 1985), 27.

32. Freud, 1894, in Gay, *Freud*, 56.

33. Freud, 1896, in Masson, ed., *Complete Letters*, 158.

34. Gay, *Freud*, 125.

35. Peter M. Newton, *Freud: From Youthful Dream to Mid-Life Crisis* (New York: Guilford Press, 1995), 142.

36. Newton, *Freud*, 142.

37. Sigmund Freud, *Interpretation of Dreams, SE IV*, xxvi, quoted in Gay, *Freud*, 89.

38. Wilhelm Fliess, "Les reflexes d' origine nasale," quoted in George Makari, *Revolution in Mind: The Creation of Psychoanalysis* (New York: Harper Perennial), 86–87.

39. Newton, *Freud*, 142.

40. Schur, *Freud*, 80.

41. Schur, *Freud*, 80.

42. Schur, *Freud*, 80.

43. Freud, *Interpretation of Dreams*, 87.

44. Freud, *Interpretation of Dreams*, 91.

45. Sigmund Freud, 1896, in Masson, *Complete Letters*, 186.

46. Freud, in Masson, *Complete Letters*, 186.

47. Freud, in Masson, *Complete Letters*, 186.

48. Gay, *Freud*, 58.

49. Bernard D. Fine and Burness E. Moore, eds., *Psychoanalytic Terms and Concepts* (New Haven, CT: American Psychoanalytic Association and Yale University Press, 1990), 196.

50. Fine and Burness, *Psychoanalytic Terms and Concepts*, 196.

51. Gay, *Freud*, 59.

52. Gay, *Freud*, 61.

53. Gay, *Freud*, 61.

54. Ernest Jones, *The Life and Work of Sigmund Freud*, vol. 1, *The Formative Years and the Great Discoveries 1856–1900* (New York: Basic Books, 1953), 315. Otto Weininger's book *Sex and Character: An Investigation of Fundamental Principles* (Bloomington: Indiana University Press, 2005) was at the center of the argument. Fliess was upset that Weininger made Freud's theory of bisexuality the center of the book without crediting Fliess. Freud spends most of the January 27 letter offering a series of explanations as to why he is not indebted to Fliess for the bisexuality theory. For example, he states that "there is so little of bisexuality or of other things I have borrowed from you in what I say, that I can do justice to your share in a few remarks."

55. Sigmund Freud, 1906, in Masson, *Complete Letters*, 466–67.
56. Jones, *Life and Work*, 1:315.
57. Freud, 1904, in Masson, *Complete Letters*, 467.
58. Freud, 1904, in Masson, *Complete Letters*, 467.
59. Jones, *Life and Work*, 1:314.
60. The abandonment of the seduction theory is an important and controversial event in the development of psychoanalysis. In terms of Freud's metapsychology, it signaled his shift from a focus on real-life traumatic events, such as the sexual abuse of children, to a focus on how such events only occur in fantasy. Also, a great deal of controversy surrounds the question of whether Freud abandoned the theory for personal reasons. Several biographers comment that Freud did not want to implicate his father by suggesting, in the theory, that all fathers seduce their children, which would suggest that Jacob Freud had seduced his children. But was it even more serious than that? Jeffrey Masson, in *The Assault on Truth: Freud's Suppression of the Seduction Theory* (New York: Farrar, Straus & Giroux, 1984) claims that Freud abandoned the seduction theory because Wilhelm Fliess was sexually abusing his son, Robert Fliess (pp. 138–142).
61. Schorske, *Fin-De-Siecle Vienna*, 186.
62. Jones, *Life and Work*, 1:324.
63. Freud, "The Dynamics of Transference," in *Sigmund Freud: Collected Papers*, vol. 2, *Clinical Papers, Papers on Technique* (New York: Basic Books, 1959), 322.
64. Freud, *Interpretation of Dreams*, 166.
65. Percival Bailey, *Sigmund the Unserene: A Tragedy in Three Acts* (Springfield, IL: Charles C. Thomas, 1965), 4.
66. Freud, *The Interpretation of Dreams*, 166–167.
67. Marianne Krull, *Freud and His Father*, trans. Arnold J. Pomerans (New York: W. W. Norton & Co., 1986), 148. Historian Daniel B. Schwartz provides information regarding the formation of the Leopoldstadt ghetto in his text *Ghetto: The History of a Word* (Cambridge, MA: Harvard University Press, 2019). According to Schwartz, the Leopoldstadt ghetto was created as a Jewish enclosure in the seventeenth century.
68. Gay, *Freud*, 9.
69. Schorske, *Fin-De-Siecle Vienna*, 172.
70. Freud, *Interpretation of Dreams*, 151.
71. Freud, *Interpretation of Dreams*, 151.
72. Lydia Flem, *Freud the Man: An Intellectual Biography*, trans. Susan Fairfield (New York: Other Press, 2003), 52.
73. Flem, *Freud the Man*, 52.
74. Flem, *Freud the Man*, 62–63.
75. Patrick Mullahy, *Oedipus Myth and Complex: A Review of Psychoanalytic Theory* (New York: Hermitage House, 1953), 29.
76. Mullahy, *Oedipus Myth and Complex*, 29.
77. Mullahy, *Oedipus Myth and Complex*, 71.
78. Newton, *Freud*, 43.
79. Newton, *Freud*, 43.
80. Max Horkheimer, "Authority and the Family," in *Critical Theory: Selected Essays*, trans. Matthey J. O'Connell (New York: Continuum, 1995), 107.
81. Jones, *Life and Work*, 1:6.
82. Freud, 1904, in Masson, *Complete Letters*, 467.

83. Sigmund Freud, "Family Romances," in *Sigmund Freud: Collected Papers*, vol. 5, *Miscellaneous Papers, 1888–1938* (New York: Basic Books, 1959), 74.
84. Freud, "Family Romances," 74.
85. Freud, "Family Romances," 74.
86. Freud, "Family Romances," 74.
87. Freud, "Family Romances," 75.
88. Ernest Jones, *The Life and Work of Sigmund Freud*, vol. 2, *Years of Maturity, 1901–1919* (New York: Basic Books, 1953), 24.
89. Freud, "Disturbance of Memory," 306.
90. Freud, "Disturbance of Memory," 307.
91. Freud, "Disturbance of Memory," 310
92. Freud, "Disturbance of Memory," 311.
93. Newton, *Freud*, 43.
94. Maynard Solomon, "Freud's Father on the Acropolis," *American Imago* 30 (Summer 1973): 152.
95. Solomon, "Freud's Father," 152.
96. Dittes, *Driven by Hope*, 4.
97. Abdul R. JanMohamed, *The Death-Bound-Subject: Richard Wright's Archeology of Death* (Durham, NC: Duke University Press, 2005), 165.
98. Michel Fabre, *The Unfinished Quest of Richard Wright*, trans. Isabel Barzun (1973; repr., Urbana: University of Illinois Press, 1993), 1.
99. Hazel Rowley, *Richard Wright: The Life and Times* (Chicago: University of Chicago Press, 2001), 1. Readers may be surprised to hear of African Americans voting in nineteenth-century Mississippi. However, due to the provisions of the Reconstruction Act of 1867, African Americans in southern states were enfranchised and played a significant role in politics. Unfortunately, by 1877, whites reversed the progress made by Reconstruction, eliminating African Americans from political participation, both the ballot and holding public office, in all southern states.
100. Fabre, *Unfinished Quest*, 1.
101. Fabre, *Unfinished Quest*, 1.
102. Fabre, *Unfinished Quest*, 1.
103. Jack E. Davis, "A Struggle for Public History: Black and White Claims to Natchez's Past" *Public Historian* 22 (Winter 2000): 48.
104. Charles Regan Wilson, *Baptized in Blood: The Religion of the Lost Cause, 1865–1920* (Athens: University of Georgia Press, 1980), 13.
105. Wilson, *Baptized in Blood*, 7.
106. Wilson, *Baptized in Blood*, 111.
107. Stewart E. Tolnay and E. M. Beck, *A Festival of Violence: An Analysis of Southern Lynchings, 1882–1930* (Urbana: University of Illinois Press, 1995), 29.
108. Tolnay and Beck, *A Festival of Violence*, 29.
109. Fabre, *Unfinished Quest*, 1.
110. Constance Webb, *Richard Wright: A Biography* (New York: G. P. Putnam's Sons, 1968), 18.
111. Rowley, *Richard Wright*, 3.
112. Allison Davis, *Leadership, Love, and Aggression* (New York: Harcourt Brace Jovanovich, 1983), 160.
113. Richard Wright, *Black Boy: A Record of Childhood and Youth* (1944; repr., New York: Harper Perennial Modern Classics, 2006), 73.
114. Wright, *Black Boy*, 10.
115. Fabre, *Unfinished Quest*, 11.

116. Wright, *Black Boy*, 11.
117. Addison Gayle, *Richard Wright: Ordeal of a Native Son* (Garden City, NY: Anchor Press, 1980), 5.
118. Gayle, *Richard Wright*, 8.
119. Du Bois, *Souls of Black Folk*, 15.
120. Clarence Snelling, "Call to Ministry," in *Dictionary of Pastoral Care and Counseling*, ed. Rodney J. Hunter (Nashville: Abingdon Press, 2005), 115.
121. Wright, quoted in Rowley, *Richard Wright*, 6.
122. Gayle, *Richard Wright*, 9.
123. Richard N. Pitt, *Divine Callings: Understanding the Call to Ministry in Black Pentecostalism* (New York: New York University Press, 2012), 9.
124. Pitt, *Divine Callings*, 9.
125. Wright, *Black Boy*, 13–14 .
126. Wright, *Black Boy*, 15.
127. Wright, *Black Boy*, 16.
128. Wright, *Black Boy*, 16.
129. Wright, *Black Boy*, 21.
130. Wright, *Black Boy*, 27.
131. Margaret Walker, *Daemonic Genius: A Portrait of the Man, A Critical Look at His Work* (New York: Warner Books, 1988), 23.
132. Constance Webb, *Richard Wright: A Biography* (New York: G. P. Putnam's Sons, 1968), 32.
133. Webb, *Richard Wright*, 32. Wright describes his attempts to run away in *Black Boy* on pp. 32–33.
134. Wright, *Black Boy*, 100.
135. Rowley, *Richard Wright*, 26.
136. Wright, *Black Boy*, 154.
137. Wright, *Black Boy*, 155.
138. Wright, *Black Boy*, 116.
139. In describing the religious atmosphere of Margaret Wilson's household, Margaret Walker states that "on the Sabbath day in Grandma Wilson's house no work-a-day activities could be done, from six o'clock on Friday until six o'clock on Saturday, not even cutting paper with scissors. . . . Moving pictures were strictly forbidden, although Wright loved films and somehow found his way to the theater week after week. Once when Wright had built a radio, his grandmother destroyed it. Dancing and card playing were strictly forbidden, and Wright never learned to dance. Bible reading and praying were daily occupations; long prayers were said morning and night. The Bible was constantly quoted, and Wright was told early that nothing good would ever come of him, that he was consigned and damned to hell and the devil" (Walker, *Daemonic Genius*, 33).
140. Wright, *Black Boy*, 144.
141. Ralph Ellison, "Richard Wright's Blues," in *Shadow and Act* (New York: Vintage Books, 1995), 83.
142. Ellison, "Richard Wright's Blues," 83.
143. Ellison, "Richard Wright's Blues," 84.
144. Ellison, "Richard Wright's Blues," 89.
145. Ellison, "Richard Wright's Blues," 91.
146. Wright, *Black Boy*, 37.
147. Robert B. Stepto, *From Behind the Veil: A Study of Afro-American Narrative* (Urbana: University of Illinois Press), 136–37.

148. Wright, *American Hunger*, 20.
149. Allison Davis, *Leadership, Love, and Aggression* (New York: Harcourt Brace Jovanovich, 1983), 155.
150. Wright, *Black Boy*, 34.
151. Wright, *Black Boy*, 34.
152. Wright, *Black Boy*, 34.
153. Wright, *Black Boy*, 35.
154. Davis, *Leadership, Love, and Aggression*, 167.
155. Wright, *Black Boy*, 35.
156. Davis, *Leadership, Love, and Aggression*, 170.
157. Davis, *Leadership, Love, and Aggression*, 171.
158. Dittes, *Driven by Hope*, 4.
159. Dittes, *Driven by Hope*, 4.

Chapter 3: Ghetto Grown

1. Jeff Chang, *Can't Stop Won't Stop: A History of the Hip-Hop Generation* (New York: St. Martin's Press, 2005), 229.
2. Adam Bradley, *Book of Rhymes: The Poetics of Hip-Hop* (New York: Basic Civitas, 2009), 133.
3. Kurt Loder, "Grandmaster Flash, The Message," *Rolling Stone* (September 16, 1982).
4. Loder, "Grandmaster Flash, The Message."
5. Grandmaster Flash and the Furious Five, "The Message" (Sugar Hill Records, 1982).
6. Cheryl L. Keyes, *Rap Music and Street Consciousness* (Chicago: University of Illinois Press, 2004), 213.
7. Keyes, *Rap Music*, 212.
8. Grandmaster Flash and the Furious Five, "The Message," https://www.azlyrics .com/lyrics/grandmasterflashandthefuriousfive/themessage.html.
9. Grandmaster Flash and the Furious Five, "The Message."
10. Bradley, *Book of Rhymes*, 135.
11. Bradley, *Book of Rhymes*, 134.
12. Paul A. Jargowsky, *Poverty and Place: Ghettoes, Barrios, and the American Inner City* (New York: Russel Sage Foundation, 1997), 91.
13. Jargowsky, *Poverty and Place*, 91.
14. Jargowsky, *Poverty and Place*, 92.
15. Economist Nicholas Eberstadt argues that American men, regardless of race, are leaving the workforce at an alarming rate, and because of this "these men have become essentially dispensable" (p. 5). He says that as the America male can no longer be the breadwinner, the family structure is also being undone. See Nicholas Eberstadt, *Men Without Work: America's Invisible Crisis* (West Conshohocken, PA: Templeton Press, 2016).
16. William Julius Wilson, *When Work Disappears: The World of the New Urban Poor* (New York: Vintage Books, 1996), 75.
17. Jargowsky, *Poverty and Place*, 107.
18. Jargowsky, *Poverty and Place*, 108.
19. Sara F. Jacoby, Laura Tach, Terry Guerra, Douglass J. Wiebe, and Therese S. Richmond, "The Health Status and Well-being of Low-resource, Housing-unstable, Single-parent Families Living in Violent Neighborhoods in Philadelphia, Pennsylvania," *Health and Social Care in the Community* 25 (March 2017): 12.

20. Jacoby, et al., "Health Status and Well-being," 17.
21. Jacoby, et al., "Health Status and Well-being," 17.
22. *Merriam-Webster*, s.v., "ghetto," https://www.merriam-webster.com/dictionary/ghetto.
23. Sandra Debenedetti-Stow, "The Etymology of 'Ghetto': New Evidence from Rome," *Jewish History* 6 (1992): 79.
24. Debenedetti-Stow, "Etymology of 'Ghetto,'" 79.
25. Debenedetti-Stow, "Etymology of 'Ghetto,'" 83.
26. Daniel B. Schwartz, *Ghetto: The History of a Word* (Cambridge, MA: Harvard University Press, 2019), 21.
27. Schwartz, *Ghetto*, 1.
28. Schwartz, *Ghetto*, 1.
29. Schwartz, *Ghetto*, 27.
30. Schwartz, *Ghetto*, 28.
31. David Vital, *A People Apart: The Jews in Europe 1789–1939* (New York: Oxford University Press, 1999), 32.
32. Vital, *People Apart*, 32.
33. Vital, *People Apart*, 32.
34. Vital, *People Apart*, 22.
35. Vital, *People Apart*, 22.
36. Schwartz, *Ghetto*, 97.
37. Schwartz, *Ghetto*, 98.
38. Herbert J. Gans, "Involuntary Segregation and the Ghetto: Disconnecting Process and Place," *Symposium on the Ghetto* 7 (December 2008): 353–54.
39. Gans, "Involuntary Segregation," 353.
40. Gans, "Involuntary Segregation," 354.
41. Louis Wirth, "The Ghetto," *American Journal of Sociology* 33 (July 1927): 57.
42. Wirth, "Ghetto," 61.
43. Wirth, "Ghetto," 61.
44. Wirth, *The Ghetto* (Chicago: The University of Chicago Press, 1928), 179.
45. Wirth, *Ghetto*, 180.
46. Wirth, *Ghetto*, 192.
47. Wirth, "Ghetto," 68.
48. Wirth, "Ghetto," 68.
49. Wirth, "Ghetto," 71.
50. John R. Logan, Wei Wei Zhang, Richard Turner, and Allison Shertzer, "Creating the Black Ghetto: Black Residential Patterns before and during the Great Migration," *Annals of the American Academy of Political and Social Science* 660 (July 2015): 19.
51. Logan, et al., "Creating the Black Ghetto," 20.
52. Logan, et al., "Creating the Black Ghetto," 26.
53. Thomas J. Sugrue, *Urban Crisis: Race and Inequality in Postwar Detroit*, rev. ed. (1996; repr., Princeton, NJ: Princeton University Press, 2005), 23.
54. Gilbert Osofsky, *Harlem: The Making of a Ghetto, Negro New York, 1890–1930*, rev. ed. (1966; repr., Chicago: Elephant Paperbacks, 1996), 7.
55. Osofsky, *Harlem*, 17.
56. Osofsky, *Harlem*, 128.
57. Osofsky, *Harlem*, 136.
58. St. Clair Drake and Horace R. Cayton, *Black Metropolis: A Study of Northern Life in a Northern City* (New York: Harcourt, Brace, and Co., 1945), 174.

59. Drake and Cayton, *Black Metropolis*, 204.
60. Drake and Cayton, *Black Metropolis*, 184.
61. Mitchell Duneier, *Ghetto: The Invention of a Place, The History of an Idea* (New York: Farrar, Straus & Giroux, 2016), 75.
62. Drake and Cayton, *Black Metropolis*, 209.
63. Elijah Anderson, "Iconic Ghetto," *Annals of the American Academy of Political and Social Science* 642 (July 2012): 9.
64. Anderson, "Iconic Ghetto," 9.
65. Anderson, "Iconic Ghetto," 9.
66. Anderson, "Iconic Ghetto," 14.
67. Tony L. Whitehead, "The Formation of the U.S. Racialized Urban Ghetto," Cultural Systems Analysis Group Special Problems Working Paper Series in Urban Anthropology (Sept. 15, 2000), 17, https://hiphoprepublican.com/files /documents/workingpapers/rugone.pdf).
68. Whitehead ("Racialized Urban Ghetto") defines racialized urban ghettoes as "not only urban areas wherein the majority of the residents are African American who are poor, in poverty, or in extreme poverty, but the residents of these are physically isolated from non-poor residential areas" (p. 5). He goes on to add that these areas are characterized by high rates of poverty and unemployment (p. 7), high incidence of female headed households (p. 11), social disorganization (p. 13), and social and cultural isolation (p. 19).
69. Weber, *Economy and Society*, 1:43.
70. Weber, *Economy and Society*, 1:43.
71. Wacquant, *Urban Outcasts*, 46.
72. Max Weber, *Economy and Society*, vol. 2, ed. Guenther Roth and Claus Wittich (Berkeley: University of California Press, 1978), 1212.
73. Weber, *Economy and Society*, 1:361.
74. Weber, *Economy and Society*, 1:42.
75. Gertrud Neuwirth, "A Weberian Outline of a Theory of Community: Its Application to the 'Dark Ghetto,'" *British Journal of Sociology* 20 (June 1969): 148.
76. Neuwirth, "A Weberian Outline," 154.
77. Neuwirth, "A Weberian Outline," 156.
78. Elijah Anderson, "Against the Wall: Poor, Young, Black, and Male," in *Against the Wall: Poor, Young, Black, and Male*, ed. Elijah Anderson (Philadelphia: University of Pennsylvania Press, 2008), 6.
79. William H. Grier and Price M. Cobbs, *Black Rage* (1968; repr., New York: Basic Books), 56.
80. Grier and Cobbs, *Black Rage*, 56.
81. Grier and Cobbs, *Black Rage*, 57.
82. Grier and Cobbs, *Black Rage*, 59.
83. James T. Patterson, *Freedom Is Not Enough: The Moynihan Report and America's Struggle Over Black Family Life—from LBJ to Obama* (New York: Basic Books, 2010), 13.
84. Darryl M. Scott, *Contempt and Pity: Social Policy and the Image of the Damaged Black Psyche, 1880–1996* (Chapel Hill: University of North Carolina Press, 1997), 77.
85. U.S. Department of Labor, *The Negro Family: The Case for National Action* (Washington, DC: United States Government Printing Office, 1965), 5.
86. U.S. Department of Labor, *The Negro Family*, 5.
87. E. Franklin Frazier, *The Negro Family in the United States*, rev. ed. (1939; repr., Chicago: University of Chicago Press, 1966), 32.
88. U.S. Department of Labor, *The Negro Family*, 16.

89. U.S. Department of Labor, *The Negro Family*, 16.
90. Kenneth Clark, *Dark Ghetto: Dilemmas of Social Power* (New York: Harper's Torchbooks, 1965), 1.
91. Duneier provides information on the relationship between Clark and Moynihan. As a young man, Moynihan was a student of Clark's at the City College of New York (CUNY). See Duneier, *Ghetto*, 88–113.
92. Clark, *Dark Ghetto*, 70.
93. Clark, *Dark Ghetto*, 63.
94. Duneier, *Ghetto*, 119.
95. Wilson Julius Wilson, *More than Just Race: Being Black and Poor in the Inner City* (New York: W. W. Norton & Co., 2009), 100.
96. Wilson, *More than Just Race*, 100.
97. Wilson, *More than Just Race*, 103.
98. Duneier, *Ghetto*, 157.
99. Elijah Anderson, *Code of the Street: Decency, Violence, and the Moral Life of the Inner City* (New York: W. W. Norton & Co., 1999), 91.
100. Anderson, *Code of the Street*, 33.
101. Anderson, *Code of the Street*, 33.
102. Anderson, *Code of the Street*, 36.
103. Anderson, *Code of the Street*, 49.
104. Anderson, *Code of the Street*, 49.
105. Wacquant, *Urban Outcasts*, 175.
106. Wacquant, *Urban Outcasts*, 175.
107. Wacquant, *Urban Outcasts*, 175.
108. Sean Joe, "Suicide Patterns among Black Males," in *Against the Wall: Poor, Young, Black, and Male*, ed. Elijah Anderson (Philadelphia: University of Pennsylvania Press, 2008), 231.
109. Cornel West, *Race Matters* (New York: Vintage Books, 1993), 5.
110. Charles Wright Mills, *The Sociological Imagination*, rev. ed. (1959; repr., New York: Oxford University Press, 2000), 7.
111. Mills, *Sociological Imagination*, 23.
112. David Martin, "Sociology and Theology: With and Against the Grain of 'the World,'" *Implicit Religion* 18 (May 2015): 160.
113. Martin, "Sociology and Theology," 160.
114. Martin, "Sociology and Theology," 168.
115. Martin, "Sociology and Theology," 169.
116. Martin, "Sociology and Theology," 169.
117. Frederick L. Ware, *African American Theology: An Introduction* (Louisville, KY: Westminster John Knox Press, 2016), 61.
118. Ware, *African American Theology*, 61.
119. Albert J. Raboteau, *Slave Religion: The Invisible "Institution" in the Antebellum South* (New York: Oxford University Press, 1980), 309.
120. Raboteau, *Slave Religion*, 310.
121. Raboteau, *Slave Religion*, 311.
122. Theophus H. Smith, *Conjuring Culture: Biblical Formations of Black America* (New York: Oxford University Press, 1994), 254.
123. Smith, *Conjuring Culture*, 254.

Chapter 4: The Wilderness

1. Max Oelschlaeger, *The Idea of Wilderness: From Prehistory to the Age of Ecology* (New Haven, CT: Yale University Press, 1991), 1.

2. Robert Marshall, "The Problem of the Wilderness," *Scientific Monthly* 30 (February 1930): 141.
3. Marshall, "Problem of the Wilderness," 141.
4. Marshall, "Problem of the Wilderness," 141.
5. Marshall, "Problem of the Wilderness," 141.
6. Marshall, "Problem of the Wilderness," 144.
7. Marshall, "Problem of the Wilderness," 145.
8. Marshall, "Problem of the Wilderness," 148.
9. Marshall, "Problem of the Wilderness," 148.
10. Oelschlaeger, *Idea of Wilderness*, 14.
11. Oelschlaeger, *Idea of Wilderness*, 15.
12. Oelschlaeger, *Idea of Wilderness*, 17.
13. Oelschlaeger, *Idea of Wilderness*, 33.
14. Oelschlaeger, *Idea of Wilderness*, 61.
15. Walter Brueggemann, *The Land: Place as Gift, Promise, and Challenge in Biblical Faith* (Philadelphia: Fortress Press, 1977), 2.
16. Brueggemann, *Land: Place as Gift*, 5.
17. Brueggemann, *Land: Place as Gift*, 8.
18. Brueggemann, *Land: Place as Gift*, 9.
19. Shemaryahu Talmon, "The Desert Motif in the Bible and in Qumran Literature," in *Literary Studies in the Hebrew Bible: Form and Content, Collected Studies* (Jerusalem: Magnes Press, 1993), 216.
20. Robert Barry Leal, *Wilderness in the Bible: Toward a Theology of the Wilderness* (New York: Peter Lang, 2004), 36.
21. Leal, *Wilderness in the Bible*, 40
22. Laura Feldt, "Wilderness and Hebrew Bible Religion—Fertility, Apostasy, and Religious Transformation in the Pentateuch," in *Wilderness in Mythology and Religion: Approaching Religious Spatialities, Cosmologies, and Ideas of Wild Nature*, ed. Laura Feldt, Religion and Society 55, ed. Gustavo Benavides, Kocku von Stuckrad, and Winnifred Fallers Sullivan (Boston: De Gruyter, 2012), 65.
23. Feldt, "Wilderness and Hebrew Bible," 65.
24. Feldt, "Wilderness and Hebrew Bible," 68.
25. Feldt, "Wilderness and Hebrew Bible," 69.
26. Feldt, "Wilderness and Hebrew Bible," 72.
27. Feldt, "Wilderness and Hebrew Bible," 75.
28. Feldt, "Wilderness and Hebrew Bible," 81.
29. Feldt, "Wilderness and Hebrew Bible," 81–88.
30. Brueggemann, *Land: Place as Gift*, 8.
31. Brueggemann, *Land: Place as Gift*, 33.
32. Brueggemann, *Land: Place as Gift*, 33.
33. Brueggemann, *Land: Place as Gift*, 33.
34. Brueggemann, *Land: Place as Gift*, 34.
35. Walter Brueggemann, *Theology of the Old Testament: Testimony, Dispute, Agony* (Minneapolis: Fortress Press, 1997), 68.
36. Brueggemann, *Theology*, 68.
37. Brueggemann, *Land: Place as Gift*, 35.
38. Brueggemann, *Land: Place as Gift*, 40.
39. Brueggemann, *Land: Place as Gift*, 41.
40. Brueggemann, *Land: Place as Gift*, 40.
41. Brueggemann, *Land: Place as Gift*, 43.
42. Brueggemann, *Land: Place as Gift*, 44.

43. Brueggemann, *Genesis: Interpretation, A Bible Commentary for Teaching and Preaching* (Atlanta: John Knox Press, 1982), 183–84.
44. Leal, *Wilderness in the Bible*, 101.
45. Leal, *Wilderness in the Bible*, 101.
46. Claus Westermann, *Genesis 12–36: A Commentary*, trans. John J. Scullion SJ (Minneapolis: Augsburg Publishing House, 1981), 23.
47. Westermann, *Genesis 12–36*, 23.
48. Westermann, *Genesis 12–36*, 24.
49. Westermann, *Genesis 12–36*, 24.
50. Blenkinsopp, *Abraham: The Story of a Life* (Grand Rapids: Wm. B. Eerdmans Publishing Co., 2015), 23–24.
51. Blenkinsopp, *Abraham*, 24.
52. Jon D. Levenson, *Inheriting Abraham: The Legacy of the Patriarch in Judaism, Christianity, and Islam* (Princeton, NJ: Princeton University Press, 2012), 3.
53. Levenson, *Inheriting Abraham*, 36.
54. Blenkinsopp, *Abraham*, 78.
55. Blenkinsopp, *Abraham*, 48.
56. Joel S. Kaminsky, *Yet I Loved Jacob: Reclaiming the Biblical Concept of Election* (Nashville: Abingdon Press, 2007), 33.
57. Kaminsky, *Yet I Loved Jacob*, 33.
58. Kaminsky, *Yet I Loved Jacob*, 34.
59. Exum gets this term from feminist psychoanalyst Julia Kristeva's *Power of Horror: An Essay of Abjection* (New York: Columbia University Press, 1980), 4.
60. J. Cheryl Exum, "The Accusing Look: The Abjection of Hagar in Art," *Religion and the Arts* (2007): 144.
61. Exum, "The Accusing Look," 145.
62. Victor P. Hamilton, *The Book of Genesis, Chapters 18–50* (Grand Rapids: Wm. B. Eerdmans Publishing Co., 1995), 78.
63. Hamilton notes the various ways that playing can be interpreted, from innocent clowning to acts of a sexual nature to some other form of physical abuse (*Book of Genesis*, 78–79).
64. Gerhard von Rad, *Genesis: A Commentary* (Philadelphia: Westminster Press, 1961), 227.
65. Von Rad, *Genesis*, 79.
66. Esther Fuchs, "The Literary Characterization of Mothers," 136, quoted in Alice Ogden Bellis, *Helpmates, Harlots, and Heroes: Women's Stories in the Hebrew Bible* (Louisville, KY: Westminster John Knox Press, 1994), 69.
67. Bellis, *Helpmates, Harlots, and Heroes*, 70.
68. Bellis, *Helpmates, Harlots, and Heroes*, 75.
69. Nyasha Junior, *Reimagining Hagar: Blackness and the Bible* (New York: Oxford University Press, 2019), 38.
70. Junior, *Reimagining Hagar*, 87.
71. Phyllis Trible, *Texts of Terror: Literary-Feminist Readings of Biblical Narratives* (Philadelphia: Fortress Press, 1984), 1.
72. Trible, *Texts of Terror*, 2.
73. Brueggemann, *Theology*, 99.
74. Trible, *Texts of Terror*, 27.
75. Trible, *Texts of Terror*, 28.
76. Renita Weems, *Just a Sister Away: A Womanist Vision of Women's Relationships in the Bible* (San Diego: LuraMedia, 1988), 2.

77. Weems, *Just a Sister Away*, 12.
78. Renita Weems, "Reading Her Way through the Struggle: African American Women and the Bible," in *Stony the Road We Trod: African American Biblical Interpretation*, ed. Cain Hope Felder (Minneapolis: Fortress Press, 1991), 58.
79. Weems, "Reading Her Way," 63.
80. Weems, "Reading Her Way," 75.
81. Weems, "Reading Her Way," 76.
82. Weems, "Reading Her Way," 76.
83. Delores S. Williams, *Sisters in the Wilderness: The Challenge of Womanist God-Talk* (Maryknoll, NY: Orbis Books, 1993), 196.
84. Williams, *Sisters in the Wilderness*, 108.
85. Williams, *Sisters in the Wilderness*, x.
86. Williams, *Sisters in the Wilderness*, xii.
87. Nyasha Junior argues that Williams makes the mistake of conflating the biblical Hagar with the Aunt Hagar found in African American culture. Junior states that Hagar "is not a prominent figure with African American biblical scholarship, including scholarship that focuses on the significance of Africa within the biblical texts" (p. 106). As for the absence of the biblical Hagar in African American culture, Junior offers an in-depth critique of Williams's "fusion of biblical Hagar within Aunt Hagar" (p. 118). See Junior's analysis of *Sisters in the Wilderness* in her text *Reimagining Hagar*, 115–23.
88. Williams, *Sisters in the Wilderness*, 3.
89. Williams, *Sisters in the Wilderness*, 3.
90. Williams, *Sisters in the Wilderness*, 6.
91. Hermann Gunkel, *Genesis*, quoted in in Westermann, *Genesis*, 246.
92. Gregory Mobley, "The Wild Man in the Bible and the Ancient Near East," *Journal of Biblical Literature* 116 (Summer 1997): 220.
93. Mobley, "The Wild Man," 220.
94. Mobley, "The Wild Man," 227.
95. Williams, *Sisters in the Wilderness*, 22.
96. Williams, *Sisters in the Wilderness*, 25.
97. Thomas Booij, "Hagar's Words in Genesis XVI 13B," *Vetus Testamentum* 30 (January 1980): 2.
98. Booij, "Hagar's Words," 6.
99. Booij, "Hagar's Words," 6.
100. Booij, "Hagar's Words," 7.
101. Yael Avrahami, *The Senses of Scripture: Sensory Perception in the Hebrew Bible* (London: Bloomsbury, T. & T. Clark, 2012), 275.
102. Avrahami, *Senses of Scripture*, 240.
103. Williams, *Sisters in the Wilderness*, 26.
104. Westermann, *Genesis 12–36*, 79.
105. Westermann, *Genesis 12–36*, 79.
106. Westermann, *Genesis 12–36*, 80.
107. Westermann, *Genesis 12–36*, 109–10.
108. Hamilton, *Book of Genesis*, 82.
109. Ed Noort, "Created in the Image of the Son: Ishmael and Hagar," in *Abraham, the Nations, and the Hagarites*, ed. Martin Goodman, George H. van Kooten, and Jacques van Ruiten (Boston: Brill, 2010), 38.
110. Noort, "Created in the Image," 38.
111. Noort, "Created in the Image," 38.

112. Hamilton, *Book of Genesis*, 83.
113. *Merriam-Webster*, s.v., "gift," https://www.merriam-webster.com/dictionary /gift.
114. Williams, *Sisters in the Wilderness*, 31.
115. Von Rad, *Genesis*, 229.
116. Von Rad, *Genesis*, 229.
117. Brueggemann, *Land: Place as Gift*, 29.
118. Brueggemann, *Land: Place as Gift*, 43.

Chapter 5: Talking about Our Gifts

1. Richard Wright, *Rite of Passage* (New York: Harper Trophy, 1994), 22.
2. W. E. B. Du Bois, *The Souls of Black Folk* (1903; repr., New York: Barnes & Noble Classics, 2003), 8.
3. Earlise Ward and Maigenete Mengesha, "Depression in African American Men: A Review of What We Know and Where We Need to Go from Here," *American Journal of Orthopsychiatry* 83 (April 2013): 386.
4. John Head, *Standing in the Shadows: Understanding and Overcoming Depression in Black Men* (New York: Broadway Books, 2004), 2.
5. Head, *Standing in the Shadows*, 4.
6. Head, *Standing in the Shadows*, 8.
7. Head, *Standing in the Shadows*, 8.
8. Head, *Standing in the Shadows*, 11.
9. Head, *Standing in the Shadows*, 5.
10. Head, *Standing in the Shadows*, 13.
11. Head, *Standing in the Shadows*, 119.
12. Head, *Standing in the Shadows*, 121.
13. Head, *Standing in the Shadows*, 120.
14. Daniel O. Black, "Spiritual Deprivation and the Legacy of Black Fathers," *Journal of African American Men* 5 (September 2000): 4.
15. Black, "Spiritual Deprivation," 16.
16. Black, "Spiritual Deprivation," 17.
17. Ed Noort, "Created in the Image of the Son: Ishmael and Hagar," in *Abraham, the Nations, and the Hagarites*, ed. Martin Goodman, George H. van Kooten, and Jacques van Ruiten (Boston: Brill, 2010), 35.
18. Noort, "Created in the Image," 35.
19. John T. Noble, *A Place for Hagar's Son: Ishmael as a Case Study in the Priestly Tradition* (Minneapolis: Fortress Press, 2016), 1.
20. Gerhard von Rad, *Genesis: A Commentary* (Philadelphia: Westminster Press, 1961), 26.
21. Von Rad, *Genesis*, 26.
22. Noble, *Place for Hagar's Son*, 7.
23. Noble, *Place for Hagar's Son*, 7.
24. Walter Brueggemann, *Theology of the Old Testament: Testimony, Dispute, Agony* (Minneapolis: Fortress Press, 1997), 366.
25. Brueggemann, *Theology*, 367.
26. Brueggemann, *Theology*, 480.
27. The third chapter of Noble's text provides an analysis of Ishmael's status in relation to the Abrahamic covenant. He considers the particularity and ambiguity of the covenant, specifically that the covenant is not the exclusive preserve of a single nation but in P a multitude of nations (see Noble, *Place for Hagar's Son*, 79–80).

28. Thomas B. Dozeman, "The Wilderness and Salvation History in the Hagar Story," *Journal of Biblical Literature* 117 (Spring 1998): 42.
29. Dozeman, "Wilderness and Salvation History," 42.
30. Dozeman, "Wilderness and Salvation History," 42.
31. Victor P. Hamilton, *The Book of Genesis, Chapters 18–50* (Grand Rapids: Wm. B. Eerdmans Publishing Co., 1995), 85.
32. Hamilton, *Book of Genesis*, 85.
33. Claus Westermann, *Genesis 12–36: A Commentary*, trans. John J. Scullion SJ (Minneapolis: Augsburg Publishing House, 1981), 343.
34. Hugh C. White, "The Initiation Legend of Ishmael," in *Zeitschrift für die Alttestamentliche Wissenschaft* 87 (January 1975): 18.
35. David D. Gilmore, *Manhood in the Making: Cultural Concepts of Masculinity* (New Haven, CT: Yale University Press, 1990), 11.
36. Gilmore, *Manhood in the Making*, 11.
37. Hamilton, *Book of Genesis*, 79.
38. *Merriam-Webster*, s.v. "wean," https://www.merriam-webster.com/dictionary/wean.
39. Hamilton, *Book of Genesis*, 80.
40. Erik H. Erikson, *Childhood and Society*, rev. ed. (1950; repr., New York: W. W. Norton & Co., 1985), 248.
41. Joseph M. Kramp, "Religion and Erik Erikson's Life Cycle Theory," in *Encyclopedia of Psychology and Religion*, ed. D. A. Leeming (Boston: Springer, 2010), 1495.
42. Erik H. Erikson, *Identity: Youth and Crisis*, rev. ed. (1968; repr., New York: W. W. Norton & Co., 1994), 97.
43. Erikson, *Childhood and Society*, 249.
44. Erikson, *Childhood and Society*, 249.
45. Ana-Maria Rizzuto, *The Birth of the Living God: A Psychoanalytic Study* (Chicago: University of Chicago Press, 1979), 204.
46. According to Donald Winnicott, the transitional object belongs to the sphere of illusion: "This intermediate area of experience, unchallenged in respect to its belonging to inner or external (shared) reality, constitutes the greater part of the infant's experience and throughout life is retained in the intense experiencing that belongs to the arts and to religion and to imaginative living, and to creative scientific work" (See D. W. Winnicott, "Transitional Objects and Transitional Phenomena," quoted in J. Laplanche and J.-B. Pontalis, *The Language of Psychoanalysis*, trans. Donald Nicholson-Smith (New York: W. W. Norton & Co., 1973), 465.)
47. Rizzuto, *Birth of the Living God*, 204.
48. Rizzuto, *Birth of the Living God*, 208.
49. J. Gerald Janzen and John T. Noble, "Did Hagar Give Ishmael Up for Dead? Gen. 21.14–21 Re-visited," *Journal for the Study of the Old Testament* 44 (May 2020), 519.
50. Janzen and Noble, "Did Hagar," 528.
51. Janzen and Noble, "Did Hagar," 528.
52. White, "Initiation Legend of Ishmael," 271.
53. White, "Initiation Legend of Ishmael," 287.
54. White, "Initiation Legend of Ishmael," 301.
55. White, "Initiation Legend of Ishmael," 303.
56. White, "Initiation Legend of Ishmael," 303.
57. White, "Initiation Legend of Ishmael," 303.

58. Ryan P. Bonfiglio, "Archer Imagery in Zechariah 9:11–17 in Light of Achaemenid Iconography," *Journal of Biblical Literature* 131 (January 2012): 509.
59. Bonfiglio, "Archer Imagery," 510.
60. Bonfiglio, "Archer Imagery," 526.
61. Richard H. Wilkinson, "The Representation of the Bow in the Art of Egypt and the Ancient Near East," *Journal of the Near Eastern Society* 20 (January 1991): 83.
62. Wilkinson, "Representation of the Bow," 83.
63. Wilkinson, "Representation of the Bow," 83.
64. D. W. Winnicott, "The Place Where We Live," in *Playing and Reality* (New York: Routledge Classics, 2005), 141.
65. Winnicott, "Place Where We Live," 146.
66. Margaret Clark, *Understanding Religion and Spirituality in Clinical Practice* (London: Karnac Books, 2012), 37.
67. Clark, *Understanding Religion*, xii.
68. Clark, *Understanding Religion*, xiv.
69. Clark, *Understanding Religion*, 37.
70. D. W. Winnicott, "Living Creatively," in *Home Is Where We Start From* (New York: W. W. Norton & Co., 1986), 40.
71. A comprehensive definition of the reality principle is offered in Jean Laplanche and Jean-Bertrand Pontalis's *The Language of Psycho-analysis* (New York: W. W. Norton, 1973). They explain that the reality principle is tied to the pleasure principle, thereby noting the two principles that control our mental functioning in Freudian metapsychology. Freud observed that the reality principle took over from the pleasure principle, thereby forfeiting hallucination in order to "form a conception of the real circumstances in the external world and to endeavor to make a real alteration in them" (p. 380). Laplanche and Pontalis add that "as a regulatory principle of mental functioning, the reality principle emerges secondarily, modifying the pleasure principle which has been dominant up to this point; its establishment goes hand in hand with a whole series of adaptations which the psychical apparatus has to undergo" (p. 380).
72. Winnicott, "Living Creatively," 44.
73. Winnicott, "Living Creatively," 51.
74. Clark, *Understanding Religion*, 34.
75. D. W. Winnicott, "Morals and Education," in *The Maturational Process and the Facilitating Environment* (New York: Karnac Books, 1990), 93.
76. Clark, *Understanding Religion*, 35.
77. D. W. Winnicott, "Playing: Creative Activity and the Search for the Self," in *Playing and Reality* (New York: Routledge Classics, 2005), 71.
78. Winnicott, "Playing," 86.
79. Winnicott, "Playing," 86.
80. Jaco Hamman, "Toys: A Man Has His Reasons. Winnicottian Perspectives on the Playing of Men," *Pastoral Psychology* (February 2001): 92.
81. Hamman, "Toys," 92.
82. Hamman, "Toys," 103.
83. Dozeman, "Wilderness and Salvation History," 32.
84. Dozeman, "Wilderness and Salvation History," 33.
85. Noble, *Hagar's Son*, 46.
86. Jon D. Levenson, *The Death and Resurrection of the Beloved Son: The Transformation of Child Sacrifice in Judaism and Christianity*, quoted in Noble, *Hagar's Son*, 46.

87. Westermann, *Genesis 12–36*, 397.
88. An alternative interpretation of Ishmael's return is given in Old Testament scholar Ekaterina E. Kozlova's "Abraham's Burial (Genesis 25:9): An Idyllic Burial or a Dispute Over Inheritance?" (*Journal for the Study of the Old Testament* 42 [November 2017]: 177–97). She interprets Abraham's burial as a scene where the dispute over inheritance takes place. "After Abraham's death," Kozlova writes, "Ishmael may well be seeking to seize the benefits due the first born by performing the duty of an heir for his deceased father" (p. 182).

Chapter 6: Warning

1. Delores S. Williams, *Sisters in the Wilderness: The Challenge of Womanist God-Talk* (Maryknoll, NY: Orbis Books, 1993), 4.
2. Williams, *Sisters in the Wilderness*, 5–6.
3. Raymond Gunn, "David's Story: From Promise to Despair" in *Against the Wall: Poor, Young, Black, and Male*, ed. Elijah Anderson (Philadelphia: University of Pennsylvania Press, 2008), 31.
4. Walter Brueggemann, *The Land: Place as Gift, Promise, and Challenge in Biblical Faith* (Philadelphia: Fortress Press, 1977), 28.
5. Ricard Wright, *12 Million Black Voices* (1941; repr., New York: Basic Books, 2008), 106.
6. Wright, *12 Million Black Voices*, 108–9.
7. Wright, *12 Million Black Voices*, 110.
8. Williams, *Sisters in the Wilderness*, 108.
9. Williams, *Sisters in the Wilderness*, 112.
10. Erik Nielson, "'Go in de Wilderness': Evading the 'Eyes of Others' in Slave Songs," *Western Journal of Black Studies* 35 (March 2011): 112.
11. Nielson, "Go in de Wilderness," 114.
12. Melvin Dixon, *Ride Out the Wilderness: Geography and Identity in African American Literature* (Chicago: University of Illinois Press, 1987), 2.
13. Dixon, *Ride Out the Wilderness*, 57.
14. Dixon, *Ride Out the Wilderness*, 64.
15. Dixon, *Ride Out the Wilderness*, 65.
16. Dixon, *Ride Out the Wilderness*, 65.
17. Dixon, *Ride Out the Wilderness*, 68.
18. Dixon, *Ride Out the Wilderness*, 62.
19. Richard Wright, *The Man Who Lived Underground: A Novel* (1942; repr., New York: Literary Classics of the United States, 2021), 63.
20. James Baldwin, "Many Thousands Gone," in *Baldwin: Collected Essays*, ed. Toni Morrison (1955; repr., New York: Library Classics of America, 1998), 27.
21. Baldwin, "Many Thousands Gone," 27.
22. Baldwin, "Many Thousands Gone," 27.
23. Baldwin, "Many Thousands Gone," 28.
24. Baldwin, "Many Thousands Gone," 27.
25. Victor Anderson, *Creative Exchange: A Constructive Theology of African American Religious Experience* (Minneapolis: Fortress Press, 2008), 11.
26. Anderson, *Creative Exchange*, 21.
27. The Notorious B. I. G., "Suicidal Thoughts," 1994, from *Ready to Die* (Bad Boy Records).
28. Daniel B. Schwartz, *Ghetto: The History of a Word* (Cambridge, MA: Harvard University Press, 2019), 1.

29. Notorious B. I. G., "Suicidal Thoughts."
30. Danielle Taylor-Gutherie, ed., *Conversations with Toni Morrison* (Jackson: University Press of Mississippi, 1970), 40.
31. Toni Morrison, *The Bluest Eye* (New York: Alfred A. Knopf, 1970), 205–6.
32. Morrison, *Bluest Eye*, 204.
33. Morrison, *Bluest Eye*, 206.
34. Morrison, *Bluest Eye*, 206.
35. Richard Wright, "How Bigger Was Born," in *Native Son* (1940; repr., New York: Harper Perennial Modern Classics, 2005).
36. Elijah Anderson, "Against the Wall: Poor, Young, Black, and Male," in *Against the Wall: Poor, Young, Black, and Male*, ed. Elijah Anderson (Philadelphia: University of Pennsylvania Press, 2008), 15.
37. James Dittes, *Pastoral Counseling: The Basics* (Louisville, KY: Westminster John Knox Press, 1999), 18.

Index

abandonment, 43, 61–62, 63, 84, 105, 116, 118, 130–31
Abraham, 94–97, 103–4, 115–16
    and Abrahamic covenant, 93, 124, 154n27
Achaemenid iconography, 120
Adam (biblical figure), 97
African American. *See entries at Black*
Ahmad, Aubrey, 4
Akbar, Na'im, 38–39
Anderson, Elijah, 69, 77–78, 79, 82–83, 106, 133
Anderson, Victor, 129–30
Andrews, William L., 33
anthropocentrism, 89
Aunt Hagar figure, 98, 153n87
Auschwitz concentration camp, 29
authority. *See* father-son relationships; leadership
Avrahami, Yael, 103

Baker, Ella, 39
Baldwin, James, 1, 6, 128–29
Barrow, Bennet, 27
Barth, Karl, 21, 22
Bauman, Zygmunt, 2
beauty, 23–24
Beck, E. M., 59
Bellis, Alice Ogden, 97–98
Bernays, Martha, 51
Bettelheim, Bruno, 29
Bible. *See* Hebrew Bible
biblical interpretation
    African American, survival/quality of life tradition, 101–2, 105–6
    feminist and womanist, 96, 97–99

biblical symbolism, 85–86. *See also* wilderness
Bigger Thomas (*Native Son* character), 7–9, 14–15, 112, 128–29
Biggie Smalls (Christopher Wallace), 130–31
bisexuality theory, 51, 143n54
Black, Daniel, 112
Black churches
    classification of urban poor and ghettoes, 5–7
    leadership in, 36, 60–61
black face, 28
Black men
    depression, 109–11
    Ishmael's story compared to, 14–15, 106, 125–26
    no human involved classification, 2–4
    state-sanctioned violence against, 1–2, 4
    See also Black messiah figure; ghettoes; manhood
Black messiah figure
    charismatic authority, 37–39
    co-option of, 39–40
    leadership types, 35–36
    manhood, 33, 36–37, 38–39
    messianism, types of, 33–34
    and the New Negro, 34–35
Black women
    and charismatic manhood, 39
    communal spirituality, 10–11, 136n53
    Hagar's story compared to, 98–101, 125
    and single-parent households, 62–64, 71, 80–81, 82, 110
Blanton, Thomas R., 12–13
Blassingame, John W., 30, 32

159

CPSIA information can be obtained
at www.ICGtesting.com
Printed in the USA
LVHW010349250922
729083LV00008B/11